The Complete Idi

Quick Steps to C
with Easy CD (

Copying a CD (Audio or Data)

1. Click Start, Programs, Roxio Easy CD Creator 5, CD Copier.
2. Select the source CD-ROM and destination CD-RW drives using the appropriate drop-down menus (don't forget to insert the discs, too!).
3. Use the Advanced tab if you want to change any settings, such as the speed at which the disc is recorded or the number of copies to be burned.
4. Click the Copy button.

Creating a CD Using Easy CD Creator (Audio or Data)

1. Click Start, Programs, Roxio Easy CD Creator 5, Easy CD Creator.
2. In Easy CD Creator, open the File menu, select New CD Project, and choose the type of CD you want to make.
3. Use the Explorer pane to locate audio or data files on the hard drives in your computer, your CD-ROM drives, etc.
4. Click and drag the files (or tracks) you want to record into the Layout pane.
5. Watch the Space/Time Remaining indicator to ensure that you're not adding more data than the CD can hold.
6. When you're ready to start burning, click the Record button.
7. Use the Record CD Setup dialog box to choose the recording method, speed, whether or not to perform a test burn, etc.
8. Insert a blank CD-R or CD-RW disc and click the OK button to begin recording.

Formatting a Disc for Use with DirectCD

1. Insert the CD-R or CD-RW disc into your CD-RW drive.
2. If DirectCD is not set to automatically load when you boot your PC, click Start, Programs, Roxio Easy CD Creator 5, Applications, DirectCD Format Utility.
3. Double-click the DirectCD icon (located in your computer's system tray) to bring up the main DirectCD interface window.
4. Click the Format button.
5. If you want, choose a name for the disc and whether or not it should have compression enabled.
6. Choose the format type (Full or Quick). If this is the first time the CD-R or CD-RW disc has been formatted, you must choose Full.
7. Click the Start Format button (a Full format can take more than 30 minutes).

ALPHA

tear here

Quick Steps to Creating Your Own CDs with NTI CD-Maker 2000

Copying a CD (Audio or Data)

1. Click Start, Programs, NTI CD-Maker Professional 2000/NTI CD-Maker Professional 2000.
2. Insert a blank CD-R disc in the burner. Select the source CD-ROM and destination CD-RW drives using the appropriate drop-down menus.
3. Select the checkbox to copy disc to image file first if making multiple copies.
4. Click the Step 2 button to bring up the Write CD dialog box. Change settings to make multiple copies or change the burning speed.
5. Click the Start button.

Creating a CD Using NTI CD-Maker (Audio or Data)

1. Click Start, Programs, NTI CD-Maker Professional 2000/NTI CD-Maker Professional 2000.
2. Select the type of CD (Audio or Data) from the menu.
3. Use the Explorer pane to locate audio or data files on the hard drives in your computer or CD-ROM, and drag them to the Layout pane.
4. Watch the Space/Time bar at the bottom of the window to keep track of how much data you've selected to burn. Overburning is allowed but not recommended, because it can ruin some burners!
5. When you're ready to start burning, click Step 2.
6. Use the Write CD dialog box to choose the recording method, speed, whether or not to perform a test burn, etc.
7. Insert a blank CD-R or CD-RW disc and click the Start button to begin recording.

Formatting a Disc for Use with FileCD

1. Insert the CD-RW disc into your CD-RW drive.
2. Click on Start, Programs, FileCD, FileCD or place your cursor over the CD icon in the system tray, then select OpenFileCD from the menu that appears.
3. From the Disc menu select Format. When the Format disc dialog box appears, select either ISO 9660 or UDF for the disc format. Also select a Quick or Full (erase) format. If you want, select the Verify after full format checkbox to check the integrity of the disc.
4. Fill in the Label field with a label for the CD-RW disc and click Start. Formatting can take from just a few minutes if you use the Quick method or up to 20 to 40 minutes if you use the Full format, which erases any previous data on a disc.

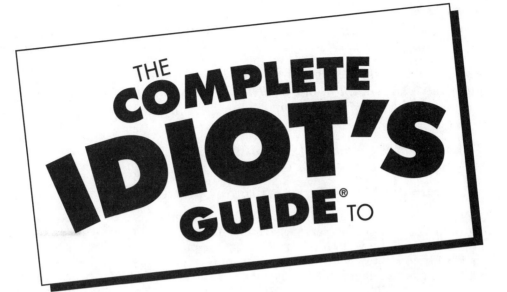

THE COMPLETE IDIOT'S GUIDE® TO

Creating Your Own CDs

NEW ENGLAND INSTITUTE
OF TECHNOLOGY
LIBRARY

Second Edition

By Terry William Ogletree and Todd Brakke

ALPHA

A Pearson Education Company

For Angie,
"You truly are my 'sun and stars.' Thank you for sharing your life and love with me."

And for Jan and the rest of the Keeler family,
"Every day you remain in our thoughts, hearts, and prayers. Know that you have any support we can offer."
—Todd

"To my parents, Gordon and Billie Jean Ogletree, of course!"
—Terry

Copyright © 2002 by Terry William Ogletree

International Standard Book Number: 0-02-864291-0
Library of Congress Catalog Card Number: 2001095866

04   03   02   8   7   6   5   4   3

Interpretation of the printing code: The rightmost number of the first series of numbers is the year of the book's printing; the rightmost number of the second series of numbers is the number of the book's printing. For example, a printing code of 02-1 shows that the first printing occurred in 2002.

Printed in the United States of America

Publisher
Marie Butler-Knight

Product Manager
Phil Kitchel

Managing Editor
Jennifer Chisholm

Acquisitions Editor
Eric Heagy

Development Editor
Clint McCarty

Senior Production Editor
Christy Wagner

Copy Editor
Abby Lyon Herriman

Illustrator
Jody Schaeffer

Cover Designers
Mike Freeland
Kevin Spear

Book Designers
Scott Cook and Amy Adams of DesignLab

Indexer
Angie Bess

Layout/Proofreading
Susan Geiselman
Brad Lenser
Michelle Mitchell

Contents at a Glance

Contents

Introduction

CD Recording in the Home—Who Woulda Thunk It?

In the past few years, the black art of CD burning has gone from an ultra-expensive, low-payoff method corporations use to store data backups to unreliable PC drives, still priced outside all but those with limitless disposable income, to a standard, dependable feature on desktop PCs and even laptops.

Don't believe me? Take a look at the weekly circulars from Best Buy and CompUSA. Without fail, the majority of PCs they advertise have some form of CD-burning capability. Let's face it, if the price-cutting, low-performance mass market PCs at Circuit City consistently come with CD-RW drives, then they're officially a standard.

Nowadays, DVD recorders are where CD-R drives were a few years ago. Few units are available, there are competing incompatible standards, and the costs compared to the next best thing (CD-RW drives) are astronomical.

We do touch on DVD technology in Chapter 1, "The Digital Revolution!" However, as it is still outside the grasp of John Q. Public, we do not cover recording to DVD in this book. Soon, though … very soon. Today, CD-RW drives are primarily used for three purposes:

➤ Creating backup copies of existing CDs

➤ Backing up data from your PC to a more permanent, reliable, and easily protectable medium

➤ Creating custom compilation or "best of" music CDs that allow you to listen to just the music you want to hear

What Once Was Lost Can Now Be Found

Things come and go. Here today, gone tomorrow. For those who have a huge collection of vinyl phonograph records or cassette tapes, those words have an ominous meaning: It's time to buy all your favorite music all over again on CD. You can still buy a phonograph player, or supplies such as a needle or cartridge, at stores that sell higher-quality audio equipment. However, this does not solve the problem of the slow degradation of the record or tape over time as it is played or as it succumbs to the elements.

While the CD has all but replaced the phonograph record, cassette tapes have managed to endure for just a while longer. I would suspect this has been due to the fact that cassettes are convenient (especially in a car), and you can always put together a tape of your own design by recording on a blank cassette tape. Until recently, tape was the only way to go if you wanted to "copy" music.

Tape's advantage had always been that it allowed you to make a complete copy of your favorite album (or CD). It also enables you to pick and choose which songs you want and the order in which you want to hear them. If it weren't for the fact that cassette tapes are analog, most people would be satisfied using them to back up their audio collections.

In the computer world, don't forget that tape has been, and in some circles still is, the method of choice for backing up large amounts of computer data. Heck, in those olden days of yore, tape was a primary method of storing any kind of data. Anyone remember using the Commodore PET?

Now that the digital revolution has taken off, the price of a CD recorder drive has dropped dramatically (as little as $150), along with the price of blank recordable CDs (less than a buck a disc these days). Instead of the slow, tedious process of recovering computer data off a tape drive backup, backup CD-Rs offer nearly instant access to their data. A quick click and drag in Windows, and it's right back on your hard drive!

Instead of having to settle for a second- or third-generation tape copy of your favorite songs, you can now create almost perfect copies using digital recording. CD recording provides the same capabilities tape does when it comes to mixing and matching songs from various sources to create your own dream sequence. It gives you the same crystal clarity that you'd get if you were playing the source itself.

To make matters even better, this book shows you how to record not just from other CDs, but also from your collection of vinyl records and tapes.

Thanks to the CD-RW drive going mainstream, no piece of data is unsafe, and no song from a one-hit wonder must wallow on a disc with lesser music (just copy it to your own custom compilation disc)!

Creating Your Own CDs, Version 2.0

The book you're now holding is the second edition of *The Complete Idiot's Guide to Creating Your Own CDs*. While the first book was a solid piece of work, there were certainly areas that could be improved. After all, it covered the use of Roxio's Easy CD Creator 4 Deluxe software, which Roxio soon replaced with Easy CD Creator 5 Platinum. (Their first revision of the software in years … go figure.)

So with this second edition we're taking a second look at Easy CD Creator. Most of the existing chapters have been completely redone to reflect the significant changes the program has undergone. And because we understand that most folks don't like being tied into using one program, we've also added complete coverage of NTI's CD-Maker 2000. If you don't like Easy CD Creator, for whatever reason, this is a program well-worth checking out. It won't blow you over with flash, but from a usability standpoint, it can easily go toe-to-toe with Easy CD Creator.

We've also included a chapter on using MusicMatch Jukebox, which, if you're just getting into creating audio CDs, is one of the best programs you can have at your disposal. You really can turn your PC into a desktop jukebox and record a limitless number of CDs for the car, work, vacations, or whatever!

Different Tracks: What's in the Book

Like the first edition, this book starts out with a brief introduction to CD recording. We could have written more on CDs and how they actually work, but as my editor points out, readers of this book are more interested in jumping into the fray and starting to create CDs than worrying about photoreflective layering and other words that can't be pronounced without the aid of a physics professor.

We'll still touch on some of that stuff in the first part of this book, though, because it can help you understand some of the basic necessities. Certain concepts such as the differences between recordable discs, how a CD-writer writes discs differently from a disc you would buy at your local music shop, and much more can ease you safely into those shark-infested CD-burning waters. To help you find out where to start in this book—and it doesn't have to be at the beginning—we offer the following summaries of the various parts you'll find herein.

In **Part 1, "So You Want to Create Some CDs, Do You? An Essential CD Technology Primer,"** we'll talk about how recording audio and video has progressed over the last hundred years to a point that, with digital recording techniques, it is possible to preserve a particular audio or video event forever. Digital recordings can be transferred bit by bit to your computer, to CDs, and even to portable devices. Chapter 1, "The Digital Revolution!" talks about how far we've come.

If you've ever wondered how a CD is actually manufactured, how recordable and rewritable discs you can burn on your computer differ, or what a multisession disc is, then you'll like Chapter 2, "The Machine Behind the Curtain: How CDs and Recordable CDs Work."

In this book, we use Roxio's Easy CD Creator 5 Platinum and NTI's CD-Maker 2000 as the applications for most examples. In **Part 2, "Quick and Painless: Duplicating CDs,"** you'll find chapters on copying CDs.

First we'll start things simply by showing you how to duplicate an audio or data CD using Roxio's acclaimed program in Chapter 3, "Easy Copying with Easy CD Creator." From there it's on to Chapter 4, "Using NTI CD-Maker to Copy CDs," to show you how to do it with NTI's claim to fame.

In **Part 3, "Digital Jukeboxes and PC Life Insurance: The Zen of Making Audio or Data CDs,"** we'll take a look at the meat of creating your own CDs by covering the core Easy CD Creator 5 Platinum and NTI CD-Maker 2000 programs.

If you want to burn a music CD with tracks from other CDs, MP3 files, and WAV files, or a data CD with backups of your most important documents and records, you can learn to become a master of the burn with Chapters 5, "Drag and Drop with Easy CD Creator," or 6, "NTI CD-Maker: Says What It Does and Does What It Says."

From there, we dig into more advanced methods you can use to record audio to CDs. If you want to take your audio further, such as extracting music from other sources (for example, vinyl records, cassettes, radio, or almost any other source that uses standard audio jacks), then check out Chapter 7, "Your Very Own Recording Studio: Using Easy CD Creator SoundStream."

Most folks know you can record audio and data to CD. Ever thought about video? Surely you must have some decaying video tapes at home that you'd like to preserve on a digital medium?

Aspiring video producers should check out **Part 4, "Eat Your Heart Out, Mr. Spielberg: Creating Video CDs,"** especially Chapter 8, "Pre-Production: What Any Home Video Producer Needs," for the basics on desktop video that you can apply regardless of the authoring program you use. Chapters 9, "Toss Your VCR: Using Video CD Creator to Create Video CDs," and 10, "Using NTI CD-Maker for Video CDs and Super Video CDs," are the ones to look at once you're ready to actually record your video.

Just because you can use the main Easy CD Creator and CD-Maker 2000 programs to record data, doesn't mean you should. Both of these packages come with the ability to record to a CD just like it was another disk on your computer. **Part 5, "Limitless Real Estate for Your Data: Using a CD Recorder Like a Hard Disk,"** tells you how. Chapter 11, "Dial Direct with Easy CD Creator DirectCD," shows you how to do it with Roxio's program, while Chapter 12, "Using NTI's FILECD," gets things done with NTI's version.

Part 6, "Picasso Was Overrated: Creating Great-Looking CD Labels and Jewel Case Inserts," covers making jewel case inserts and CD labels. Get your feet wet with Chapter 13, "What Do I Need to Make Great Labels and Inserts?" for the scoop on how these labels work and what you need to create them. In Chapter 14, "Making Killer Labels with Easy CD Creator CD Label Creator," we step through the basics of creating great labels with Roxio's program. In Chapter 15, "Using NTI JewelCase Maker," we go into doing killer labels using NTI's tools.

With the meat all out of the way, **Part 7, "Wait! There's More, So Buy Now: More Fun Software and Utilities!"** takes the time to fill in the gaps. First off we'll cover one of the best PC audio players, which also can burn audio CDs, in Chapter 16, "MusicMatch: Making Your PC the Ultimate Jukebox."

In Chapters 17, "Using NTI Music Café Lite," and 19, "Roxio's Sound Editor," you'll find out how to edit audio files and get rid of parts of a track you could live without (like the artist talking politics in a live recording), adjust the recording volume level, and even apply special effects.

In Chapter 18, "Making Digital PhotoAlbums with Roxio's PhotoRelay," you'll find out how to put your family photographs on CD. And your relatives thought they were safe from pictures of your vacation because you were three states away! Scan your pictures, burn 'em to a self-playing CD, and stick them in the mail!

No matter how well you prepare, there is always the possibility that something will go wrong. That's what Chapter 20, "I Ain't Got No CDs, but You Should See All My New Coasters: Troubleshooting CD Recording," is all about. If you run into trouble spots in your CD-burning adventure, this is your survival guide.

Finally, we've included a series of appendixes for some of the miscellaneous information you might require. For installing Roxio's or NTI's programs see either Appendix A, "Installing Roxio Easy CD Creator," or Appendix B, "Installing NTI CD-Maker." If you're interested in learning about the different recording standards that make CD recording on your PC possible, check out Appendix C, "The Colorful Books of CD Standards."

Other Junk You'll Find Herein

Similar to a child, we like to write in the margins and all over the page. In this book, you'll find some examples of this in the following forms.

Don't Get Burned

Caution! Caution! Caution! Can I make it any plainer? These notes point you away from potential pitfalls and help you keep from spending hours working on your pet project only to have something go wrong in the process.

Between Tracks

These small bits of text are inserted here and there to provide tips, notes, and extra information that aren't in the main body of the text. You might find a shortcut or possibly a topic you may want to explore further in another chapter of the book.

Arcane CD Speak

Sometimes words just say too much—so much that they don't make sense. In these little text bites, we explain some of this terminology. You don't need to know these words to get the job done, but they'll make you sound smarter when you're spouting off to friends about how clever you are.

Cross Reference

Need more information? These cross references will point to other locations in the book where further discussion takes place.

Start Having Fun!

Read this book fast! Why? Because the Internet and the music industry are moving faster than you are! Make backups of your precious CDs. Put your family photographs on CD for long-term digital storage. Scour the Internet for new songs, new files, and new programs. After you get started with your CD recorder, you'll wonder how you ever got along without it. CD recording for the home user really is a *digital revolution!*

About the Authors

Todd Brakke has been around PCs since he was tall enough to tug on his dad's pant-leg and ask how to boot a *Star Trek* game on the family Apple II. Since then, he grew (physically, anyway) and went on to be a published reviewer, columnist, and editor for various online and print PC game publications. After helping lay the groundwork for the dot-bomb implosions as the editor-in-chief of a PC gaming Web site, he became a development editor for a major computer book publisher. There, among many other projects, he helped develop the first edition of Terry Ogletree's *The Complete Idiot's Guide to Creating Your Own CDs* while also penning several articles for *Computer Games Magazine* (formerly *Computer Games Strategy Plus*). For this second edition of *The Complete Idiot's Guide to Creating Your Own CDs*, Terry has enticed (i.e., bribed) him to step out from behind the curtain to help co-author the book.

Terry W. Ogletree currently works as a technical consultant for The Computer Merchant. He has worked with computers for more than 20 years. Terry has thoroughly trained and worked with OpenVMS, UNIX, and TCP/IP platform systems. He has also had extensive experience with all flavors of Windows NT. He is the lead author for *Upgrading and Repairing Networks, Third Edition, Windows XP Professional Unleashed,* and *Practical Firewalls* (Que).

Acknowledgments

I would first like to thank all of you who purchased the first edition of this book. I think you'll find this second edition covers more territory and will be helpful when you start to burn your own CDs. If you did read the first edition, you will remember me saying that Todd Brakke, the development editor for that edition, really deserved to be a co-author because of the tremendous input and editing skills he provided. Well, this time around I'd like to acknowledge him for being the co-author of this second edition! As things go, most of what you read in this second edition is Todd's work, and I thank him for helping out.

Eric Heagy of Alpha Books also deserves a lot of praise. I've never been one to meet deadlines, and his patience is greatly appreciated! He's also just a down-right fun person to talk to—just call him up at Alpha, and you'll see!

Until the next edition …

—Terry Ogletree

First off, I'd like to thank my many parents (Gayle, Jim, John, and Nancy) for the years of infinite patience and unwavering support. Some are lucky to have one parent who cares, while I've been blessed to have been raised by four very special individuals. Speaking of special, a very heartfelt thanks to my wife, Angela, for putting up with the phantom husband I became while co-authoring this book. You're the best that's ever happened to me.

Obviously, no book gets written without *a lot* of help. Thanks to Eric Heagy, the acquisitions editor, for his help and patience in getting this book turned in. Let's do this again sometime. Also, thanks to development editor, Clint McCarty, for all the input he's given. This is a much better book than it would've been without his help and insight.

Additionally, be sure to look through the entire list of credits for this book. From senior production editor Christy Wagner who made sure we didn't sluff off during the review process, and copy editor Abby Herriman who made us sound like educated folk, on down to all the talented professionals who handled laying out the book, designing the cover, and more. Alpha has put together a top-notch team who deserve a well-earned thanks for their efforts.

Finally, I'd like to thank my co-author, Terry Ogletree, for bringing me in to help author this book with him. You've given me a very unique opportunity to jump out from behind an editor's desk, and for that I owe you a lot. Thanks for all your professionalism as an author and your encouragement and support as a friend!

—Todd Brakke

Special Thanks to the Technical Reviewer

The Complete Idiot's Guide to Creating Your Own CDs, Second Edition, was reviewed by an expert who double-checked the accuracy of what you'll learn here, to help us ensure that this book gives you everything you need to know about creating your own CDs. Special thanks are extended to Bonnie Jaye Biafore.

Trademarks

All terms mentioned in this book that are known to be or are suspected of being trademarks or service marks have been appropriately capitalized. Alpha Books and Pearson Education, Inc., cannot attest to the accuracy of this information. Use of a term in this book should not be regarded as affecting the validity of any trademark or service mark.

Part 1

So You Want to Create Some CDs, Do You? An Essential CD Technology Primer

I know that many of you reading this book are mostly interested in just getting right to the fun part—burning CDs! In this first part, however, you'll find a quick look at the technology behind CDs and recordable CDs. You'll learn about how a CD you buy at the store differs from a CD-R disc or a CD-RW disc. After you read the chapters in Part 1, you'll be better prepared to understand the remaining chapters in this book. Understanding how the laser literally burns holes in a dye layer and the precise timing involved makes for good bedtime reading.

Chapter 1

The Digital Revolution!

In This Chapter

➤ Analog is out! Digital is in!

➤ Digital methods provide superior audio and video quality

➤ Digital methods allow you to transfer information from fragile and decaying media to something more stable

➤ You can store computer files and programs, as well as audio files, on a CD using a CD burner

➤ Roxio's Easy CD Creator and NTI CD-Maker are both comprehensive packages that can do what it might take several other products to do

If you're one of those whippersnappers born in the 1980s or sometime after that, you will never know the time that some people devoted to protecting their music collection before CDs came along. Analog phonograph records were fragile platforms to hold music and—other than various forms of magnetic tape, such as cassettes or reel-to-reel—there was no alternative. Music was recorded as an audio signal that was laid down onto tape by magnetically manipulating atoms on the tape, or it was etched into the surface of the master that would eventually lead to stamped phonograph records.

Such fragile things are subject to quick deterioration. All you have to do to damage a record is walk across the floor not-too-softly, making the needle skip across the record. There's the first scratch. And it will show up in the playback. When the compact disc was finally released, its capability to store audio digitally was heralded as a great leap forward in the music industry. And, indeed, it has come to prove itself to be just that ... not just for music, but for storing data as well.

Recordable CDs and DVDs: A Revolution in Data Storage

Digitally recording music on a CD improves on the analog record in two major areas. First, the actual sound quality is much better on the CD than on the record. The digital recording method used to sample music at thousands and thousands of times per second almost guarantees that you won't miss a beat.

Between Tracks

You might wonder why CDs were developed first to store 74 minutes of audio information. The "urban folklore" answer is that it was selected because it could hold the entire performance of Beethoven's Ninth Symphony. This is, however, not true, at least as far as this author has been able to determine. The amount of audio data was more likely determined by the technological capabilities available at the time the compact disc was first introduced. As technologies are further developed, we are able to fit more and more information on a much smaller amount of disc (or disk) real estate. Thus, we now have 80-minute CDs and, even more importantly, DVDs (digital video disks) that can hold much more information than CDs—even though both are the same physical size.

The second area in which CDs can be said to excel is in their durability. Now, I'm not saying you can take your CDs and use them to play Frisbee with your dog. However, in normal everyday use, CDs are much more durable than records. Record needles continually scratch away a small amount of the surface each time a record is played. Basically, you damage your precious music collection just by listening to it! With audio tape a similar process of deterioration occurs as the magnetic surface of the tape is passed over the tape head when it is played. And don't even think about getting a magnet near a magnetic tape! You might say that with vinyl and tape, it's downhill from the very start!

The laser used in audio playback devices for CDs does no damage to speak of to the CD itself. It simply points the laser at the disc and processes the amount of light reflected back. Nothing touches the surface of the CD other than a clamping device, which holds the CD in the drive by clamping onto the very center of the disc, where there is no recording surface. The wear and tear factor for CDs, when compared to vinyl and tape, is almost nonexistent.

Digital versatile discs, or DVDs, are pretty much an evolution of the CDs. These discs, however, can hold a lot more information. Up to this point, DVD has mostly served to replace your videotape collection, but a related format, called DVD-audio, is taking aim at revolutionizing the music CD industry as well. Comparing the advantages of DVD movies over videotape isn't much different from the advantages of CDs over vinyl records. DVDs give you a much clearer picture and better sound, and, because of the large amount of space available for data, DVDs also allow for other options that videotape cannot provide, such as the capability to select from multiple languages or subtitles.

Arcane CD Speak

As you already know, CD stands for "compact disc." So what is this DVD thing? Originally, the term was considered an acronym for "digital video disc." Later, when it was realized that the DVD, like the CD, could have other uses, such as in the computer industry, many began referring to them as digital versatile discs. In the end, no one really agreed on one name, meaning that DVD doesn't really stand for anything anymore (depending on who you talk to).

Digital vs. Analog: Analog Gets Its Butt Kicked

After you get past the physical advantages of the CD itself, the digital method used for recording audio needs to be considered. Vinyl and older tape machines used analog methods to encode sound. When a copy was made, the sound quality was degraded a little each time. Lost sound quality comes about partly because of the wear and tear on the original and the condition of the recording equipment. And let's not even get into making copies of copies with analog music. Have you ever made a photocopy and then tried to copy that copy, and copy the copy after that, and so on? The same gradual demise of the image you see in a photocopy also happens to your music when making copies of copies using a cassette tape. Major bummer! Of course, it makes one wonder if, when it comes to cloning human beings (something that could, even now, be a reality), we can expect the same results?

Digital recording writes audio on the CD in a digital format that is similar to the way your computer stores its data. As a matter of fact, you can, using the right program, extract songs from your favorite CDs and store them as files on your hard drive.

Because the music is stored in a digital format, it is even possible to do a little error correction to help ensure that the sound quality is up to par.

When using CDs to store computer data, the error correction scheme used is even more powerful than that used on audio CDs. This is because there is less tolerance for a mistake in a computer program or the data it uses than there is in an audio file. You probably wouldn't even notice if one zillionth of a second of music got screwed up while burning your favorite CD. Having your CD-RW drive flub those few bits when burning a computer program or word processor file, however, could cause a complete disaster!

Duplicating and Creating Your Own CDs

As this digital revolution has progressed from the 1980s when CDs were first introduced, we've come to a sort of mini-revolution: recordable CDs. The terms generally applied to these discs are *CD-R,* which are blank CDs you can burn once (and only once), and *CD-RW,* which are discs that can be used, erased and used again many more times.

Don't Get Burned

When choosing which blank CD-R media to buy, you'll find that you can get it a lot cheaper when you buy in bulk. Most computer stores and electronics discount stores regularly put these large bulk packages on sale for really cheap prices.

Since the first edition of this book was written, I haven't paid more than 29 cents for a blank CD, and many times much less. If jewel cases are important to you, you can usually find them in bulk also, and the slim jewel cases that are now very popular are also inexpensive (although creating labels for them can be a bit more tricky).

One important thing to remember is to save your receipt. Not all burners will get along with just any generic CD-R. So watch those sales papers that come in your Sunday newspaper for CD-R bargains. Try them, and if they start producing lots of coasters, take them back for a refund!

CD-R technology, with high prices, started to take off around 1996, and prices have since dropped dramatically. More significantly, the price of the blank media—the blank CDs—has dropped a lot, too. You can expect to pay around a buck a disc if you buy them in jewel cases, or less if you find them on sale. At the expense of just a dollar, you can make a copy of your favorite CD so that you have one for the car and one for home. Or, use only the copy for listening and put the original away for safekeeping.

Because CD burners can also be used to store not just audio information, but computer data files also, their use is becoming more widespread. Using a program such as DirectCD or FileCD, which are discussed later in this book, you can write to a CD-RW disc just as if it were a hard disk on your system. The new Windows XP operating system also includes a drag-and-drop feature that allows you to treat CD burners like an ordinary disk drive. And if you happen to use Microsoft's Media Player version 7 or newer, well, that can also be used to burn CDs.

For Computer Nerds, as Well as Aspiring Musicians!

As you can see, buying a CD burner gives you the chance to get a lot more out of your computer. If you follow this book's lead and use Roxio's Easy CD Creator 5.0 Platinum, or NTI's CD-Maker Version 5, for your CD-burning pleasure, the sky is very nearly the limit. If, for example, you happen to be someone who has a large collection of LPs just sitting around the house, you're going to find it impossible not to use SoundStream to clean up the sound and make CDs from those LPs. After waiting all these years, you could even put the songs in the order in which *you* think they should be. To heck with those dopey record producers!

When you're finished copying all your LPs and making backup copies of your CDs, you can get started scanning and storing all your family photographs on CD. Want to annoy relatives and friends? Create video CDs or video postcards and send everyone the family movies of Junior dropping an ice cream cone in Grandma's hair that you so excellently taped over the last holiday.

And for those of us who are also computer nerds, there are even more reasons for using a CD burner. All your software CDs can be backed up so you don't have to re-purchase them or wait weeks to receive a new copy from the vendor when one screws up or gets played with by the cat. Important data can be stored on CDs, again at less than a buck a disc. If you are a programmer, you can distribute copies of your software using a CD burner and make professional-looking labels and jewel box booklets to go with them.

And, at the risk of sounding like a poorly produced infomercial, there's more, more, *more!*

Between Tracks

One thing I should make perfectly clear here at the beginning of this book is that, as president, I am not a crook. Oh, sorry, my mind is slipping again. What I meant to say is that *you* should not be a crook. The Internet, much less new computer technology such as recordable CDs, has made a quagmire of existing copyright laws, even though they've been updated during the past few years to try to cover new technology.

As this author understands it, you are allowed "fair use" copying privileges to make back-ups of CDs or other recordings you already own—for your own use. This means you can't, legally, make copies and sell them. Whether you can give away copies to friends is a hot topic of debate. Of course, those "people" who run the Hollywood media machine have introduced copy protection encryption on DVDs and have fought others in court who have merely tried to give us the tools to make copies of what we already own! In my opinion, what they are trying to do is judge you a criminal just because you want to make a copy. This situation did not exist when home tape recording came along. Of course, people were a lot friendlier back then!

The point here is that you shouldn't get yourself in trouble until all these legal arguments settle down and the government (at least in the United States) can tell you what you really can and cannot do—which they can't right now. So when reading this book please note that ***the authors and Alpha Books*** do in no way mean to encourage the breaking of any laws, no matter how silly or ambiguous they are.

For the record, I'm holding on to my Napster stock. From here on out, you're on your own!

When Will I Be Able to Record to DVD?

Since the first edition of this book the price for recordable DVD drives has dropped dramatically. When I first looked at prices for these new drives I found that they were priced more expensively than my computer itself! However, there has recently been a lot of movement in this market. While I wouldn't recommend you buy one yet, I can tell you three things. First, there is a drive that now sells for less than a thousand dollars. Second, there are three competing standards, so there's another reason to wait. It's like the VHS versus BetaMax competition, only it's even more complicated. You don't want to pay a lot for a DVD burner (and a lot for the media) only to find out a year later that you bought the wrong one.

For the record, however, there are several kinds of DVD burners you'll find on the market right now. Three general types are DVD-RAM (Apple and Compaq offer this as an option on some of their high-end computers), DVD-RW and DVD+RW. The latter two are newer technologies and some manufacturers offer drives that allow you to create discs that can be read by a standard DVD drive. The discs used by the DVD-RAM drive can only be read in another DVD-RAM drive. Additionally, some of the DVD-RW and DVD+RW drives allow you to burn CDs also, which is a plus. By combining CD-burning and DVD recording into a single drive, you can better justify the cost of the drive, and use up only one drive slot in your PC.

However, the prices for recordable DVD media run from $10 to $30 right now, so it's not exactly cheap. If you want to record a movie off of your cable box, you might find it cheaper to just buy the DVD instead!

Unless you have an overwhelming need to store lots of data on removable discs, I'd wait at least another year before looking at buying a recordable DVD drive. By then the marketplace will force prices to drop further (especially for the media), and as standards emerge and are adopted by other manufacturers, the odds of getting stuck with a drive that is incompatible with others that are more popular is less. To keep yourself informed about DVD-recordable technology, check out the Web site www.dvdforum.com.

What to Look for in a CD Burner

So, how do we get to this wonderful world in which we can copy most anything and store it on a CD? Well, if you haven't already, go buy yourself a CD burner. Today, you can get a very good one for under $200 (watch for the sales and rebates). Things to look for include:

➤ The drive should support CD-RW discs as well as CD-R discs that can be burned only once (nearly all recent drives do).

➤ The drive should support *packet-mode writing* so that you can use software such as DirectCD (again, nearly all recent drives do).

➤ Does the drive support Sanyo's BurnProof technology?

➤ The drive should support *multisessions*.

Quite frankly, the speed at which the drive records shouldn't concern you too much if you're working with a newer drive. At 1× speed, recording a CD will take a little longer than 74 minutes. At 2×, that drops to 37 minutes, more or less. Today's 12× and 16× drives can burn a disc in less than 8 minutes. For drives that claim to burn at 12× rates or higher, you must carefully choose which media you use for your CD-R blanks. Sometimes bigger and faster isn't better. One of the main troubleshooting tips you'll find throughout this book is this: If you're having problems, drop back to a slower speed (relative to your drive) and see if that works. However, for media that is rated at 16×, you might find just the opposite to be true! With drives rated 16× or better, as a rule of thumb, start with the highest speed your recorder supports, use media that is rated for that speed, and drop down to a slower speed if you start producing coasters.

Arcane CD Speak

If you don't know what the word **multisession** means or what **packet-mode writing** is, don't worry. Just make sure any new drive you buy supports it (pretty much all of them do). If you want to know more now, check out Chapter 11, "Dial Direct with Easy CD Creator DirectCD," for the scoop on packet writing. Or for the dish on multisession CDs, see Chapter 2, "The Machine Behind the Curtain: How CDs and Recordable CDs Work."

If you buy a new drive today, it will most likely meet the previously mentioned requirements, so don't worry about this stuff too much. Just don't go buy a bargain somewhere like a flea market and expect it to perform up to the standards set by today's products. Besides, for the price, you might as well get a good one. A poorly made drive will ruin so many discs trying to record properly that you'll end up spending more money on blank CDs than you did on the drive itself!

If you got your CD burner with a new computer, it should be installed and set up already. If you have just purchased—or are about to purchase—a new drive, you need to follow the drive's instructions to install it properly. If you're just terrified of popping open that computer case of yours, call that computer nerd friend on your speed dial or see if the place you bought your drive can install it for you (for a price).

Feeling the Need for Speed (the X-Factor)

While the speed at which a CD burner can write a CD is the speed that most manufacturers advertise, you need to keep in mind several other speed factors. For example, when you want to extract tracks from CDs to store them on disk, you need to be aware of whether or not your CD-ROM drive supports digital audio extraction (DAE), and at what speed it can rip the track from the drive. So, you need to check the speed at which you can extract digital audio data for both your ordinary CD-ROM drive (which probably came installed in your PC if you bought one in the last few years), as well as the speed at which your CD burner drive can perform this function. Easy CD Creator, which is one of the applications you'll learn to use in this book, performs a test on your CD-ROM drive the first time it is used. This test tells you if the CD-ROM drive supports DAE, and judges the speed at which it can rip the track from a CD.

Recording speeds have been increasing dramatically this past year. While 16× seems to be the current standard, which can burn a CD in just about 4 minutes, you can expect that the technology will advance and we'll see faster CD burners. However, as discussed earlier, make sure the media you buy matches the speed at which you want to record!

BurnProof Technology (Having Your Cake and Eating It, Too!)

A new technology developed by Sanyo is called BurnProof. If your drive supports BurnProof technology, then you should probably not worry too much about the major contributor to creating coasters in the past—buffer underruns. BurnProof itself is an acronym and comes from "Buffer Under RuN-Proof." Traditionally, a burning process can't stop in the middle of a track if the burner runs out of data (the buffer is empty), and then pick up again when data does become available. Because of this, on lower-powered PCs (say, one with a Pentium II CPU of 350MHz or less), one way to avoid creating coasters is to close all other programs on the PC while the CD burner software is doing its job. However, drives that do support this new BurnProof technology, such as drives from Sanyo (obviously!), Plextor, and several others, are virtually immune to this CD-burning disaster.

Basically, BurnProof allows the software to suspend recording when the buffer starts to drop to a low value. The recorder (which must support this technology) is then put into a suspend mode. When the buffer is again filled, the software can then use a seek feature to reposition the laser close to the spot where it stopped recording, so it can continue.

Between Tracks

Easy CD Creator 5 also features built-in support for BurnProof technology for those who own drives that use it.

However, another thing to keep in mind about BurnProof technology is that there will still be a small gap on the CD-R where recording stopped and was restarted. The Orange Book Specification (see Appendix C, "The Colorful Books of CD Standards") states that there can be a gap of no longer than 100 milliseconds between data writes on the CD-R. BurnProof technology can leave a gap of about 40 to 45 milliseconds, so this should be no problem. Note that this is not a perfect solution to buffer underruns. When the CD is played back, error correction built into the CD-ROM drive comes into play to correct for this small gap in the recorded track. Yet, it seems like BurnProof technology will be a new feature that most manufacturers will incorporate since it eliminates one of the major problems associated with recording CDs.

Psst! Hey, Mr., You Got Any Cache?

When you hear about the buffer underrun problem these days, first you think about getting a new drive with BurnProof technology, but if that's not an option, you should think of cache memory. Just as modern CPUs have on-chip cache memory, so do disk drives. When looking at a CD burner, be sure to check the documentation to determine the size of the on-drive cache memory. You should expect to see at least 2MB, with some drives containing as much as 8MB. As explained in the previous section, if your drive supports BurnProof technology—and if your recording software also supports this feature—then you might think that the cache memory on your CD burner is no longer something to worry about. However, you should also consider that BurnProof does indeed leave small gaps when it is employed, and having a larger drive cache can help keep your drive buffer from ever running out of data. It's always best to try to produce the best CD you can, so, if you are comparing CD-recordable drives, check to see what the documentation says about the drive's cache memory. More is always better!

Cross Reference

For broader information on the features contained in Easy CD Creator and NTI CD-Maker 2000, including how to get these applications installed, see Appendixes A, "Installing Roxio Easy CD Creator," and B, "Installing NTI CD-Maker."

Software Applications Used in This Book

Every CD burner I've ever purchased came with one version or another of Roxio's Easy CD Creator. Because it's the most common one out there, that's one of the applications that you'll learn how to use in this book. However, the version of this software most commonly found in CD-RW drive packages is usually not the most up-to-date version of Easy CD Creator software (and if it is, it usually is missing the extra features of the full-blown Easy CD Creator 5 Platinum edition).

Another popular product we cover in this book is NTI's CD-Maker 2000. CD-Maker 2000 Professional Edition boasts a similar suite of applications and functions as Easy CD Creator. This includes the ability to copy discs, create audio or data CDs, create video CDs, and much more. Both of these products sell for about the same price and can be found at larger software retailers.

In this book, we use Easy CD Creator Version 5 Platinum and NTI CD-Maker Version 5. If you have an older version of Easy CD Creator (version 4 or earlier), note that most of the examples in this book will work for basic functions. However, if you want to use advanced features, such as Easy CD Creator's SoundStream (formerly Spin Doctor) to accomplish more specialized tasks, like recording from those old vinyl records you keep in your basement, you'll need to purchase the most recent version.

Other Software Choices

A lot of other software applications are out there that can be used to acquire and organize your music files, or to burn CDs, or both. As discussed earlier, we chose Roxio's and NTI's software for this book because they're both comprehensive in their capabilities, very widely available (often coming in some form with new CD-RW drives), and easy to use. When learning something new it's always best to start with what you know, and then go on to more complex programs! While not quite as common as Easy CD Creator, we chose NTI's CD-Maker 2000 because it's an excellent complement to Easy CD Creator and, as a consumer, it's best to see the variations between different products. This gives more information when making a choice as to which product you want to buy, and as the old Saturday morning cartoons used to tell us, "Knowledge Is Power!"

That doesn't mean, however, that there might not be a better package for you. Nero, for example, is an excellent CD-burning package in terms of offering lots of options and control over how you burn CDs. It's also quite difficult to use for those new to the CD-burning process (which is why it's not covered here). The best way to find out which is the best product for you is to look for information about new software on the Internet after you've seen the package in the store. You can go to a company's Web site and find technical information that might be of some help in making a purchasing decision. For example, what kind of audio or video file formats does the software support? You can also stay tuned to various products by subscribing to several e-mail mailing lists, described in Chapter 20, "I Ain't Got No CDs, but You Should See All My New Coasters: Troubleshooting CD Recording."

Where Do You Go from Here?

In the next chapter, we're going to take a very quick look at how CDs work. That is, how ordinary CDs you buy in the store are manufactured, and how they differ from the recordable CDs you buy and record using a CD burner. Heck, we'll even talk about how that CD recorder of yours burns that darn CD!

The obvious question then becomes, if the process works, why worry about how? Well, as easy as it should be, burning a CD can be a frustrating process if and when you run into problems. If you understand how a recordable CD works, you will be better empowered to troubleshoot any problems that do come up. After all, not all recorders or playback devices work the same. Although they're all round and shiny on one side, minor differences do exist in the recordable CDs you buy. There are also

Between Tracks

You can also find a lot of tips for troubleshooting common problems in Chapter 20.

factors, such as the recording speed and the way you decide to write to the CD, that need to be considered.

Or if you're like me and just want to get right to it, just skip the next chapter and go have some fun in Chapter 3, "Easy Copying with Easy CD Creator," where you can start using your CD Recorder to copy CDs! You can always come back to the "boring" Chapter 2 later if you find yourself scratching your head trying to figure out what went wrong!

Make sure, of course, that the first CDs you back up are the ones that come with your CD software, and the CD that comes with this book!

The Least You Need to Know

➤ Yes, you really can make copies of those darned expensive audio CDs you've been buying—for backup purposes, of course.

➤ Yes, you can become your own DJ and mix and match CD and audio files on your hard drive to create your own CDs.

➤ Yes, you can preserve your family memories, both photos and videos (and of course, sound), on CDs to pass on to future generations—in a digital format!

➤ Yes, this book uses Roxio's Easy CD Creator 5.0 Platinum and NTI's CD-Maker 2000 Professional. These were chosen because they have lots and lots of features, are widely available, often coming in demo versions with new CD-RW drives, and are user-friendly.

➤ Yes, there are other software packages that might be better suited for you. Read this book and find out!

➤ Windows XP and Windows Media Player both support limited CD-burning functions, but you may find that you're better off using another software package if you plan to really get into CD recording!

Chapter 2

The Machine Behind the Curtain: How CDs and Recordable CDs Work

In This Chapter

➤ Commercial CDs are similar to phonographic records in many ways

➤ The tracks on a CD are different from the ones on a computer hard disk

➤ Understanding why CDs shouldn't cost so much!

➤ Using multiple sessions to record a CD

➤ Putting audio and data onto a recordable CD

In this chapter, we take a quick look at how ordinary CDs are made and how they differ from recordable CDs that you can burn using your home computer. When you buy music CDs in retail stores, the kind of CD you get is not the same as the kind of CD that you record to. They work in a similar manner, which is why most CD readers can read most of the CDs you will write. However, some of them won't work. Some will work in one drive, but not another, and some will not work at all. It can be a big confusing mess that this chapter, and this book in general, will make much clearer.

Understanding how a regular compact disc is made, and how that compares to recordable discs, can help you figure out whether you are doing something wrong or if your CD reader is just the type that won't work with the disc you just created.

In addition, there isn't just one kind of compact disc. The typical audio CD you purchase at the mall is usually referred to as a *CD*, or more properly, *CD-DA*. The *DA* stands for digital audio. Those last two letters must now be tacked on much more often than in previous years because of all the other kinds of compact discs that are available, each of which is intended for a particular kind of use. For example, a CD-ROM is a compact disc that is used to store computer data and cannot be written to. Other formats also are available—for audio, video, photos, and combinations of all these kinds of data.

Snakes, Snails, and Puppy Dog Tails; What Are CDs Made Of?

CDs and CD-ROM discs have something in common: They are manufactured products, much like the now old-fashioned phonograph record. As a matter of fact, although phonographic records use analog recording methods and CDs (and CD-ROMs) use digital recording methods, they have a whole lot in common.

For example, one important aspect that phonographic records and CDs share is the way the actual tracks of data are laid out on the media. This is in stark contrast to how data is laid out in the more common magnetic components of your PC, like a floppy or hard disk drive. In a typical magnetic hard disk (or floppy disk, for that matter), the data is laid out in a set of concentric rings. That is, circles within circles, as you can see in Figure 2.1.

Figure 2.1

Ordinary computer hard disks store data on separate tracks that are not connected. The closer to the middle of the disk, the shorter the track is.

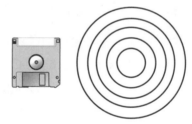

Each of these circular tracks is divided into sectors, which means the closer you get to the outside of the hard disk, the more sectors of data you can place on a track because a greater surface area exists to hold more sectors.

CDs do not use this method. Instead, similar to a phonographic record, a continuous spiral track is used, as shown in Figure 2.2.

Figure 2.2

CDs, like phonographic records, use one long, continuous, spiral track to record data, unlike a computer's hard disk.

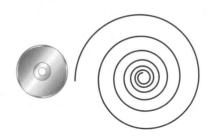

However, even though both use this spiral method for tracking, phonographic records are played by starting at the outer portion of the spiral and then following the spiral inward to the center of the record. *CDs are played in just the opposite manner,* by starting where the spiral begins in the center of the CD and continuing to the outermost portion of the disc.

For those who are interested in the technical details, along this spiral track is a series of *pits* and *lands*. Each pit is about 0.6 micrometers wide, and the distance between each track on the disc is about 1.6 micrometers. So basically, they're very small. But so what, right? What are they? Well, a land is just a continuous smooth section between pits that reflects the CD player's laser back to a detector. These changes in reflections are the equivalent of transitions between bits of data (from "1" to "0" or vice versa).

If you were to take the spiral track and stretch it out into one long line, it would go on for about three miles. Now that's a lot of room to record data! In most cases, however, the entire disc is not used. If the CD holds the maximum amount of data possible, it will be recorded up to about three millimeters from the outer edge of the disc.

Between Tracks

The last few millimeters at the edge of the CD are generally not used. In addition, many CD manufacturers deliberately do not use the entire 74 (or 80) minutes that are available on a compact disc. By leaving a few minutes unused, a small area exists at the outer edge of the disc that contains no audio data. This is done for two reasons. First, this makes it easier to control the quality of the CD. Second, it gives the end user a little leeway when handling the CD. This means that for some CDs, you don't have to worry too much about getting fingerprints or very small scratches on them, so long as these occur at the very outer portion of the CDs, which is where you are most likely to handle them.

Both phonograph records and compact discs are created from masters and then made into mass-produced copies by a stamping or molding method. However, before we go into describing the process by which a CD is manufactured, let's first look at what the darn thing is actually made of and how data (including music) is stored digitally on the disc.

It's All About Pits and Lands?

Computers, no matter how complex they appear to be, are really just sophisticated electronic adding machines. While I sit here and type this chapter on my computer, the actual background processes going on inside the computer involve moving around a bunch of 0s and 1s. At first glance, there doesn't seem to be much you can do when using just 0s and 1s, does there? The truth, however, is that you can digitize music and create a CD using 0s and 1s. You can compute the trajectory and flight path to send a rocket to the moon and back. In fact, 0s and 1s, or the binary numerical system, can actually be used to do a whole lot of things.

So to put music—or data, or whatever—on a CD or CD-ROM, a method of recording 0s and 1s and reading them back again must exist. When your favorite CD is playing, what is really going on behind the scenes is that a laser beam (very tightly focused) is pointed at the CD and, depending on the amount of light that is reflected back, 0s and 1s are detected.

When the CD is played, a laser is directed from the bottom of the CD—the opposite side from the label—to the reflective surface that is encased in a protective plastic layer. The reflective coating that lies beneath the surface of the disc reflects light back to the laser pickup device differently, depending on whether the light strikes a pit or a land. The reflective layer can be made of gold, silver, or another reflective material, such as aluminum.

The laser simply follows this spiral of data and passes on to other electronic components of the data it gathers from the light reflected. Because the laser beam must first pass through the protective plastic coating on the bottom of the CD, you might think that fingerprints, dust, and other contaminants would cause the disc to be unreadable. In the extreme case, this is true. However, because the laser beam is focused to a point past the surface of the CD to the reflective layer (about a millimeter past the bottom surface of the CD), it usually doesn't detect these minor imperfections—major defects, yes, but not the minor ones. To understand how this works, try this the next time it rains. Look out the window. If it's a light rain, you don't see it, or at least you don't see it very clearly. If you take a minute to focus your eyes past the window to try to see the rain, you'll find you don't see the window as well as you did before, if at all.

Between Tracks

With a CD, you can get away with a lot more than you can with a phonograph record! Because the *audio* CD employs an error-correction and detection-coding scheme, it also can recover more easily from minor defects or errors. With a phonograph record, one scratch becomes part of the music!

How Are the 0s and 1s Encoded on the Disc?

Although it might seem that the most logical way to record 0s and 1s on a CD is to have a pit represent a 1 and a land represent 0, that is not the case. As a matter of fact, even magnetic media, such as your computer's hard drive, doesn't use such a simple method. Instead, 0s and 1s are encoded by detecting the *change* from a pit to a land, and vice versa. As long as the surface of the CD remains constant, the reader records a stream of 0s; however, when the CD reader detects a change from a pit to a land, it interprets this as a 1 bit. The same is true when a change is detected from a land to a pit. It doesn't matter which direction the state change takes. It just matters that a change occurs at all. Figure 2.3 shows this a little more clearly.

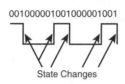

State Changes

Figure 2.3

The encoding scheme encodes 1s as a state of transition, no matter which direction.

As you can see from Figure 2.3, every time the laser detects a change from one to the other (pit/land), it assumes that a binary bit with a value of 1 has been detected. Everything else is interpreted as a 0 bit. It should become quickly obvious that, for this scheme to work, *the laser must read the spiral track at a constant speed*—timing is very important when reading CDs. If a constant speed is not maintained, the CD reader has no way to interpret how many 0 bits existed between state changes.

Now, as any phonograph audiophile knows, on a phonographic record, the closer to the center of the record that the stylus gets, the faster it travels in the groove of the record. Or, more precisely, the more surface area of the record passes beneath the needle during a particular amount of time. If this *were* the case with a compact disc, this state change from pit to land would not work. No method would exist to detect the number of 0s if the area being covered by the laser was continuously becoming slower as the CD was read from the center to the edge. To remedy the situation, the CD reader actually increases the rotation speed as it approaches the outer edge of the disc. Thus, a constant speed is always being maintained so the state changes that the laser experiences can be accurate.

Mastering the Mastering Process

To mass-produce CDs, like the ones you buy in music stores, you first must create a *master,* which contains the data image you want to *impress* onto a number of blanks. Several methods are available for producing a master and its family of discs, which are eventually used to mold the conventional CD.

One of the most frequently used processes starts with a glass disc that has been specially treated and examined (using a laser) to ensure that no imperfections exist which might cause problems with recording. Most of this mastering process is done in a *clean room,* so that particles of dust cannot interfere with the microscopic pits that get burned into the disc.

After the glass master has passed all tests, it can be prepared for recording. It is first coated with an adhesive material and then a photoresist material. The photoresist coating is the part of the master will be subjected to a burning laser that is much more powerful than the type used in the CD-RW recorders we have in our PCs. The laser etches away portions of the photoresist material to create the pits and lands of the CD. To finish the process, the glass master is cured in a special oven. It can then either be used immediately or stored for a few weeks.

After the glass master has been developed, the photoresist side of the glass is covered with a metal to further strengthen it and prepare it for the next step in the process. In many cases, silver is used for the master disc.

The master disc is then put through a plating process that, in most cases, plates the recorded surface with nickel. After this has successfully been done, *the nickel surface is separated from the glass disc* and the metal portion is called a *father*. This father is then subjected to an arcane process called electroplating, the results of which are separated from it. This can be done several times, creating a host of *mothers*. And then it's done yet again to create *sons,* which are the actual media used to produce the CDs you purchase at the store.

Note that because the actual CD you buy is created by a simple injection molding technique, the actual cost of the CD is minimal. I can remember when CDs were first produced. It was promised that the "high cost" would eventually come down as more were sold. That doesn't seem to be the case. As it is, manufacturing the recordable CD blanks probably costs more than mass-producing the commercial CD! Yet you can buy a set of blank CD-R discs for under a buck per disc, while a new music CD can cost you upward of $17 (as expensive today as they were in the 1980s)!

Drawing the Property Lines: How Information Is Arranged on a CD

The compact disc is not simply a continuous stream of bits that contain audio or data. Instead, certain areas are set aside for such things as storing a table of contents. Other areas are used for certain control aspects of the disc as it is played. In this discussion, we are talking about only simple audio CDs. More complicated formats use these same techniques, but variances are made depending on the use of the CD and the kind of data stored.

Who Leads in This Dance: Lead-In and Lead-Out Areas

For most ordinary audio compact discs, a lead-in and a lead-out area exist. These special areas on the disc are usually situated on the innermost and outermost areas of the disc, respectively. The *lead-in* area is made up of all 0s and is used to indicate the start of music data. Directly after the lead-in area, there is a field called a start flag, which takes up two or three seconds of time before the actual audio tracks begin.

You can probably guess by now that the *lead-out* area comes after the last audio track. However, directly before the lead-out area there is another start flag of two or three seconds. This flag is used to indicate to the player that the lead-out section is about to follow.

You Mean CDs Have a Table of Contents?

The table of contents on the CD works much like a table of contents in a book. This area contains information that can be used to locate other tracks on the CD. For example, the table of contents contains such things as:

➤ The number of audio tracks on the CD (up to 99 total tracks).

➤ The starting time of each track. This timing information is used to locate specific tracks on the disc. This is what makes it possible for you to just push the skip button on a CD player to get past a song you don't want to hear.

➤ The specific track number of a selection (usually one song) on a CD.

The table of contents is one of the first things a CD player reads when you insert the disc. This is why most modern players can show you the number of tracks, using an LED display, before the CD has actually been played. You also can use this information on most modern CD players to program a sequence in which the tracks will be played—or repeated, if you have a track you particularly like.

Recordable CDs Are a Burning Issue!

Now that we've spent most of this chapter telling you how CDs, in general, are manufactured and how they work, it's time to talk about a burning issue—recordable CDs, or CD-R and CD-RW discs. Because most of us can't afford to spend millions creating the clean-room environment necessary to create CD masters the hard way, we instead use CD recordable technology to make our own CDs at home, using an inexpensive laser burner.

If you'll remember back at the start of the process, the master CD is a glass disc coated with a material that is later subjected to the laser treatment. This burns through the material to create pits in the surface, which is later coated with a metallic layer and used to create molds.

CD recordable technology isn't nearly so complicated. It's a rather dyed-in-the-wool simple process.

What Kinds of Different Media Are There?

You'll find that there are many kinds of CD-R and CD-RW discs available on the market today. The most common are the same size as a commercial CD. Yet, you'll also find "business card" CD-R discs as well as mini-discs that are much smaller and meant for playing in portable players. However, for all practical purposes, the main two differences between discs, other than size and capacity, are whether the CD blank disc can be recorded once, or if it can be erased and used again.

So How Are CD-R and CD-RW Discs Different?

Instead of using a powerful laser to blast away at a hard surface, as is done when making a master CD, the laser in your CD recorder drive has a much easier task. It needs only to poke holes in a very thin layer of dye that makes up part of the CD-R disc. Underneath this layer of dye is the reflective metal layer of the blank disc. When the laser needs to create a pit, it burns a small hole in the dye layer. Then, when the result is played back, the light that bounces off the dye layer—or the reflective layer underneath—determines the pits and lands that make up the information stored on the disc. The laser mechanism in your PC is also less complicated in its mechanics. The blank CD you record, unlike a manufactured CD, has grooves impressed into the plastic that make it easier for the laser to track the spiral track, so to speak. There is no need for complicated circuitry to calculate coordinates or complicated mechanics to position the laser.

The Size Does Matter: How Much Can a Recordable CD Store?

A rather "new" recordable disc has been available for about two years now that claims to enable you to store up to 80 minutes on a recordable CD. These 80-minute discs, however, suffer from significant limitations that affect whether you can actually use them. Some hardware (and burning software) is programmed to stop at 74 minutes. *If this is the case with your hardware or software, these CDs won't work for you when you try to burn them.*

Because some publishers are using 80-minute discs, you might find that, when running a CD copier program to copy a CD, you get a prompt telling you the 74-minute blank you've inserted for copying can't hold the all the data the disc you want to copy contains. In this type of situation, you have no choice but to either buy the 80-minute CD blanks or use your CD burner software to select a number of tracks from the original that will fit on a 74-minute CD without exceeding the time limit.

Either way, it always pays to keep up with the technology. If you are going to use 80-minute blanks, be sure your CD recorder hardware will work with them. You also might want to test your CD player(s) to ensure that it can also read these discs.

Do All Those Different Colors Make a Difference?

Although various dyes are used and manufacturers might use different metals for the reflective surface, that's the only thing about a CD-R that differs from a manufactured CD.

Between Tracks

For those who care to know, several kinds of chemicals are used for the dye layer on recordable CDs. The most commonly used are cyanine and phthalocyanine, but I'm sure that more are already in use that we don't know about. When you look at the bottom of the CD-R blank, if it's a greenish color, then most likely there's a gold metallic layer underneath. If it is more of a bluish color, silver is probably being used instead for the metallic reflective layer. This isn't a guarantee, but I just mention it to let you know different kinds of recordable CD blanks exist.

Another kind of recordable CD is also available. It's called *CD-RW,* which, as you can guess, stands for "CD-rewritable." These discs are more expensive than ordinary CD-R blank discs, but they can be erased and reused. This can be done because, unlike CD-R discs that use a layer of dye to burn-in a recording, CD-RW discs use a layer of metal alloy. Instead of burning a hole through this layer, the laser changes the state of the metal from amorphous to crystalline (each of which reflects the laser light differently). When read back by the laser, the changes made to this layer cause the light reflected back to the detector to change, once again creating the illusion of the pits and lands that a manufactured CD uses.

A caveat of CD-RW discs is that they will most likely not be playable in other, older CD-ROM drives and most audio CD players. However, because their use is generally to back up data that frequently changes, this should generally not be a problem.

Don't Overburn!

Some CD burner software applications allow you to *overburn* a CD. That is, they let you record a few minutes of additional audio or a few extra megabytes of data. This can be a risky process, however. Recently there have been reports in Internet

Between Tracks

Although most recordable drives on the market today are CD-RW—capable of reading both CD-R and CD-RW discs—that doesn't mean your drive will. If you have an older drive, make sure that it is not just a CD-R drive that can only write—one time—to a blank CD-R disc. These drives won't recognize a CD-RW disc no matter how much you beg, plead, or bribe.

newsgroups that some CD-RW drives can actually be damaged if you try to use them for overburning. So while your software application may allow this feature, use it at your own risk! If you want to record 80 minutes, buy 80-minute CD-R discs! Don't try to put a few extra minutes on a 74-minute CD-R disc!

Which Is the Best CD-R Disc to Use?

There is an easy answer to that question: Use the discs that work best in your recorder! Because several combinations of dyes and metallic reflecting materials are used, what works well in one recorder or player might not work well in another. Furthermore, because several brands exist on the market—even though there is only a handful of manufacturers—you can not even be sure many times that when you continue to buy the same brand, you're getting the same disc. The brand-name distributor might be buying batches of discs from other manufacturers based on whoever has the lowest price at the moment!

Now that makes for a confusing situation! So buy first in small quantities, find a brand that works, and stick with it until it doesn't! Also, be sure you use a recording speed for which the media is rated. You'll usually see them rated for various speeds, such as 1×, 2×, 4×, and now up to 16×. If higher speeds don't produce good results, try the standard 1×. If that fails then try a different brand of discs. Also, try to buy media that is rated at the speed of your CD burner. If you have an old burner that records at 1× to 4×, you may or may not get good results using media rated at 16×. Instead, it's time to upgrade that old CD burner, since prices have never been lower!

The Murky Waters of Multisession CDs

As you've probably already found out (or soon will), burning CDs isn't always a straightforward process. Many times, you might want to add more data to a CD you've already burned to once (but that still has space for more). Or, you might want to put music and data on the same disc. This is done by writing multiple sessions to a CD. A *multisession* CD is one that groups tracks together into *sessions*. Each session has its own table of contents and is essentially a mini-CD on a CD.

Sessions are basically just collections of tracks written in a single pass of the laser. A CD can be burned using several methods. One of them is the *track-at-once* (*TAO*) method, which allows you to write one track at a time, pausing in between. Note, however, using that method requires a two-second gap between each track for synchronization purposes. TAO offers more flexibility when you are putting together an audio CD because you can record a few songs and then add a few more later, closing the CD when you are ready to play it. However, if you don't want those mandatory two-second gaps, you need another method for recording the CD, such as session-at-once (SAO) or disc-at-once (DAO).

The *session-at-once* (*SAO*) method, which enables you to add groups of tracks that can, on the appropriate player, be played before the CD is closed. After you've decided not to add more sessions (or you just run out of space), you can close the CD so that it plays in a wider variety of players. The SAO method avoids the mandatory two-second gap between each track. This does not, however, remove any silence that might be inherent in the actual start or finish of the track itself.

Between Tracks

One thing you should note when using multiple sessions on a CD is that there is an over-head cost to bear. Each session is like its own CD to the reader and has a lead-in and a run-out track. This overhead is about 20MB for the first track and 13MB for the remaining sessions you add. For an audio CD, this translates into losing about nine minutes worth of space for each session. For even an 80-minute CD, that's a lot of time to lose!

Finally there's the disc-at-once (DAO) method, which writes the entire disc in one session and closes it, so it can be read in a wider variety of CD-ROM drives and, for music CDs, most home CD audio players. Like SAO, this method does not enforce a mandatory two-second gap between tracks.

How Do Sessions Work?

Because each session is kind of its own disc, when inserting a multisession data CD-R in a CD-ROM drive, the drive must pick a session to read first. Most drives first read the last session written to the disc, the idea being that if you use the same CD-R disc to back up the same data several times, the last session contains the most up-to-date information. In this case, reading the last session first makes the most sense. However, you might be recording some tracks now and some later and need access to all sessions on the disc.

Fortunately, you can tell your CD-ROM drive which session you want to read (how depends on your software). Of course, this won't overcome the fact that you won't be able to play all sessions on

Don't Get Burned

Although you can have multiple audio sessions on a CD-R, most home/car stereo CD players see only the first session on the disc and ignore the rest.

an ordinary audio player. But, if you use the CD-R to back up important data, or if you use it for music and play it back on your computer, using multiple sessions can be very helpful.

Where Can You Use Multisession CDs?

Where you can play or use a multisession CD depends on the player and the composition of the CD. Older players can usually read only one session and no others. Most newer CD-ROM drives will look at the last session first (this can be overcome depending on which software you use).

If you record audio in the first session on a multisession CD, your ordinary CD player will probably play this first session. Don't expect it to play any more than that, though. If you have audio on a second or third session, for example, you can easily play any session's audio tracks back using your computer.

There are variations on multisession CDs, though. It is possible to use programs in one session to control the playback of audio or other multimedia content located in another session. The two methods for doing this are called writing CD-extra CDs or writing mixed-mode CDs and are covered in the next chapter.

Best of Both Worlds: CDs with Data and Audio

Today, the term *multimedia,* when it comes to computers, generally means a presentation that includes both audio and video, under the control of computer programs. Some are interactive and some are not. To burn a multimedia presentation onto a CD—in other words, using audio and data—usually requires burning a CD with multiple sessions. The two standard methods for doing so are called CD-extra and mixed-mode.

CD-Extra CDs

A CD-extra disc has two sessions—one to hold data and one to hold audio files. Because the first session holds the CD-DA (digital audio) tracks, you can play this kind of CD in your ordinary CD audio player to listen to just the music. The second session is written using the CD-ROM/XA data CD format. To use the programs or other data stored in the second session, you need a computer with a CD-ROM drive that supports multisessions. Don't worry about it, though, because most new drives do.

Because this is a multisession CD, the last session is activated and used by the CD-ROM drive first. Programs and data found in this session can be used with the audio session to present a multimedia presentation to the viewer. Although you won't see the packaging saying so, several CDs in your local CD shop were created using the CD-extra method. Do you have any music CDs that also include "CD-ROM" features? Odds are those are done using CD-extra.

Mixed-Mode CDs

Unlike CD-extra, a mixed-mode CD is not a multi-session CD. Instead, the audio and data are put into one single session. The first track contains the data. It also instructs your CD-ROM drive on how to read the audio (CD-DA) tracks that come next. This first track can be in either the CD-ROM format or CD-ROM/XA.

The important thing to remember about recording mixed-mode versus CD-extra discs is that one method uses a single session on the CD, whereas the other method uses two sessions. Of these types of CDs, the CD-extra is generally more popular because of its capability to be used in any ordinary CD player without incident. On the other hand, if there's no chance that you're going to put the disc in a standard CD player, then you might prefer a mixed-mode CD that allows you access to all data on the disc without having to switch between multiple sessions.

Don't Get Burned

One caveat of a mixed-mode CD is that if you put it in an older audio player (or a cheaper new one), it might attempt to play the first track with disastrous results! Like what, you ask? How about frying your speakers with a shrill siren call that could wake up Elvis? In other words, don't try this at home.

The Least You Need to Know

➤ CDs manufactured using a simple molding process are highly overpriced.

➤ Even though a CD is much more tolerant of fingerprints and scratches than a phonographic record, you should still treat them carefully. Error correction and detection codes can only do so much to preserve the original data. CD-ROMs employ additional methods to ensure that the data can be read and delivered to the program with no errors.

➤ Don't use overburning if your software supports it. It can damage not just the blank CD you're trying to record, but your CD burner also!

➤ CD-R and CD-RW discs can be recorded in multiple sessions.

➤ The techniques used for recording a CD are track-at-once, session-at-once, and disc-at-once. Each method has its own strengths and drawbacks.

➤ You can burn two types of multimedia CDs that contain both audio and data. The preferred method to use is CD-extra because ordinary audio CD players can play these kinds of CDs. With mixed-mode CDs, most old and some newer audio CD players can't read the discs at all.

Part 2

Quick and Painless: Duplicating CDs

The fun begins in Part 2. What follows are chapters that tell you how to easily duplicate both audio and data CDs so you'll never have to worry about losing or damaging a CD again. Keep a copy in your car and leave the original at home! Or make copies of new CDs and play the copies at home so you always have the original stored away just in case. The same is true for data CDs—it's much easier to have a copy on hand if an application CD goes bad. The chapters in this part will guide you through these processes.

Chapter 3

Easy Copying with Easy CD Creator

In This Chapter

➤ What you can and cannot copy with Easy CD Creator's CD Copier

➤ Copying disc to disc!

➤ Using only your CD-RW drive for copying CDs

➤ Advanced options that can help fine-tune the copying process

One of the simplest Easy CD Creator Platinum programs to use is also the one most record executives would rather you didn't have: CD Copier.

The Spin Doctor and Easy CD Creator programs make it an easy task to select audio tracks or data files, create a CD layout, and then use the layout to burn a CD using your CD-RW drive.

If all you want to do is make a straight copy of a CD, though, you don't have to go through all that trouble. You don't have to create a CD layout, and you don't have to worry about editing tracks or using special effects such as fade in, fade out, or cross-fade. Indeed, making a copy is much simpler. To sum it up in just a few words, launch Easy CD Copier, insert the CD you want to copy and the blank recordable disc into the correct drives, and click OK—then you're on your way.

So, why devote a chapter to such a simple process? Well, there are a few twists to this process, and there are some tips I will show you that can make the job easier. However, it really is a simple matter to make a copy of almost any CD, unless it has some sort of copy-protection scheme encoded into the data, or unless your particular CD-RW drive has some problems with the CD-R blank media you have purchased.

What Kinds of CDs Can You Copy?

In Chapter 2, "The Machine Behind the Curtain: How CDs and Recordable CDs Work," we discussed the various types of CDs you can create using programs like CD-Maker 2000 and Easy CD Creator. This included not only your garden-variety audio and data CDs, but also some of the more "exotic" varieties like mixed-mode and CD-extra CDs. Generally speaking, regardless of the type of CD you have, CD Copier can duplicate it for you. That does not mean, however, that CD Copier can duplicate any CD you throw at it.

Confused? Well, if you've read a newspaper or watched a news program in the past 10 years you're probably hip to the fact that digital content publishers are a bit touchy about consumers making copies of their products. They're convinced they've lost millions, perhaps billions, of dollars to piracy of content they own. In truth, they've got a right to be worried. However, it's also difficult to feel much pity for major record publishers and executives from operating system makers when they're yelling their complaints out over a high-tech cell phone from some beach resort on the island of Kauai.

Nevertheless, laws tend to favor those with the bucks (lose in court, buy a congressman) so the unquestionably illegal works of the few make impossible the right to fair use for the many who just want to make backup copies of expensive programs. I'm speaking of course of copy-protection schemes. Already seen in abundance in the PC game industry, using advanced encryption schemes, digital content publishers are using every method they can think of to prevent programs like CD Copier from, well, copying CDs (and don't kid yourself, eventually this will become common practice in the music CD industry, too). Unfortunately, other than by reputation, there's no way to tell if a CD is copy-protected until you actually try to duplicate it.

Don't Get Burned

Unless you're already reading this book from your jail cell, you might want to check the "terms and conditions" or other such text that comes with any CD you buy. Although the copyright laws do allow "fair use" copying for audio CDs, the licensing terms for game or software application CDs might prohibit you from doing so. I'd hate to tell you how to create CD copies and then have you send me e-mail from the pokey. Whether you agree or not, the bottom line is that the law is the law, so you'd better not break it.

Between Tracks

Some copy-protection schemes involve simply screwing up the table of contents on a CD. If the original program or application knows that the table of contents isn't necessarily correct, but knows how to read it, the original CD works just fine. When copying the CD, however, this kind of thing can make the copy unusable.

For audio CDs, you can try to get around this scenario. Try extracting each audio track to a separate WAV file on your hard disk and then use Easy CD Creator to re-create the CD. Using Easy CD Creator instead of CD Copier enables the program to create its own table of contents and other formatting information on the blank CD, rather than copying the original's table of contents.

You will know that you have a CD that cannot easily be copied when one of the following things occurs. First, you make a copy, and the copy process appears to succeed. However, when you try to use the copied CD, it just doesn't work. This type of problem is particularly frustrating for those of us with slower CD-RW drives (2× or less) because the process usually takes more than an hour. Second, you try to make a copy of a CD and find that CD Copier is incapable of reading the CD, or perhaps just one track on the CD.

A third kind of problem you might run into when trying to copy a CD has nothing to do with copy-protection schemes. Some commercial CDs have also been recorded past the 74-minute limit that is the standard. If CD Copier detects that the disc you wish to backup does not, at least, match the source's capacity, it will eject the disc and tell you to insert a blank disc with a higher capacity.

To solve this problem, you can find 80-minute CD-R blanks at most computer stores. Whether or not they will work in your CD burner depends on your drive, as well as the software you are using. Roxio's CD Copier that is included with the 5.0 Platinum version will gladly make copies to 80-minute blanks. However, just because CD Copier will work past the 74-minute limit, *that doesn't mean your CD recorder will!* This is a hardware and software issue!

Between Tracks

Why would a drive not support an 80-minute disc? Some CD recorder vendors simply assumed that 74 minutes was always going to be the maximum amount of time on a CD and built their drives to operate in that manner.

33

Finally, there is one other speed bump on the road to copying a CD. As covered in Chapter 11, "Dial Direct with Easy CD Creator DirectCD," DirectCD is a packet-mode program that enables you to write to CD-R and CD-RW discs a little at a time (rather similar to how you write to a hard disk). However, when you make a copy of a CD that was written this way, it might or might not work. Roxio recommends you look for a CD-ROM drive that has multiread capabilities if you want to copy these sorts of discs (pretty much any new or recent drive does support multiread).

Copying from a CD-ROM Drive to a CD-RW Drive

Once you've sorted out your own views on what you do and don't have a right to duplicate, the hard work is complete. Actually, using CD Copier is an exercise in simplicity. To start up the CD Copier, simply double-click the Easy CD Creator icon that appears on your desktop after installing Easy CD Creator 5 Platinum. This brings up the menu shown in Figure 3.1.

Figure 3.1

The Project Selector gives you access to all of Easy CD Creator's programs.

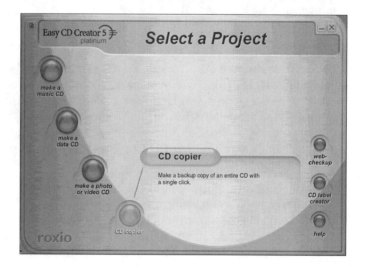

From this menu, briefly hover your mouse pointer over the CD Copier button and then click the second CD Copier button that appears in the middle of the window. If this is your first use of CD Copier, a warning dialog box pops up on the screen, essentially reminding you to use the program responsibly. To keep it from popping up every time you use CD Copier put a check in the Don't Show This Again check box and click OK. From there CD Copier launches and it's time to start copying CDs!

Between Tracks

If you removed the desktop icon (no one wants a cluttered desktop), you can also use the Start menu, by clicking Start, Programs, Roxio Easy CD Creator 5 and Project Selector.

If you hate having to add an extra mouse click to your day (who doesn't?), instead of clicking Project Selector, select Applications and you'll see a listing of all the installed Easy CD Creator programs (just click the one you want to go right to it).

Prepping for the CD-Copying Process

Because you don't have to select audio tracks, files, or folders, CD Copier is one of the simplest ways to make use of your CD-RW drive. When used in conjunction with a CD-ROM drive, you also don't have to insert more than one CD, since your PC can read from one drive and write to the other. To gear up for the big burn, place the CD you want to copy (your source) into your regular CD-ROM drive and insert a blank CD-R or CD-RW disc into your CD-RW drive. Figure 3.2 shows an example of the main CD Copier window.

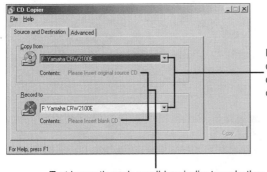

Down arrows in the drive scroll-box let you change the Copy from or Record to drive.

Text beneath each scroll-box indicates whether a suitable source or destination disc is present.

Figure 3.2

Insert two discs and click Copy. The CD Copier program is much simpler than other programs in this suite.

In Figure 3.2 you can see that neither drive has a CD (or a CD-R blank) inserted. If you have just started up the program, this is normal. It will take a few seconds or perhaps a minute, depending on how powerful your computer is, before the CDs are detected. If, however, you have yet to put the CDs in the appropriate drives, now is a good time to do it!

Also note in this figure that both the source and the destination drives use the same drive letter: F. Since we're looking to copy with both a CD-ROM drive (source) and a CD-RW drive (destination), this is incorrect. After you have inserted the CDs in the right drives, use the down arrow located on the right of each device display to select the correct drive. Note that the Copy button is grayed out because the program knows it is not possible to make a copy given the current situation.

Between Tracks

CD Copier will not let you select a nonrecordable drive as the Record To device.

When you do have the CDs inserted in the correct drives, and have ensured that the Copy From and Copy To drives have been selected correctly, the program tests the drive that holds the CD-ROM to be copied (see Figure 3.3). It performs this test only once to be sure that the drive can support audio extraction and data copying at the rate necessary to write the CD-R disc. This happens whenever you use one of the Easy CD Creator 5 Platinum programs for the first time, or after you add new CD hardware. After the initial test, the program stores the results so it won't happen again.

Figure 3.3

Because no two drives are equal, CD Copier likes to test yours to see what it can and can't do.

Finally, in Figure 3.4 you can see that we are set up now to make a copy of a CD. Both source and destination drives are now properly selected and both have the correct CD media inserted. In this figure, note that the first disc we will make a copy of is, of course, Easy CD Creator itself! Making backup copies of all your important software CDs, protects you if the original becomes corrupted or otherwise unusable because you will still have a copy from which to work.

Figure 3.4

The first CD we will copy is the Easy CD Creator disc itself.

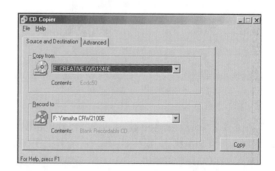

Because most software costs so much these days, keeping an extra copy around is not only a good idea, it's almost a necessity. When you spend several hundred dollars on an office suite of applications, wouldn't you rather have a copy laying around in case of an emergency? Sure, you can register the software and then wait for a few days for the vendor to mail you a new CD, but people's time is often critical and days can be an eternity (not to mention they'll probably charge a handling fee for the replacement). Making copies of all your important software CDs is a very good idea from a time and economic standpoint.

Another way to think of your copy is not as a backup copy, but as the original instead. Why? Because the original is a precious commodity. You can always make one or more copies of it, but the best copies always come from the original, not from another copy. I would suggest that whether you are copying audio or data CDs, you use the copy as your working CD and put the original itself away for safekeeping.

After all, if you're using the copy, you really don't have to be as careful as you would with the original—you can always make another copy. And, because the fair use clause in the newest copyright act allows you to make copies for your own personal use, you can make copies of audio CDs for both your home CD player and your car. Going to the beach this summer? Why take a CD along that cost $16 when you can take a copy that cost less than $1 to make?

Start Copying

After all, the media is ready to go, CD Copier will know it and enable the Copy button. Give that button a click when you're ready to take the plunge! After you do, another program window appears, called the CD Creation Process.

If you've already skipped ahead to chapters on using Easy CD Creator to make audio or data CDs, this window should look familiar. One of the niceties of using Easy CD Creator programs is that most of them show you the types of dialog boxes when creating CDs. The CD Creation Process dialog box, shown in Figure 3.5, is probably the most common.

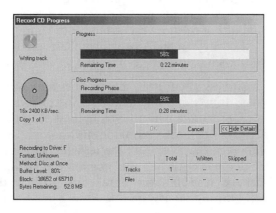

Figure 3.5

You can follow the progress as the CD is written. Notice the small bug indicating this CD will take another 28 minutes to complete. In reality it was only 28 seconds.

Over the course of burning a data CD, it goes through several steps. These steps include the following:

➤ **Prepare Data.** Because this is a data CD, during this phase, the program examines the CD that will be copied.

➤ **Writing Table of Contents.** Because the CD starts at the center of the disc and is written from there toward the outer portion of the disc, the table of contents is the first thing that must be written after the CD Copier prepares the data.

➤ **Writing Track.** In this phase, CD Copier begins copying the actual data of the CD to the CD-RW recorder. Because this is a data CD, only one large track is written that will contain several files and folders.

➤ **Closing CD.** When CD Copier begins closing a CD, that means it is setting the data so that it can be read in CD players of any kind (mainly so music CDs can play in normal audio CD players).

You can also gather some more information from the display shown in Figure 3.5. On the top left are two icons. The upper one lists the current stage in the burn process. The other is a visual depiction of the copy's progress (with only one track to copy, the disc pictured remains shaded until the copy is complete). On the upper-left of the dialog box are two progress indicators. The upper one indicates the time to completion for the current stage in the burn, while the other indicates the time remaining until the burn is complete.

To get the most from this dialog box, be sure to click the Details button. Here you get some more advanced information about the burn in progress. For example, since this is just a straight disc copy, the process being used is disc-at-once (described in Chapter 2). There is also a buffer indicator, which is very important for drives that lack BurnProof technology in letting you know if you're likely to experience a buffer underrun.

Cross Reference

If you're not sure what a buffer underrun is or what BurnProof technology does, be sure to take a look back at Chapter 1, "The Digital Revolution!"

Ideally, you want the buffer to remain as close to 100 percent as possible. For some drives, the ideal range is in the 90 percent area, but it can vary based on the amount of memory cache built into your drive. In the case of my Yamaha 16×, which boasts an impressive 8MB cache, an 80 percent buffer level isn't too shabby.

Regardless, the further this number dips, the more likely it becomes that a buffer underrun will occur. If it drops to zero percent, you're toast unless using a CD-RW drive with BurnProof technology. Do note, however, that it doesn't matter whether the buffer is at zero percent when the program is preparing the data because all that stuff takes place before the CD-burning process begins.

Crossing the Finish Line

As you can see, this is hardly a time-consuming process (unless you're recording at 4× or less, of course). Figure 3.6 shows the dialog box that appears when CD Copier has finished copying a CD. It's not particularly exciting, but it does let you know that the process was completed successfully.

From here you can select the CD Label Creator button at the bottom if you want to make a label for the CD and create inserts for the jewel case. Chapter 14, "Making Killer Labels with Easy CD Creator CD Label Maker," can give you more information on that creative endeavor. Or, if you want to do that at a later time, just click the Close button and then click OK Record CD Progress dialog box to return to the main CD Copier screen.

Cross Reference

If you are having problems, such as a buffer underrun, that prevent this process from successfully completing, consult Chapter 20, "I Ain't Got No CDs, but You Should See All My New Coasters: Troubleshooting CD Recording," for some troubleshooting tips.

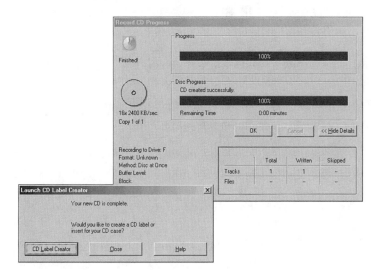

Figure 3.6

CD Copier tells you when the CD has been successfully copied. Notice the dialog box in the background indicating that 1 out of 1 tracks were successfully copied.

Using Advanced Copying Features

Now that we've made a simple copy, let's look at the advanced features you can use to control the copying process a little more precisely. For the most part, you can use the procedures we've just discussed to make all your copies. However, if you plan to make several copies and want to speed up the process, you might want to use the advanced features of CD Copier to change the speed at which the copying is performed.

Figure 3.7 shows the CD Copier program with the Advanced tab selected. Since this tab doesn't have a ton of features to choose from, you might want to consider trying each one, just to see what works best for you.

Figure 3.7

The Advanced tab of CD Copier enables you to more precisely control the copying process.

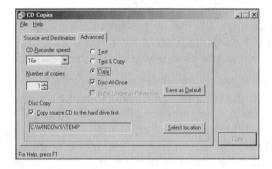

The advanced features include ...

➤ **CD-Recorder Speed.** If your CD-RW drive can write at a faster rate, you can select it here. CD Copier will display only speeds at which your drive is capable of performing. Thus, you might see higher speeds on one computer than on another.

➤ **Number of Copies.** If you want to make more than one copy of the disc, select the number of copies here.

➤ **Copy Source CD to the Hard Drive First.** This option is a good one to use if you are making more than one copy of the CD. This is because the program can usually extract data from a temporary image file on your hard disk much more quickly than it can from the CD-ROM drive in your computer. Click the Select Location button if you want to select a new temporary location to store CD data.

➤ **Test.** Use this option if you want to test whether or not the CD can be successfully written. When you select this option, CD Copier performs the copy process, but no data is actually copied to the CD-R blank disc. Use this option if you are having problems copying a CD or if you have just installed a new drive and want to ensure it is in working order.

➤ **Test & Copy.** Similar to the preceding option, this one enables you to perform the test first, and then, if the test is successful, automatically begin burning the CD.

Arcane CD Speak

An image file, in terms of burning CDs, is a file stored on your hard drive that contains the entire contents of an audio or data CD that you want to copy to a recordable disc. Only your CD-burning software can work with this file, so don't expect to be playing audio tracks from a music CD you copied to an image file.

➤ **Copy.** This is the default. Just go ahead and make the copy without any of that sissy testing stuff!

➤ **Disk-At-Once.** This is a good selection to make especially if you have an audio CD that has more than one track—and how many don't? It prevents the mandatory two-second gap between each track from occurring. For some CDs, where tracks just blend together, this is something you absolutely need to do if you want an exact copy of the disc.

➤ **Save as Default.** If you make changes to these options and want to make your changes the new default settings for when the program is started up again, click this button.

As you can see, there aren't many options to worry about, and for the most part they are self-explanatory. However, you should consider a few things when making a copy of a CD.

The Disk-at-Once option won't work when copying a data CD that has more than one session on it. Also, your CD-RW drive must support this mode. Don't worry, however, because most of the newer drives do. If you have more than one physical hard disk drive installed on your computer, you should probably select your secondary drive as the location for the temporary file (unless that drive is an older one that may have slower performance). Even though you might not be using any other applications while the copying is occurring, the operating system (Windows for most readers of this book) still uses the C: drive. Putting the temporary file on another disk can avoid any possibility of the hard disk becoming a choke point.

If you find that CD Copier is not finishing successfully, it might be that the blank CD-R media you are using doesn't work well with high recording speeds. I've had trouble recording at 12× with media that specifically said it would work at that speed. It just goes to show you that you can't always trust the manufacturer to give you all the facts. If this happens, try dropping the recording speed down to 8× or 4× (depending on the speed of your drive, you may have to resort to 1×) and see if that works. If it doesn't work at a significantly lower speed, then you have some other problems. If it does work at that speed, try increasing the speed a notch at a time with other copies until you find out how well that particular brand of media works with your CD-RW drive.

Why Make an Image Copy First?

Of all the advanced options we just went over, copying the source CD data to the hard disk first—before making the CD-R copy—is one of the more important ones. Why? For several reasons, one of which we have already mentioned: The hard disk in your computer is faster than the CD-ROM drive you have installed in your computer. At the rate technology is advancing, this isn't likely to change in the near future.

Another good reason is for making multiple copies. After the CD has been read the first time, and copied to the temporary file, the remaining copies should be made more quickly because the CD won't have to be read each time. Instead, the program uses the copy made on your hard disk. Then, provided you aren't using a bunch of other programs that hog memory or make a lot of use of your hard drive, the program will be able to keep the buffer full while it writes the remaining copies. By keeping the buffer full, and by selecting a fast write speed, you can save yourself a lot of time when making multiple copies.

Dancing Alone: Copying Using Only the CD-R Recorder

Using your hard drive as a temporary place to store the CD data brings up another interesting subject. Suppose, for some reason, you can't use your CD-ROM as a source drive. Perhaps it has stopped working or had some other, gremlin-caused problems. You can still use CD Copier to copy discs.

Instead, just use the CD-RW drive to read the source CD and copy it to the hard drive first. This way you can bypass using your CD-ROM drive entirely! It might take a little longer (having an extra step), but at least you can make copies. After the program has finished reading the original CD and has copied its data to the hard disk in your computer, it then prompts you to replace the source CD with a blank recordable one.

The following are a few things to think about when using your hard drive as a staging ground for the data to be written to a CD:

➤ Make sure enough space is available on the hard disk! A full CD-ROM can hold up to 650MB of data, 700MB if it was written on an 80-minute blank. Since all this data is going to your hard drive you must have at least that much space available, and preferably more.

➤ Keep your hard disk in good shape. Windows has a variety of system tools you can use to keep things running smoothly, but you'll need a book tailored to your version of Windows (9x/Me, NT4/2000, XP) to get the most out of them. However, the main two programs to look for are Disk Defragmenter and ScanDisk. Getting to these utilities varies based on the operating system, but generally, look in your Start menu under Programs, Accessories, System Tools. Once there, look for icons named after these programs.

➤ Don't use your hard disk extensively while the CD Copier is working. Oh, you can try, but don't be surprised if you end up with a coaster when all is said and done. (Even if you have a drive with BurnProof technology, why tempt fate?)

The Least You Need to Know

➤ Use CD Copier, not Easy CD Creator, when you want to make a copy of a single CD.

➤ You can't use CD Copier to create a CD that has tracks from multiple sources.

➤ Use the advanced options to copy the CD to your hard disk when making multiple copies or having troubles with buffer underruns. This speeds up the copying process and makes it more reliable.

➤ You don't have to have two CD drives in your computer to use CD Copier. You can use the CD-RW drive as both the source and destination.

➤ Make copies of your software and music CDs for normal everyday use. Save your originals as the precious commodities that they are. If the copy takes some abuse and becomes unusable, you can always make a new copy from the original.

➤ Some CDs simply cannot be copied. These are usually games, but some newer audio CDs also employ various protection schemes. With audio CDs, try extracting single tracks to your hard disk and re-creating the CD from there instead of using CD Copier.

➤ The ability to make backup copies of audio and data CDs is in jeopardy because of digital content publishers' desire to protect their pocket books from people and groups who illegally distribute pirated software. Be responsible and don't let yourself become part of the problem!

Chapter 4

Using NTI CD-Maker to Copy CDs

In This Chapter

➤ Copying CDs Using NTI CD-Maker is as simple as Step 1, 2 and 3, only there's no Step 3!

➤ Copying directly from CD-ROM to CD-R drives

➤ Creating CD image files and using those to burn CDs at another time

➤ Using the Compare feature to make sure you get a good copy

In the last chapter, you learned how to use Easy CD Creator to make a copy of a CD. In this chapter, you'll learn the steps involved for making a copy of just about any kind of CD you can imagine. The copying process will make copies of audio or data CDs. Think of it as similar to the MS-DOS **diskcopy** command. Unless the CD has some copy protection mechanism to keep you from making a copy (and most don't), then you should be able to use NTI CD-Maker to duplicate the CDs in your collection.

Again, as suggested in Chapter 3, "Easy Copying with Easy CD Creator," the first thing you should do if you are using NTI's CD-Maker is to make a backup copy of the NTI CD-Maker disc! After all, if you don't have a backup of your CD burner software, then you have a useless CD burner.

I always recommend that you make a backup copy. Keep your originals safely stored away and play or use the copies! That way when some friend accidentally uses your CD for a coaster, you'll always have your original to go back to so that you can create a new copy. Save the originals! Play copies of your music CDs! Install programs using copies of your CDs! Make a copy of the CD that comes with this book!

Selecting the CD Copy Function

To start, you first need to bring up the NTI CD-Maker menu. Click on Start/Programs/ NTI CD-Maker 2000 Professional and then choose NTI CD-Maker 2000 Professional from the submenu that appears. Or, if you put an icon on the Desktop when you installed the software, just double-click the icon.

In Figure 4.1 you can see the window that NTI CD-Maker puts on your screen. As you move your cursor over each of the disc icons, the little guy on the left side of this menu tells you what the button is used for. From the options offered, click on Copy CD. Now what could be easier?

Figure 4.1

You can start the NTI CD-Maker copying function by simply double-clicking on the CD Copy icon on the NTI CD-Maker graphical menu!

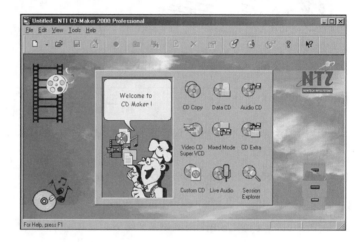

Between Tracks

There is a third way to start the CD Copying function. In Figure 4.1, look at the first button you see on the toolbar. It looks like a sheet of paper with a corner folded. Next to it is a smaller button that has an arrow pointing down. If you click on this arrow, you'll get a menu that offers the same options you already see in the GUI display on the screen. From the menu, select CD Copy, of course!

You can copy a CD using one or two CD drives. If you have a CD burner and a CD-ROM drive, then you can copy directly from the CD-ROM drive to the CD burner. If you only have a CD burner drive, NTI's software will allow you to create an image copy of the CD you want to copy, and then turn around and copy that image back to a recordable CD. And, if you have a slower computer that may suffer from "buffer underrun" as you learned about in the previous chapter, you can still select to copy from the CD-ROM drive to a temporary file, and then burn the CD, all in one step.

First, let's look at using two drives: your CD-ROM drive for the source you want to copy and your CD burner to use for creating the new CD.

Choosing the Source and Target Drivers

Once you select the CD Copy function from NTI's main Graphical menu, you'll get a display that looks like Figure 4.2. Here you can see that this computer has a CD-ROM drive (the top box, that has the text *Pioneer DVD-Rom DVD-116 (1.07) (F:)* in it. That's just Windows 98 (or whatever your operating system is) telling you that you have a CD inserted in the CD (or in this case a CD/DVD) drive. The second field in Figure 4.2 shows the CD burner drive, which in this figure is called a *PLEXTOR CD-R PX-W1610a (1.01) (E:)*. Wow, all you'd think they'd need to display is that one is a CD burner and the other is a CD-ROM drive!

As you can probably guess, the last parts of both of these fields are simply telling you what the drive letters are for each drive that will be used in the copying process. If you're familiar with the drives on your system (and who isn't?), you'd think all that the program needs to display are the drive letters and the title of the CD (if any) inserted in the drive! Yet, NTI does give you this additional information, so if you're really into CD burning, you know what you're working with.

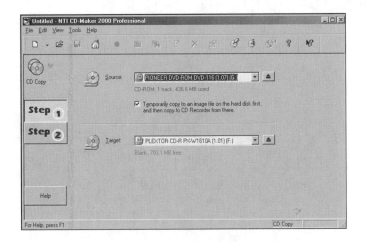

Figure 4.2

To copy from your CD-ROM drive to your CD burner drive, make sure the appropriate source and target drives are selected in this dialog box!

Last, notice that right under the Source field is a check box that tells CD-Maker to make a temporary image copy on your hard disk drive before copying to the CD burner. Why would it want to do that? Well, if you have a slower CD-ROM drive, then it might not be able to keep up with the speed of the burner. Hard disk drives are much faster than today's CD-ROM drives, so this check box is enabled by default. If you are sure of your CD-ROM drive's capabilities, then you can deselect this check box and the copy will be made directly from your CD-ROM drive to your CD burner.

Don't Get Burned

If you have two drives on your computer—a CD-ROM driver and a CD burner—and both show up in both of these fields, use the down-arrow associated with the field to select the correct drives. The Top field, labeled *Source*, should match the drive letter associated with your CD-ROM drive, while the second field, labeled *Target*, should be the drive that is your CD burner! If you're not sure, bring up Windows Explorer (Start/Programs/Windows Explorer in Windows 98) to check on the drive letters!

Get Ready to Copy!

Once you've established that you have your source CD in the right drive, and the blank recordable CD in the CD burner drive, then just click on the Step 2 button on the left side of Figure 4.2. However, let's look a little closer. NTI's CD-Maker is a very versatile program. When you click on the Step 2 button, another dialog box appears that has a button labeled Start. You could just click that button and start the copying process, but you wouldn't get a good copy. Why? Well, click the Advanced button and you'll see a larger dialog box, shown in Figure 4.3.

Figure 4.3

After you click on Step 2, the Write CD dialog box appears, shown here with the Advanced button clicked.

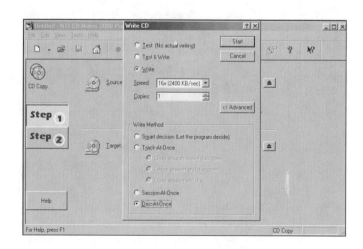

Since NTI's CD-Maker software does a lot of things (like make multisession CDs, which we'll get into in another chapter), don't click the Start button yet! If you don't make the selection to close the CD, you can add additional sessions (a multisession CD) and at this point you don't want to do that. We're saving that feature for a later chapter you can read after you've gotten past these basic steps for making a simple copy of a CD. This is a standard dialog box used throughout the NTI CD-Maker program, so some of the options you'll see here are appropriate for other uses, and not appropriate for making a copy of a CD. For now, to simply make a copy of a CD, click on the radio button labeled *Disk-At-Once*. This option tells the program to copy the CD and then perform the necessary operations to close out the CD so you can play it (if it's an audio CD) or use it on your computer (if it's a data CD) without having to bother with later closing the CD.

Between Tracks

Another way to get to the Write CD dialog box is simply to click the button on the top of the window that has the big red dot on it. It's the record button. Either way, you'll get the same dialog box.

Don't Get Burned

CD-Maker can usually figure out what you want to do by the selection you make from the first menu. So when you get to the Advanced section of the Write CD dialog box you'll see a blue checkmark to the right of the selection that CD-Maker is suggesting you use. In this case, the *Disk-At-Once* option is suggested by the program, and it's also the option I chose. If you're ever unsure of which selection to make under the Write Method section, click the radio button labeled *Smart decision (Let the program decide)*. The program will then place a blue checkmark off to the right side of the Write Method it thinks you should use, and it will use that method unless you change it.

Don't believe me? Well, then click the radio button labeled *Smart decision (Let the program decide)*. When you do this it will place a blue checkmark beside the *Disk-At-Once* option!

If you are troubleshooting problems recording to certain media, you might want to use the testing buttons at the top of the dialog box. Or, at least use the Speed drop-down menu to select a recording speed that is appropriate for the media you've purchased. You can save time when making multiple copies by selecting that option here also. Every time a copy is made, CD-Maker will prompt you to insert another blank CD until it's finished making all the copies.

What Speed Should You Use for Recording?

Now let's look at the top part of this Write CD dialog box. By default the program will use the maximum write speed of your CD burner. Unless you've had problems creating CDs (in other words, you've created lots of coasters), then you might want to lower the value in the Speed menu by using the arrow key. This arrow key will show you all the speeds at which your CD burner is capable of writing a CD. It is important also to make sure you are using the correct recordable CD-R media with your burner. While most recordable CD media today is rated up to at least 16× and 24×, some may not be. In this case, you should choose a lower value. CD-Maker only knows the speed at which your drive is capable of recording. It doesn't have any idea of what kind of blank, recordable CD you've put into the burner. Check your CD-R (or CD-RW) media to see the speeds at which it's capable of recording.

If you do produce a coaster (in other words, your copying process doesn't work and you get an error), then try lowering the speed to see if this helps. This industry is progressing at a very fast rate. While it used to be a good idea to simply lower the recording speed to 1× when you have problems, that is not the case anymore. Instead, experiment with different brands of CD-R media and find one that works with your particular CD burner, and at what speed it does the be best job.

Testing First?

If you are new to CD-burning, then you might want to use the buttons labeled *Test (No actual writing)* or *Test & Write*. These buttons merely test the capabilities of your drives to make sure they can keep up with the recording process. The first selection, *Test (No actual writing)* just tests the drives. The second, a *Test & Write* might be a good idea if you've been having problems. Otherwise, simply use the *Write* radio button and click on Start to get the process of burning your CD underway!

In Figure 4.4 you can see that CD-Maker first tests the CD-ROM you've chosen for the source to see if it can extract the data at the rate required to keep up with the burning process and that it supports digital audio extraction (DAE—which some older CD-ROM drives don't support). If you receive an error message, then you may have a slower CD-ROM drive (which may be the case if you have an older computer to which you've added a new CD burner). In that case, lower the recording speed, as previously discussed, and try again.

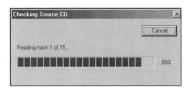

Figure 4.4

CD-Maker first tests the ability of your CD-ROM drive to keep up with the speed you've chosen for the recording process.

After it checks to be sure that it can read the tracks on your CD-ROM drive, CD-Maker then begins to copy the tracks to an image file, since we left that check box selected back in Step 1. You can watch the progress as it copies each track, as shown in Figure 4.5.

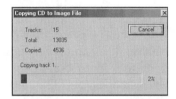

Figure 4.5

CD-Maker next copies each track to an image file on your hard drive.

When it's finished creating the image file, then the program will fire up your CD burner and start to make the copy. In Figure 4.6 you can see the dialog box that tells you that the first thing CD-Maker does is to write the table of contents for the disc. Without this table of contents, the disc would be unreadable, as you learned in Chapter 2, "The Machine Behind the Curtain: How CDs and Recordable CDs Work."

Figure 4.6

CD-Maker next writes the table of contents for the disc.

Finally, as you can see in Figure 4.7, the actual tracks of the disc are written. Watch the Cache field, as it shows you the amount of data being buffered during the writing process. Remember that unless your CD burner supports BurnProof technology, then you'll probably get a coaster if the cache becomes empty. The cache is simply data waiting in memory to be written by the laser and if the laser runs of out data to write, then the disc will be useless!

Figure 4.7

Next, CD-Maker writes the actual data to your CD burner.

When it's finished, you'll get a nice dialog box titled "Congratulations!" This simply tells you the rate at which the CD was recorded and the elapsed time that it took. In Figure 4.8 you can see that you can choose the OK button if you are finished. However, if you want to design the disc label and jewel box inserts, you can select the Jewel Case button to bring up the Jewel Case application. For now, click the OK button. You'll learn about creating jewel case stuff in a later chapter!

Figure 4.8

Congratulations, you've copied a CD.

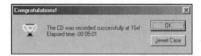

In this example, I left the check box selected in Step 1 that told CD-Maker to create a temporary image file on my hard disk as a precaution to ensure that it would be able to read the data fast enough to keep up with my CD burner. After you click the OK button, CD-Maker is polite enough to ask if you'd like to save this image so you can make other copies at a later time. You can see this dialog box in Figure 4.9.

Figure 4.9

If you selected the check box to create a temporary disk file, CD-Maker will prompt you to save it after it has copied the CD.

You can click Yes and CD-Maker will prompt you with a dialog box titled Save As. You can choose the directory to save the image file and give it a name. However, leave the type of file (the file extension) at the default that the dialog box presents to you: NTI CD Image Files (*.ncd). When you see any file on your hard disk that has the .ncd file extension, you can be sure it's an image file created by NTI CD-Maker.

Otherwise, just click OK. If you had told CD-Maker to create more than one copy, it would now prompt you to put a new blank disc in the recorder. If not, you're back at Step 1, ready to exit the program or insert another disc to copy.

Creating a CD Image File on Your Hard Disk

There are several reasons why you might want to just make an image copy of the CD instead of copying from your CD-ROM drive to your CD burner drive. The first thing that comes to mind is that you may have a CD-ROM drive in your computer that doesn't support digital audio extraction. Or your CD-ROM may not be able to keep up with the speed of your CD burner. Or perhaps you just want to save an image copy so you can quickly make multiple copies at a later date.

Oh, and there's always the case where you might have just the CD burner installed in your computer, and don't have a CD-ROM that you can use to copy from! In that case, you can create an image file using your CD burner (since it can be used just like a regular CD-ROM drive) and then turn around and burn the image back to the CD-R media.

In our first copying example, you learned that you can simply tell CD-Maker to create an image file when it does a normal copy. However, if you simply want to create an image file, you don't have to go through all that trouble of actually burning a CD.

Instead, back in Step 1, don't select the CD burner as the destination drive. In Figure 4.10 you can see I've chosen from the Target drop-down menu the entry named NTI CD Image Writer instead of a CD burner.

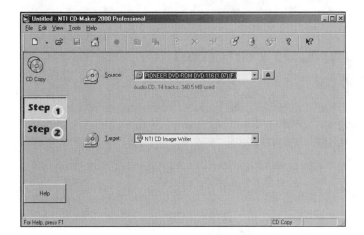

Figure 4.10

Select NTI CD Image Writer as the Target drive if you only want to create an image file for later use.

Once you click the Step 2 button (or the big red dot!), a Save As dialog box will pop up and allow you to select a location and give a name to the image, in the same manner described in the previous section. Make sure you pick a location that contains enough space for the image file! CDs, depending on their size, can hold between 650 and 800 MB of data! Once you've chosen a location and name for the image file, click the Save button.

Once you've created an image file, then you can later burn it to a CD-R or CD-RW disc by changing the drive listing in the Source field. Select NTI CD Image Reader, as shown in Figure 4.11.

When you click the Step 2 button, an Open dialog box will prompt you for the location of the image file you want to burn to the CD-R drive. To finish the process, just follow the same directions given earlier in this chapter to close the CD (*Disc-At-Once* method) and burn away!

Figure 4.11

To burn a CD from an image file, choose as the source NTI CD Image Reader.

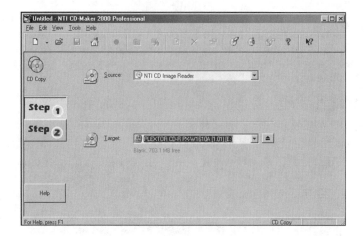

Using the Compare CDs Function to Check Your Copy

Do you want to make sure that you got a good copy without having to listen to the entire disc (or install a program if it's an application installation CD)? You can use the Compare CDs function to perform a quick check for you.

Simply leave both CDs in their respective drives—the source CD in the CD-ROM drive and the recorded CD-R media in the CD burner drive. From the Tools menu, select Compare CDs.

CD-Maker will compare the CDs and report back if any differences are found.

The Least You Need to Know

➤ You can copy CDs by using your CD-ROM and CD burner drives.

➤ You can copy CDs by using just a CD burner, and creating an image file that you can then burn to a CD-R disc.

➤ NTI's CD-Maker is smart enough to recommend the correct way to record a CD!

➤ You can compare CDs after you've recorded them to make sure you got a good copy.

Digital Jukeboxes and PC Life Insurance: The Zen of Making Audio or Data CDs

Although making a copy of a CD is always a good idea, there are more creative things you can do when burning CDs. In the next few chapters you'll learn how to create your own CDs. You can customize an audio or data CD and include just the songs or data that you want on the CD.

And that's just the beginning of what you'll find in Part 3. You'll also learn about how to use Easy CD Creator's SoundStream application, so you can save what's left of that vinyl record collection you've got stuck away in the garage. You might even be able to clean up the sound quality a bit when you record to a CD.

Chapter 5

Drag and Drop with Easy CD Creator

In This Chapter

➤ How to create and edit an audio or MP3 CD layout

➤ Creating an audio or MP3 CD with Easy CD Creator

➤ How to create and edit a data CD layout

➤ Burning a data CD with Easy CD Creator

➤ Making a CD image file and using it to burn multiple CDs

There is more than one way to skin a cat—or so I'm told. Obviously I'd never do such a thing, especially since I have nosy neighbors and no desire to explain myself to the ASPCA. There is, however, also more than one way to create an audio or data CD using Roxio Easy CD Creator software.

If you open the Roxio Project Selector (by either double-clicking its desktop icon or clicking Start, Programs, Easy CD Creator 5, Project Selector) you'll find that there are a lot of ways to skin ... err ... burn a CD. The two buttons to concern yourself with here are the Make a Music CD and Make a Data CD Buttons. Highlighting one or the other with your mouse pointer brings up a small list of programs you can use. For audio CDs, there are two key options we focus on in this chapter: MusicCD Project and MP3CD Project (see Figure 5.1).

Figure 5.1

Pick your audio poison with the Project Selector: Music CD or MP3 CD.

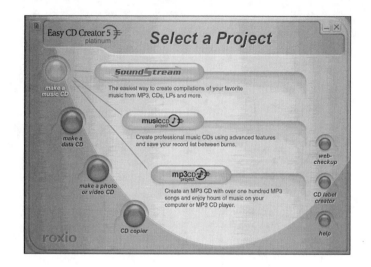

There is also a third option, using the SoundStream program, but that is covered in Chapter 7, "Your Very Own Recording Studio: Using Easy CD Creator SoundStream." If you're looking to create audio CDs from a variety of sources—such as cassettes or phonograph records or clean up audio with lots of pops, hisses, and scratches, Chapter 7 is for you.

If you highlight the Make a Data CD button you'll notice options for using:

➤ DirectCD, which is covered in Chapter 11, "Dial Direct with Easy CD Creator DirectCD."

➤ DataCD Project, which is what we'll focus on here.

➤ TakeTwo, which is not covered in this book. Browse through Appendix A, "Installing Roxio Easy CD Creator," if you're curious as to why we chose to avoid this particular program.

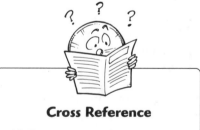

Cross Reference

If all you want to do is make a copy of an entire CD, use Roxio's Easy CD Copier, see Chapter 3, "Easy Copying with Easy CD Creator."

The interesting thing about all of the programs we cover here is that they use the same basic interface (with a few subtle variations). Which, of course, is why they're all included in a single chapter. While this chapter has sections that offer details specific to each one of these programs, the bulk of the information for interacting with Easy CD Creator, creating CD layouts and burning the disc are in the "Creating a MusicCD Project CD" section. If you skip ahead in the chapter and find that you're not seeing "key" information about the program, be sure to give it a thorough read-through. The answers you seek are likely there.

Creating a MusicCD Project CD

For your music listening pleasure, you can use Easy CD Creator to create audio CDs that can be played in your CD-ROM drive or virtually any home audio CD player (although your mileage on these may vary). Personally, I think the most fun to be had with this program is in selecting your favorite songs from various CDs for a mini-megahits collection that can get you through the commute to and from work or school. However, creating compilations that mix Tom Petty with Motley Crue are hardly the only use to draw from MusicCD Project. If it strikes your fancy, you can also select all the songs from just one CD and change the order in which they are stored or even include MP3 or WAV files located on your hard drive on the same CD.

Between Tracks

While several audio file formats can be used to store and play music on a PC, Easy CD Creator supports the two most important ones: WAV and MP3.

If you haven't heard of MP3 technology by this point you've likely not spent much time on the Web, watching TV, reading newspapers, communicating with other human beings, or certain dogs, cats, and hamsters. MP3 files are all the rage on the Internet (and in the court system), but if you really care about the quality of the sound on the finished CD, WAV files are a better format.

As with all things, there is a trade-off, however. Because they're designed to be portable (to MP3 players, PDAs and even some cell phones), MP3 files get so compressed that they lose a little quality in the process. Not a lot, but a little. Even if you convert the MP3 file to a WAV file (which Easy CD Creator does when it burns the MP3 file to a CD), you don't get back what you've lost! The WAV format, however, is almost identical to the CD-DA format used on the CD itself. That quality comes at a price, though, as these files can be extremely large and certainly wouldn't fit (in any quantity) into any MP3-compatible portable player you might have.

To get things cracking, use the Project Selector window described in the previous section to select MusicCD Project. You can also use the Start menu to open Easy CD Creator directly. Simply click Start, Programs, Roxio Easy CD Creator 5, Applications, Easy CD Creator. In the window that appears, you'll need to make sure you're in the correct mode, by clicking File, New CD Project, Music CD. In the end, you should see a screen similar to what is shown in Figure 5.2.

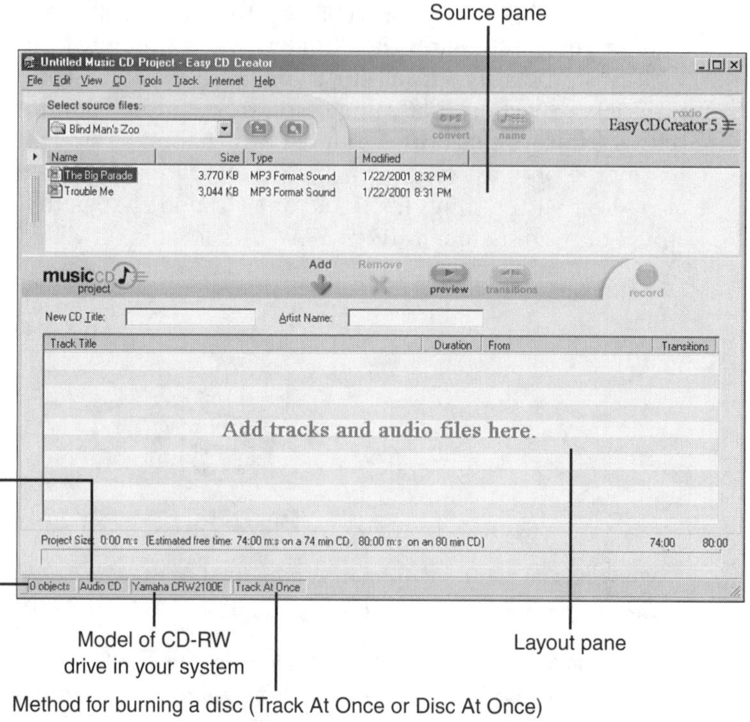

Figure 5.2

The MusicCD Project window provides a simple means for creating Audio CDs.

Source pane

Current Easy CD Creator mode (Audio CD, MP3 CD, Data CD)

Number of objects in layout (audio tracks, in this case)

Model of CD-RW drive in your system

Layout pane

Method for burning a disc (Track At Once or Disc At Once)

Typically, the mode in which Easy CD Creator opens is the one you've most recently used. You can tell which mode it's in by looking at the information bar in the middle of the window or by looking at the data in the *very bottom of the program window*. Here, you can see information about various aspects of creating a CD. These fields let you know the number of *objects* (music tracks in this case) in the current layout, which mode you're in (should say Audio CD), the type of CD-RW drive you use and the current method with which the disc will be burned.

For now, you don't need to understand these different modes. You just need to ensure that Audio CD appears in the mode section.

Creating the Audio CD Layout

The most important part of creating an audio CD is building a layout (truthfully, this applies to any kind of CD you create using Easy CD Creator). To do this, you must tell the program exactly which files or tracks you want to record, and in what order. The program then uses this information to burn the CD, rather like creating a building from a set of blueprints. You can also save the layout so that you can recall it for use at a later time.

If you refer to Figure 5.2, you can see the MusicCD Project program. The window is essentially divided into two panes. The Source pane on the upper portion of the window lists files, folders and audio tracks on your computer in a style similar to Windows Explorer (these can be located on any hard disk, or CD drive on your PC). The bottom Layout pane is used to add audio tracks you want burned to disc.

While you can use this window as is, there are some customizations I recommend making to ensure maximum usability. First of all, if you're creating an audio CD from MP3 or WAV files on your hard drive, you don't need the distraction of seeing a bunch of Windows data files and documents. On the menu bar, click View, Show Files, Audio Files Only to restrict the Source pane's listings to just audio files. Secondly, as a veteran user of both Windows and Easy CD Creator 4.0, I prefer to see a "tree" listing of folders on my disks, in addition to folder contents in the Source pane. To enable this tree, click the small black arrow in the upper-left corner of the Source pane (see Figure 5.3).

Don't Get Burned

There are two good reasons for saving the layout after it's created. First, you might want to change the order, or maybe add or delete some tracks in the future. Secondly, you also never know when disaster, like Windows crashes and power outages, might occur. Saving your layouts early and often can save you the extra work!

Between Tracks

If you are going to be doing a lot of audio CD recording and are using WAV or MP3 files, you can locate these files more easily if you keep them all in one folder or set of folders. Windows has a My Documents folder built in for this purpose. If you own Windows Me, you will find My Documents also contains a My Music folder!

Since I have two hard disks, I've created a My Music folder on my second hard drive, in which I store MP3 files in subfolders based first on the recording artist/group and then the album the actual song comes from. Some, like my wife, may find this practice to be anal-retentive, but I've discovered just how painful it can be to pick out just one file out of hundreds when lumping everything into just one Windows folder.

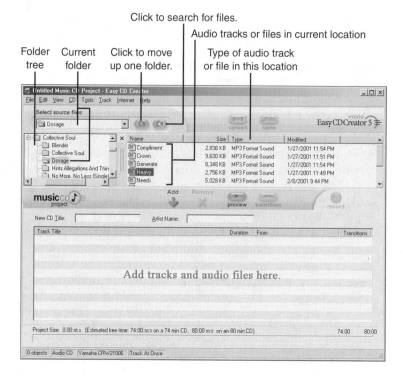

Figure 5.3

With the folder tree in view, you can select your source for audio content and view the content that source contains at the same time.

The figure labels:
- Folder tree
- Current folder
- Click to move up one folder.
- Click to search for files.
- Audio tracks or files in current location
- Type of audio track or file in this location

Between Tracks

Generally, when you insert an audio CD with Easy CD Creator open, it immediately switches the Source view to the CD drive the disc is in. If it doesn't, use the folders tree or click the Source scroll-box to manually select the drive.

In the example shown in Figure 5.3, you can see that I've opened a folder containing MP3 files from the Collective Soul CD titled Dosage (my wonderfully anal filing system at work). From here I can scroll up and down all the folders on my computer, while also being able to see which tracks are in the one I've currently selected. Using the view in Figure 5.2, all I can see is names of the tracks in the current location and the name of the current folder. Because I think the view in Figure 5.3 is much more useful, that's what you'll see used during the rest of the process.

Working with Audio CDs

Identifying an MP3 or WAV file is generally not too difficult. They're almost always named after the song or artist they represent. Audio CDs can be a bit trickier. By default, Easy CD Creator just lists songs by their track number (see Figure 5.4).

Click to convert track to an MP3, WMA, or WAV file.　　Click to get CD information from the Internet.

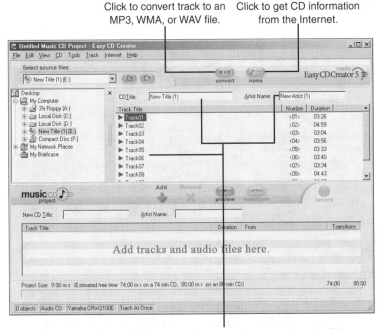

Figure 5.4

What's with this "Track 1," "Track 2" stuff?

Easy CD Creator assigns generic names to audio CDs.

Let's face it, if you had to look on the CD cover to find out which track is which when you are deciding what tracks to add to the layout, you'd probably get so frustrated you'd be thinking about climbing up to your roof to thin out the neighborhood. After all, "Track 13" is not very descriptive, especially if you're dealing with tracks from multiple CDs.

The good news is that, so long as you have an Internet connection, you probably don't have to worry. There is a Web site available that Easy CD Creator can access to download information about almost any music CD. This includes the CD title, the name of the artist, and the names of the audio tracks.

To initiate this download, click the Track option on the Easy CD Creator menu bar, and choose Name CD Tracks from the list that appears (or click the Name button in the Source pane). (Make sure you're connected to the Internet first!) This initiates the download process. Sit tight for a few seconds while Easy CD Creator connects and locates the CD information concurrent with your

Between Tracks

Rare is the CD that Easy CD Creator can't find information about on the Internet (unless it's a custom compilation). If this happens, you can enter track information manually, which we'll discuss in "Adding Artist, CD Title, and Song Title Information," later in this chapter.

disc (you may be asked to choose from a few options, if Easy CD Creator finds more than one likely candidate).

Once Easy CD Creator has located the information for your CD, you'll find that the information in the Source pane of the Easy CD Creator window has dramatically changed (see Figure 5.5).

Easy CD Creator has now properly identified this audio CD.

Figure 5.5

After the download finishes, the display makes a lot more sense!

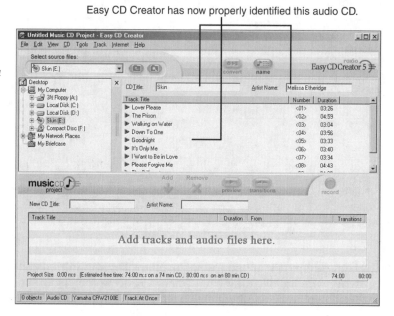

As you can see, the mystery CD from Figure 5.4 is actually the Melissa Etheridge CD, "Skin." Each track is identified by the name of the song, which makes creating the layout for the new CD much easier. The good news is that you only have to do this once per CD. Easy CD Creator remembers discs that it's already identified.

If you'd rather not have to go through this series of clicks every time you insert a new CD, you can configure this service so that it works automatically. Click Tools at the top of the Easy CD Creator and then Options to open the Easy CD Creator options dialog box shown in Figure 5.6.

Three check boxes are available here. The first, Enable Audio CD Information Download, is all you need to have Easy CD Creator get your CD's information from the Web. However, if you are connecting to the Internet through a modem, it's a good idea to also check the second check box, Prompt Me Before Attempting Internet Download, so that the program asks before performing the download, giving you a chance to establish your Internet connection if you haven't already.

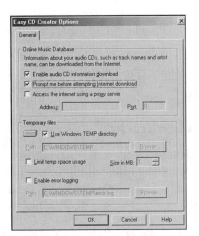

Figure 5.6

Use the Options properties page from the Tools menu to enable automatic downloading of CD information from the Internet.

If you elected to have Easy CD Creator notify you before downloading CD information, displays a quick confirmation dialog box before automatically attempting to get CD information from the Internet. After making sure you've established your Internet connection, Click OK to begin the download.

Arcane CD Speak

The third option here, Access the Internet Using a Proxy Server may not be one you need to worry about. A proxy server is a component of a firewall, which is used to protect a network from evildoers on the Internet. While some form of software firewall like Zone Alarm or Black ICE Defender comes highly recommended (especially for those with always-on connections like DSL or cable), unless you're using Easy CD Creator through an office network you probably don't need to worry about it.

If your system does access the Internet through a proxy server, check this box and give Easy CD Creator the necessary keys (Address and Port) to get through. At work, your network administrator should have this information, at home, talk to the techno-geek who set it up in the first place.

Between Tracks

If this Internet download doesn't work for your CD (or a connection is not available) you can always input CD information manually. It's a simple, but time-consuming process. At the top of the Source pane enter the CD title and artist name in the appropriate fields (you will need to highlight and delete the placeholder text they contain by default).

Changing the name of the track is a little trickier, but certainly no challenge. Just highlight the track by clicking it once, pause for a second, and then click it again. The existing track name is now highlighted in blue with a cursor at the end. Just replace the placeholder text with the correct track name. You can use this method to manually rename each track in the layout, either as you select the tracks or after you've finished the layout—which ever is easier.

This process can also be used to correct any incorrect information about a CD or track that the Internet download may have provided (like spelling errors and such).

Adding Tracks to the Layout

Now you are ready to start adding audio tracks to the layout. The easiest method is to use your mouse to drag a track from the Source pane to the Layout pane. Just select the location of your track in the Source pane and place your cursor over the track you want to add (be it an audio CD track or an MP3/WAV file), click and hold down the left mouse button, and then move the mouse until it is over the CD Layout pane at the bottom of the window. Release the mouse button and the track will show up as part of the layout.

If you despise using drag and drop methods to move tracks around, you can always highlight the tracks(s) you want in the layout and click the Add button located between the Source and Layout panes. As you can see in Figure 5.7, I've placed multiple tracks in the CD layout from both MP3 files on my hard drive, and audio tracks from a CD in my CD-ROM drive.

Click to remove selected track(s) from the Layout pane.

Click to add selected track(s).

Click to hear a selected track.

Click to start recording the CD.

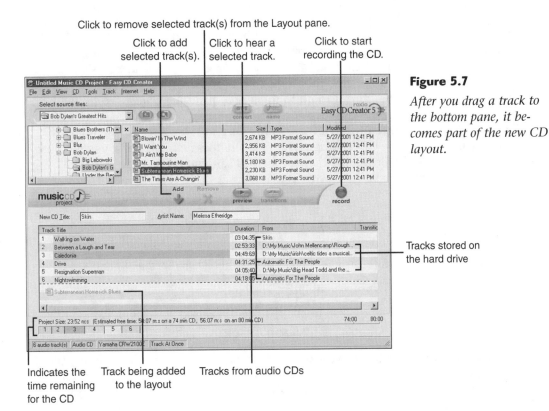

Figure 5.7

After you drag a track to the bottom pane, it be-comes part of the new CD layout.

Tracks stored on the hard drive

Indicates the time remaining for the CD

Track being added to the layout

Tracks from audio CDs

Between Tracks

If you can't see enough information in a particular Easy CD Creator pane and don't want to use scroll bars to browse through it all, you can alter the dimensions of each pane in the window. Placing the mouse cursor between the folders tree and Source pane or be-tween the Source and Layout panes changes it to a bi-directional arrow. Click and drag (left/right or up/down depending on the panes being altered) the cursor to customize the view to your tastes.

Notice that near the bottom of this figure there is a timeline which shows how much of the CD's available time you've used up and how much free time you still have available depending on whether you're recording to a 74-minute or 80-minute CD-R. Anyone who has ever tried to make audiocassettes from several sources will appreciate knowing exactly how much time they have to deal with, rather than having to guess as to whether or not they've got room to squeeze in just one more, "short," track. Here there's no running out of tape with just 30 seconds left on the last song. With Easy CD Creator (or virtually any other CD-burning software), if you use up more space than exists on the CD, the program tells you how much *overtime* you've run before the first track is ever recorded. This way, you can determine how many and which tracks you will have to remove from the layout to create the new CD layout.

Between Tracks

You can select multiple tracks or audio files to add to the layout all at once, rather than clicking them one at a time. To do so, click the first one, hold down the Shift key, and click the last file. All the files in between, including the ones you clicked, will be selected. Then, click the Add button.

You can select multiple tracks or files that aren't all in a row by using Ctrl-click. That is, click the first file you want to select; then, hold down the control button (Ctrl) and click each of the other files you want selected just once. They do not have to be contiguous in the listing, but they do have to be located in the same folder or CD. When ready, drag the selections into the Layout Pane.

Using Multiple CDs

Because you have between 74 and 80 minutes of recording time to work with, you can keep adding tracks until you've designed the CD you want or until you run out of space (time) on the CD. Sure, you can select all the tracks from the same CD, but that's only useful if you want to duplicate a single disc.

What does make sense, though, is to create a CD of songs using tracks from several CDs—a best hits CD, so to speak. To do this, just insert one CD at a time, selecting and adding the songs you want to the layout for each disc until you run out of space.

Between Tracks

While working with multiple CDs in one layout is possible, it can be a pain when it comes time to record. Even if it's only temporary, consider copying CD audio tracks to a folder on your hard drive as MP3 or WAV files. Simply select the track(s) you wish to store, select Track on the menu bar and click Convert to Audio File (or click the Convert button near the top of the Source pane).

A Convert x Audio Tracks dialog box appears, where x is the number of tracks you selected. If using one track you can customize the filename, but converting multiple tracks at once causes Easy CD Creator to generate the filenames automatically. Using the Save As Type scroll box, you can save the track as an MP3, WAV or WMA file. If you're well acquainted with audio file formats, use the Format dialog box to set this option as well. If these file types and formats are Greek to you, stick with MP3 file types and the recording format (160Kbps).

Once you've set your file location, click Save and Easy CD Creator will convert the files as you've chosen. Do so for each CD you're using tracks from. Once that's complete add the files on your hard drive to your audio CD layout, rather than using the CDs themselves.

This is where it becomes important to download CD information from the Internet. Without that download, Easy CD Creator uses its own generic naming system— Disk 1, Disk 2, and so on—instead of the actual CD and artist name. This can get really hard to keep track of if you're using a lot of CDs. Again, if the CD information is not available online, never fear, you can put the information in yourself.

Editing the Audio CD Layout

Rare is the CD layout that doesn't need a modification of one sort or another. There's always a need to modify the track order or dump a track that won't fit on the disc. After all, what if, right before recording, you realize in a spark of divine inspiration that Van Halen's "Top of the World" should come right after Eric Clapton's "Tears in Heaven," instead of before it?

No worries! Simply select the track (or tracks) you wish to move, hold down the mouse button and drag them to a different location in the layout. When you move a track around like this, the program takes care of renumbering all the other tracks.

Between Tracks

If hearing a track can help you decide where to put it in the layout (or whether or not it should be cut entirely), select it in either the Source or Layout panes and click the Preview button located between the two panes. This brings up a CD-player-like interface with which you can listen to the selected track.

Just as adding a track to the layout is easy, removing one is also an exercise in simplicity. So when you decide that Prince's "Purple Rain" doesn't work on the same CD as John Lennon's "Imagine," you can use three methods to cut one of them:

➤ Right-click the track in the layout pane and, on the menu that appears, click Remove From CD Project.

➤ Click the song once in the layout pane and click the Remove button between the Source and Layout panes. The Remove button is easy to find because it has a big "X" underneath it.

➤ Click the track (or tracks) and press the Delete key.

Changing the order of songs in a layout and removing songs from a layout are not only convenient when you are first creating the layout, but also when you decide to use a layout that was saved from a previous session.

Saving the Layout for Later Use

After creating the layout, you can then go right ahead and create the CD. However, if you think you might want to use this layout again or if you don't have time to create the CD right away, you can save it to your hard disk for later use. To save the layout simply perform these steps:

1. Click File at the top of the Easy CD Creator program.

2. Select Save Project List. Assuming this is the first time you've saved this layout, a dialog box appears that you can use to select the location on your hard disk to which to save the layout. Just give it a name, using the File Name field and click Save (see Figure 5.8).

3. Click the Save button.

Figure 5.8

Saving a project layout for later use ensures that you won't have to create the same layout twice.

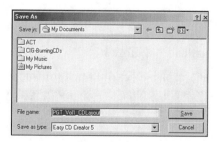

Now, whenever you choose this option, Easy CD Creator automatically overwrites the filename you just gave it. If you want to rename the layout, click Save Project List As in the File menu instead of Save Project List. Note that *saving the layout doesn't save any of the songs*—it just saves the information that Easy CD Creator uses to create a new CD. If you use a saved layout at a later time, you still must have the CDs or other files that were used to select songs to create the layout (and they must be in the same location as when you added them to it).

Creating an Audio CD

Having come this far, let's make a CD from the layout we've created. As you might guess, there are a couple of ways to do this. You can use either of the following methods:

➤ Click the Record button located between the Source and Layout panes.

➤ Select File from the menu bar and click Record CD.

Cross Reference

You can also create an image of the CD you want to create. This puts all the data for the CD into a huge file on your hard disk (unlike a layout, this includes all your music tracks' data). You can't play this file, but you can use it at a later time to burn as many copies of the CD as you like. For more about using CD images, see "Creating a Disc Image and Burning It to a CD," later in this chapter.

Either of these two methods yields the same result, so it's completely up to your personal preference. However, in either case, the first thing you need to do is make sure a blank, recordable CD is in your CD-RW drive. Don't worry; if you forget this, you'll get prompted when it comes time to start recording. Once you click the Record button, the dialog box shown in Figure 5.9 appears (click the Options button to see the full dialog box depicted here).

We'll get into each of these options over the course of this section. For now, let's focus on the first five:

➤ **Select CD-R Drive.** This somewhat misnamed option is the drive letter of the CD-RW drive that holds the blank recordable CD. If you have more than one CD-RW device in your computer, which is not likely, you can choose between the devices.

➤ **Write Speed.** The values available in this field depend on the type of CD-RW disc drive you have. Some drives are capable of writing at a faster rate than others. However, don't go out and buy a CD-RW drive based solely on its maximum speed. These days an 8× drive is more than adequate, with a 12×, in my opinion being the most desirable. Since you can burn a 12× CD-R in under ten minutes, faster drives make less and less of a difference.

➤ **Number of Copies.** What can I say? This is the number of CDs you want to create, obviously!

➤ **Write CD-Text Info.** Off to the side, you will notice this button. Not all CD-RW drives have this capability, but if yours does, you can select this option and the information about the artist, CD title, and song titles are saved on the CD you create. If played in a CD player that recognizes this kind of data, you will see this information displayed when the CD is played.

➤ **Buffer Underrun Prevention.** If your CD-RW drive supports BurnProof technology, be sure to check this box so that you don't have to worry about the occurrences of buffer underruns that create coasters from your CDs. Buffer underruns are discussed in more detail in Chapter 1, "The Digital Revolution!"

Figure 5.9

The Recorded CD Setup dialog box allows you to set the stage for the CD-burning process.

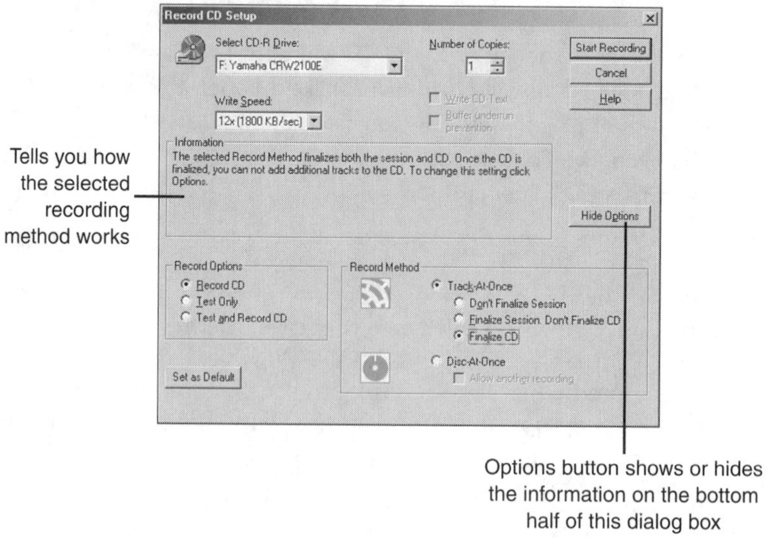

Tells you how the selected recording method works

Options button shows or hides the information on the bottom half of this dialog box

With the Options button clicked, you can see the other advanced options available for you to choose from. These fall into two categories. The first is Record Options, where you can decide whether you want to perform a test or just create the CD. The second set of options, called Record Method, gets a little more complicated, but we'll steer you through those murky waters.

From the Record Options, you can choose one of the following options:

➤ **Record CD.** This option enables you to go straight to recording the CD. If you've been using the drive for a while and are confident in its capabilities, choose this option. If you run into a problem and find you are making coasters instead of CDs, try selecting one of the next two test options.

➤ **Test Only.** This option test writes the entire CD-burning process without actually writing anything to the CD. This is a good idea if you're having problems burning discs, using a new computer, or have just installed a new CD-RW drive. If the test burn encounters any problems your CD-R won't be made into a coaster because of them. If you're not having any problems, you don't need to go through this lengthy process.

➤ **Test and Record CD.** Similar to the previous option, except that if the test is successful, Easy CD Creator automatically starts to burn your CD.

As discussed in Chapter 2, "The Machine Behind the Curtain: How CDs and Recordable CDs Work," recordable CDs work in tracks and sessions and whether or not they are open or closed. Tracks are individual chunks of information—for example, in this case, a song. A group of tracks burned in one process is called a *session*. Finally, a disc remains open and able to store more sessions until it is closed. You can choose how to write a disc from the Record Method options list:

Arcane CD Speak

You'll often hear the term *coaster* applied to a CD that didn't make it all the way through the burning process. Because you can't rewrite a CD-R disc, a failed burn leaves you with a disc that's only good for setting drinks on.

Between Tracks

If you'd rather not go back to Chapter 2 for more information on these burn methods, put yourself in the capable hands of Easy CD Creator. Selecting any of the options given here causes the Information portion of the Record CD Setup Dialog box to show a description of how that method works.

➤ **Track-At-Once.** This means that each track is written individually, with a two-second gap between each track. Under this option you can choose either:

> ➤ **Don't Finalize Session.** This leaves both the session and disc open so you can add more tracks later on. However, you won't be able to play the disc in a CD player until you at least finalize the session.

> ➤ **Finalize Session. Don't Finalize CD.** This completes the session, but leaves the disc open so more sessions can be added later.
>
> It's important to remember that most audio CD players cannot read beyond the first session of a disc, so this option isn't very useful for music CDs. Also, because the disc is left open, you'll be able to use it only in your CD-RW drive.

> ➤ **Finalize CD.** This option, naturally, closes the CD. After this is done, you can no longer add any tracks or sessions to the disc. You can, however, play it in a regular audio player.

➤ **Disc-At-Once.** This causes the entire disc to be written, as you have designed it in the layout, and then the CD to be closed. Because multiple sessions aren't of much use with a music CD, this is usually the best choice. This method also prevents the two-second gap from being created between tracks on the disc.

Don't Get Burned

Using the disc-at-once method has a few other advantages over the track- or session-at-once methods. When recording from multiple source CDs with the other methods, you don't switch between source discs until each disc has written the track according to the order of the layout. This means you must sit through the entire burning process so you can switch discs when called upon to do so.

Disc-at-once prompts you to enter each CD right away so it can extract the audio tracks you have placed in the layout. So instead of writing each track out, and making you wait while it does so, it extracts each track and creates a temporary file on your hard disk. When all the tracks have been read, it then writes the entire CD, and you can go off and tend to other matters.

Finally, if you find that the preset options Easy CD Creator uses for this dialog box don't suit your needs, you can use the Set as Default button after making the necessary changes to make the program remember the current settings.

When you are ready, click the OK button to start recording. When Easy CD Creator is first installed and used to create a CD, it tests the source CD-ROM drive to ensure that it supports digital audio extraction (see Figure 5.10). It also makes sure that the drive can keep up with the speed at which the CD-RW drive will be writing the new CD.

It is important to understand that if you selected the disc-at-once method, after the laser starts to burn the CD, it can't stop or pause for even a second until the entire CD is written (un-

Arcane CD Speak

Digital audio extraction (DAE) refers to the process of taking the data straight from the CD, still in digital format, and sending it to the program (Easy CD Creator in this case) that is "ripping" the data from the CD.

less your CD-RW drive supports BurnProof technology). The burning of a track, session, or entire disc is a continuous process that cannot be interrupted from beginning to end. If the buffer becomes empty in the middle of writing a track, which can happen for various reasons, a buffer underrun occurs and your disc becomes a coaster.

After testing your drive's capabilities (which should happen only once unless you reinstall the program or install a new CD-RW drive), the CD creation process begins. If you have one or more audio CDs for your source(s), Easy CD Creator prompts you for each CD in turn, collecting the necessary tracks from each disc before requesting the next CD it needs (see Figure 5.11).

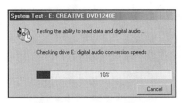

Figure 5.10

Easy CD Creator can test the digital audio extraction capabilities of a CD-ROM drive.

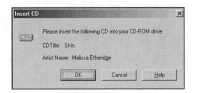

Figure 5.11

Easy CD Creator prompts you to insert each CD you have used for the layout.

Don't Get Burned

When you are using your computer to record a CD, *don't use it for anything else* unless you have a very fast CPU, have a CD-RW with BurnProof, and don't plan on making heavy use of other resources, such as memory. As a rule of thumb, leave the computer alone while it's burning the CD!

After the program reads the last CD, the next step is to write the table of contents and then begin writing each track. In Figure 5.12 you can see the dialog box named Record CD Progress (be sure to click the Show Details button for the full view of this dialog box). This display shows you where the program is in the CD-burning process.

In the upper-left quadrant of this dialog box, you can see the stage of the burn process Easy CD Creator is currently at, along with an icon below that indicates the actual burn speed. The stages you should expect to see include preparation of the audio data, writing the CD-R table of contents, writing each individual track and, depending on what record method you chose, closing the CD.

To the right of the two icons is a pair of progress bars. The upper one indicates the progress Easy CD Creator has made on the current stage in the process. If it's recording an actual audio track, the name of the track appears above the progress bar. The second bar indicates how close to completion Easy CD Creator is in making the entire CD.

Figure 5.12

The Record CD Progress dialog box shows the progress Easy CD Creator is making.

Current task being performed

Progress of entire disc

Progress at current task

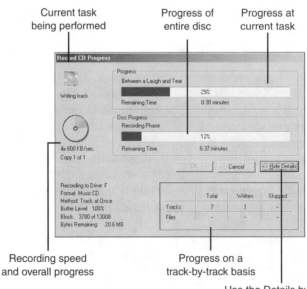

Recording speed and overall progress

Progress on a track-by-track basis

Use the Details button to show or hide the information on the bottom half of this dialog box

If percentages aren't enough for you, at the bottom-right you can see a small chart showing the number of tracks contained in the layout and the number that have been written so far. If you are having a bad day, you might also see something under the Skipped column, which means that the program could not write that particular track and moved on to the next one. If you're making more than one CD, text beneath the chart lets you know how many copies have been completed and how many are left to go.

If you get bored with the process, or decide you've made a big mistake, click the Cancel button at the bottom. This aborts the process, and regardless of what has been written to the CD, you'll have another coaster to put your drinks on.

After everything is finished, yet another dialog box pops up to let you know whether the process was successful or not. In most cases, you'll see the dialog box depicted in Figure 5.13.

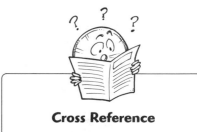

Cross Reference

For more details on the Record CD Progress dialog box, check out Chapter 3.

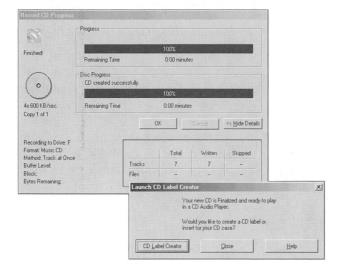

Figure 5.13

Easy CD Creator tells you when it has finished successfully.

Notice that in addition to telling you the CD was created successfully, Easy CD Creator also asks if you'd like to create CD labels or jewel case inserts. If this is something you'd like to do now, click the CD Label Creator button and check out Chapter 14, "Making Killer Labels with Easy CD Creator CD Label Creator." Otherwise click Close.

Creating a DataCD Project CD

If you're still feeling the burn from your audio CD creating workout, the good news is that it's not much different using Easy CD Creator to burn your own data CDs. You audiophiles may be wondering why you'd want to take time out to make a data CD when there's a new top 10 music CD you want to burn. Well, remember that your computer isn't infallible and accidents do happen. If you value what's on your computer, burning a good data CD to back up your important files, programs, or even your operating system (Windows for most of you) is some of the best protection you can have. No power surge is going to affect a small disc sitting on a CD rack.

Cross Reference

If problems occur during the creation process, then something has gone terribly wrong and the CD will most likely not be playable. Check out Chapter 20, "I Ain't Got No CDs, but You Should See All My New Coasters: Troubleshooting CD Recording," for help and insight as to what went wrong.

In the section "Creating a MusicCD Project CD," you learned about the many ways to start the Easy CD Creator program for the creation of audio CDs. Opening a data CD creation session isn't much different. You can open the Project Selector, highlight Make a Data CD and choose the DataCD Project option. Alternatively, you can open Easy CD Creator via the Start menu (Start, Programs, Roxio Easy CD Creator 5, Applications, Easy CD Creator) and then select the File menu, New CD Project and, finally Data CD. In either case, you're presented with the window shown in Figure 5.14.

As you can see, there's not a whole lot to distinguish this window from what you saw in the previous sections. However, this time around, the Layout pane is divided into two sections. On the left you have a tree listing of all the folders selected for inclusion on the CD (empty in this figure). On the right, is a listing of all files currently set to be stored in the folder selected in the left-most pane of the Layout.

Creating a Data CD Layout

Even though you're working with data rather than music, adding that information to the CD Layout pane is done in the same way as we just described. You can select individual or groups of files or even entire folders when creating the layout you want to use to create the CD and drag them into the Layout pane (or use the Add button).

Notice also that at the bottom of the application window you can see indicators of how much space you've used so far when you are creating the layout. Whereas with audio CDs you needed to worry about keeping less than 74 minutes of audio in your layout, data CDs work in megabytes (MB). So the progress bar running across the bottom of the Easy CD Creator window measures megabytes instead of minutes! Also, directly above this indicator you can see the amount of space you're currently using and the amount of free space still available (with different figures for 750MB and 800MB recordable CDs). Use this as a guide when adding files or folders to the data layout (see Figure 5.15). After the number hits or goes below zero, you need to scale back your layout a bit.

Layout pane now has two sections: a tree folder
(left) and a list of files in current folders (right)

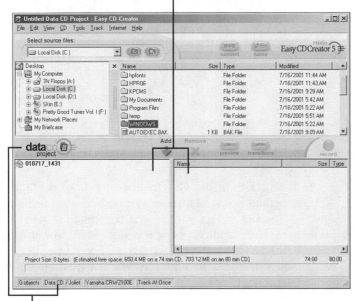

Figure 5.14

The DataCD Project window isn't much different from a MusicCD Project window.

Indicates a data CD project

Between Tracks

In this section, we are just creating an ordinary data CD—like the ones you get when you buy computer software. You can also click File on the menu bar, select New CD Project and choose to create an enhanced, mixed-mode, or bootable CD. Since these types of CDs (usually containing both audio and data) are all variations on creating CDs as described in this chapter, we don't elaborately cover specific steps for each CD type here. You can get more conceptual information on these CD types in Chapter 2.

Figure 5.15

The layout for this data CD won't fit onto a normal 650MB CD, but could be squeezed in to one that can store 700MB of data.

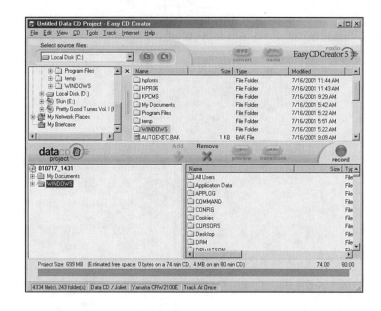

Between Tracks

Unlike creating an audio CD (which typically requires a CD-R disc for compatibility with home CD audio players), it doesn't matter much if you use a CD-RW or a CD-R disc to create your data CD. Most current CD-ROM drives can read either format, so long as there is a complete session on the disc.

Notice that Easy CD Creator gives your data CD the default name of a series of numbers akin to a serial number. If you want to change this to something more descriptive, click the label to highlight it, pause for a second and click it again. The name should now be selected with a blue highlight with a cursor at the end. Just type in the disc's new name and press Enter when complete.

If you'd like to change the name of other files and folders your data CD layout, you can use the same steps. If you find that you need to remove files or folders from your layout, just select the files or folders in question and either press Delete on your keyboard, click the Remove button between the Source and Layout panes, or right-click your selection and click Remove From CD Project.

Finally, as with music CDs, saving your layout early and often is always a good idea. Simply click File and Save Project List to give your layout a safe home on your hard drive.

Starting the Copying Process

Once your data CD layout is set, it's time to start burning the CD. Again, this is not much different from creating an audio CD. Simply put a blank recordable disc in your

CD-RW drive and, to start the copying process—
you guessed it, click the Record button between
the Source and Layout panes (or click File, Record
CD). You are once again confronted with the
Record CD dialog box that allows you to select the
target CD-RW drive and the same options you
could select for audio CDs, such as Track-At-Once
or Disc-At-Once.

Especially if the Layout pane indicates you're not
going to fill your data CD to capacity, this is one
kind of CD which it would make sense to consider
making a multisession CD. To do so, select the
Track-at-Once option for Finalize Session. Don't
Finalize CD (see Figure 5.16). This enables you to
add another session later should the need arise.
Roxio's software has a session selector that can be
used to switch between sessions, so you can use
this method to fill up a CD over time. You can find the Session Selector by clicking
Start, Programs, Roxio Easy CD Creator 5, Applications, Session Selector.

Between Tracks

If this is the first data CD you've
created, Easy CD creator may run
a data transfer rate on your CD
or hard disk drives to determine
their capabilities. This should be
a quick, error-free process that
won't cause you any problems.

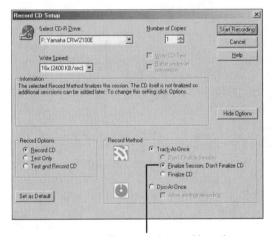

Usually, you'll want to choose this option.

Figure 5.16

*Unless you know that
you'll never want to add
more data to your CD,
only choose to finalize the
session, not the CD.*

Once you're ready, click Start Recording. The Record CD Progress display used for data
CDs pops on the screen, which looks nearly identical to the one shown in Figure
5.12.

The steps that will be performed to create a data CD, however, are a little bit different
than for an audio CD. Instead it goes through the following stages:

➤ File system generation

➤ Copying files

➤ Writing track

➤ Closing session (or closing CD)

After the program finishes creating the necessary data structures on the CD, it then starts copying files from your hard disk to a temporary location. Next, it writes a single track out to the CD-RW drive. If you chose to finalize the session, but leave the CD open, you'll see Closing Session as a step in the CD creation process. If you selected to close the CD, you'll see Closing CD in the CD Creation Process dialog box.

You can keep adding sessions to the CD until you run out of space on the disc. Even if you leave the CD open, you can use the disc in the CD recorder or in most CD-ROM drives—just as long as the *session* itself is closed. If you want to prevent any additional sessions from being added to the CD (fino, absoluto, it's all over now), you can choose to close it.

When you're ready to close a CD, just select Close CD instead of Close Session when you add the last session to the CD.

Creating an MP3 CD Project CD

The key benefit behind the popularity of the MP3 file format is that it's a very compact way to store lots of near CD quality music. That music can then be offloaded to portable MP3 players, MP3-enabled car audio players, PDAs, and even some cell phones. Heck, there have already been demonstrations of MP3 watches! (Although I haven't seen one in the flesh, so to speak.)

As the ability to read and play MP3 files begins to invade every aspect of consumer electronic devices (normal CD and DVD players are starting to get in on the act), the ability to record *a lot* of MP3s to a single CD becomes more and more valuable. After all, a 64MB MP3 player might be able to store what? 12 to 15 songs or so? Compare that to the number of tracks a 650MB can store! Even if your car's CD player or your home theater's DVD player can't read MP3 files, you could still burn a single CD full of MP3s and play it in your office computer's CD-ROM. Who needs office Muzak when you can jam to Lenny Kravitz while trying to avoid any and all on-the-job responsibilities! Not to mention the fact that you've got a better chance of not hearing the same song twice of a CD filled with MP3s than you do when listening to the radio, and without all those annoying commercials, too!

Although it's really little more than a glorified method of creating data CDs, Easy CD Creator comes with an MP3CD Project application that makes the process of producing an all-MP3 CD a simple one.

Creating an MP3 CD Layout

To get started, either use the Project Selector to select Make a Music CD, MP3CD Project or use the Start menu to open Easy CD Creator, select the File menu and choose New CD Project, MP3 CD. Either way, you'll end up with the window shown in Figure 5.17.

Just as with a data CD, you can drag and drop (or use the Add button) dozens, even hundreds, of MP3 music files from the Source pane to the Layout pane. The sky is very nearly the limit when making an MP3 CD.

Since keeping track of hundreds of MP3s on a CD can be tricky, the main reason Roxio seems to have made creating an MP3 CD its own mini-application within Easy CD Creator is to let you organize MP3 files through the use of a playlist. The Playlist in the MP3CD Project window, which has the default name of playlist.m3u, allows you to customize the order in which MP3 tracks appear on an MP3 CD (something you cannot control in the DataCD Project mini-application). However, unlike modifying track order in an audio CD, you cannot control play order in the Layout pane. Instead, you must select Edit in the menu bar and choose MP3 Playlist Editor (see Figure 5.18).

Between Tracks

If you'd prefer to have a more descriptive name for your playlist than playlist.m3u—and who wouldn't—you can change it using the same click-pause-click method discussed in the data CD section of this chapter for changing the volume name for a data CD. Unfortunately, you cannot get rid of the .m3u extension.

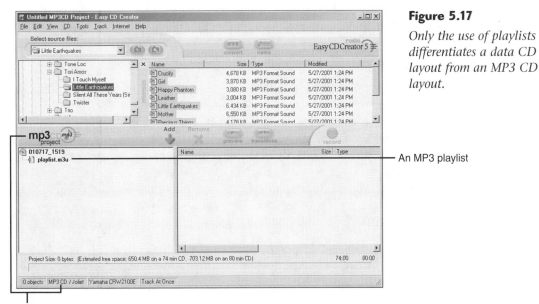

Figure 5.17

Only the use of playlists differentiates a data CD layout from an MP3 CD layout.

An MP3 playlist

Indicates an MP3 CD project

Figure 5.18

The playlist editor gives you control over the ordering of MP3s in your MP3 CD layout.

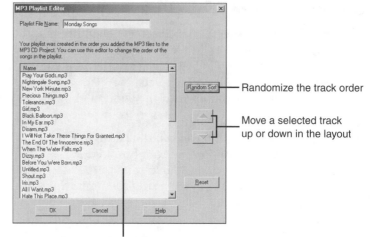

Randomize the track order

Move a selected track up or down in the layout

Current order of MP3 tracks

Don't Get Burned

In testing different MP3 layouts in the MP3CD Project application, I've discovered what can only be a bug in the way the program interprets MP3 filenames. Say you've got two song tracks from different artists that are similar, only in that they have the same first word in the song title. For example, try putting "Little White Lies" from Sammy Hagar on the same MP3 layout as "Little Earthquakes" from Tori Amos.

Easy CD Creator, for some reason, interprets these files to be one and the same. Whichever one you copy over second causes Easy CD Creator to ask you if you'd like to keep the original file or replace it with this "new" one. This would make a certain amount of sense (although not much more) if the song filenames were spot-on duplicates, but keep in mind that in this case, we're talking about just having only the same first word in their filenames.

Notice in this window that in addition to being able to rename the playlist and shift tracks up and down in the list, there is also a button labeled, Random Sort. After all, if you've got a CD jam-packed with MP3 files, do you really have the free time necessary to put them in a decent play order? (If you do, then get a job and stop loafing around, worrying about whether or not you should have a Toad the Wet Sprocket sound in front of a batch of Smashing Pumpkins tunes.) By clicking the Random Sort button, Easy CD Creator randomizes the play order of the MP3s in your layout (big surprise there). Once you're happy with the ordering of your playlist, click OK and get ready to burn.

Copying Files for an MP3 CD

Once again, creating an MP3 CD is really no different than making a data CD. However, if you want to have access to all songs at once, I do recommend that you burn only one session to a CD. You don't have to close it, if you think you might add more, but switching between CD sessions to hear more tunes is rather like having to get up to turn over a cassette tape. And who would want to go back to that dark age in home audio history?

To get the process moving, click the Record button to bring up the now familiar Record CD dialog box. After making sure that a blank recordable disc is in your CD-RW drive, click Start Recording and wait patiently for your work of digital audio art to be completed.

Between Tracks

Easy CD Creator will not let you burn a session to an MP3 CD without finalizing the session.

Upon successful completion of the burn, give your new MP3 CD a whirl!

Creating a Disc Image and Burning It to a CD

Instead of burning straight to a CD, you can use Easy CD Creator to make an image of the CD on your hard drive. I can hear the question now: Why would you do this? Well, if you want to create multiple CDs, creating a CD image on your hard disk and using the image to create new CDs as you need them is faster. Because they read and write information so much more quickly, copying from your hard drive can also be more reliable than from a CD-ROM drive.

Just like burning straight to a recordable CD, creating a CD image requires a CD layout. However, instead of using the Create CD button, use the Create CD Image option in the File menu of Easy CD Creator (see Figure 5.19).

Figure 5.19

Creating an image file of a CD layout can simplify the process of making multiple copies of a CD over a variable period of time.

Click to create a CD image file.

Click to create a CD from an image file.

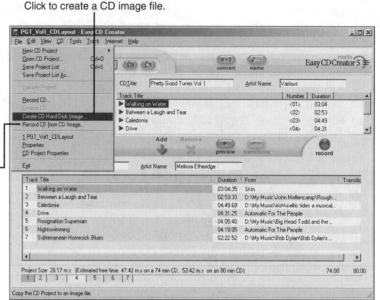

Don't Get Burned

It's important to remember, especially when creating music CDs, that image files can eat up a lot of your hard drive's real estate (up to 700MB). With hard disk capacities getting larger and larger with each passing year, this has become less of a concern than it used to be. However, if you create a lot of these image files and don't delete them when they're no longer needed, the amount of space they use can add up very quickly.

Easy CD Creator prompts you to select the location for the image file (be sure you have enough space on the hard disk!) and to give it a name. When you click the Save button, it then creates the image file. This won't take nearly as long as it does to burn a CD.

When you are ready to use an image file to create a CD, go back to the File menu and select Create CD from CD Image (refer to Figure 5.14). You are asked to select the image file on your hard drive that you want to use, and are then prompted to insert a blank recordable CD in the CD-RW drive. From there, the process works pretty much the same as for creating CDs from an audio or data CD layout (minus any of that nasty disc swapping if your layout had multiple source CDs).

The Least You Need to Know

➤ Easy CD Creator provides mini-applications that allow you to create CD-audio, MP3, and data CDs.

➤ When creating an audio CD, make sure to finalize the disc before attempting to play it in a home audio CD player.

➤ Avoid finalizing data CDs until you can no longer fit any more data onto them or you know you'll never need to add more. Just keep adding new sessions!

➤ A normal CD-R disc can store hundreds of near CD-quality MP3 files that can get you through a long work day without having to hear the same song twice.

➤ If you have to create duplicates of the same CD over an indefinite period of time, make a CD image from your disc layout. Then use the image file on your hard drive to quickly create new CDs from that layout as necessary.

Chapter 6

NTI CD-Maker: Says What It Does and Does What It Says

In This Chapter

➤ Creating an audio or data CD layout

➤ Extracting CD tracks to WAV files

➤ Changing the names of files or audio tracks when you create the CD layout

➤ Creating multisession CDs that allow you to use the CD-R disk to burn multiple sessions, each as if it were a separate CD

➤ Burning a custom CD

In Chapters 3 and 4 you learned how to copy CDs to make backups so you won't have to worry about losing or damaging the originals. In this chapter, you'll learn how to make custom CDs that contain audio files from a variety of sources, from CDs to MP3, and WAV files.

Creating a Custom Audio CD

You don't have to copy all the tracks from a particular audio CD, and in this chapter you'll learn how to create CDs made up from your own compilations of your favorite songs. You'll also learn how to create CDs that contain data files, just like having a large floppy disk! In either case, NTI CD-Maker allows you to pick and choose what you want to add to a CD layout, and then use the layout to create the CD.

Create a New Audio CD Layout

To create a new CD layout for an audio CD, you can simply click on the Audio CD button that shows up when you start the NTI CD-Maker program. Remember, you can either click on the desktop icon or use Start/Programs/NTI CD-Maker 2000 Professional and then click on NTI CD-Maker 2000 Professional. Using either method to invoke the menu, you'll then see something like what is shown in Figure 6.1. Just select the Audio CD button from this menu.

Figure 6.1

Select the Audio CD button from the main CD-Maker menu to start creating a custom audio CD.

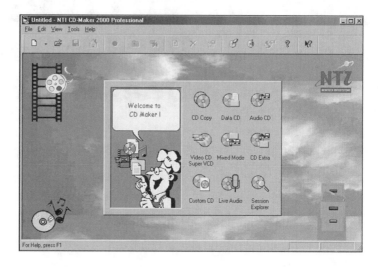

Once you've clicked on this button, you should see a display similar to that shown in Figure 6.2, but the appearance of this window will depend on the number of drives in your computer.

Figure 6.2

Once you start a new layout, you get an Explorer kind of view of your system.

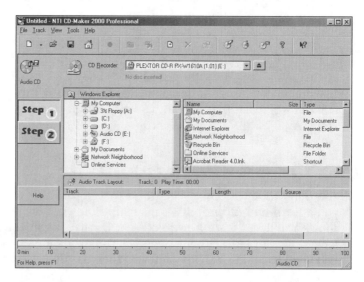

From this window, you first need to create a new CD layout. You do this by selecting audio tracks—which can be WAV files or even MP3 files—from the top portion of the screen, and adding them to the Audio Track Layout portion at the bottom of the screen.

The simplest method to use is the drag-and-drop method—you locate the files you want to record to CD and simply drag them to the Audio Track Layout.

Using the Explorer View (Drag and Drop)

In Figure 6.3, you'll notice that in the Windows Explorer pane I've clicked on drive D: and selected the directory named Frank. In this directory I've stored a lot of WAV files that I've extracted from CDs (which you'll learn about later in this chapter). Now I want to put together a compilation of songs that I like, instead of what those record producers thought best when they originally put these out on vinyl!

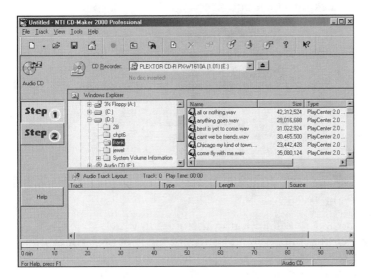

Figure 6.3

Use the pane labeled Windows Explorer to locate the drive and directory that contains audio files you want to put on your CD layout.

To add the first song, I'll just select it from the listing next to the Windows Explorer pane and drag it to the Audio Track Layout pane. In Figure 6.4, you can see that the actual name of the file shows up as part of the audio layout. This is the name of the file I extracted from a CD, not necessarily the complete name of the song. But we'll get to how you can name your songs in just a few minutes!

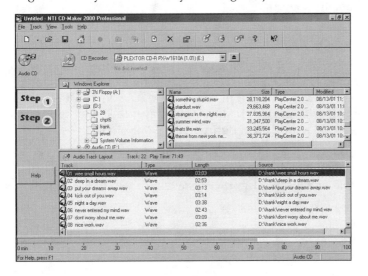

Figure 6.4

When you've dragged an audio track, the layout pane appears, showing the type, length, and source of the file that will be burned to the CD.

91

Using Add File

If you're not into dragging and dropping (which meant something entirely different when I was much younger), then you can add audio tracks to the layout pane using another method. Simply click on the Track menu at the top of the CD-Maker window and select the Add button. You'll get the standard Windows Open dialog box, as shown in Figure 6.5. You can navigate your way to the correct drive and directory, click on an audio file, then click the Open button to add it to the layout.

Figure 6.5

You can also add audio files using the Track menu by selecting the Add button.

Or if you're really in a hurry, just double-click on the audio file in the Open dialog box and it will be added to the layout.

As you continue to add songs, they will appear in the order in which you select them. You can change directories, and add different kinds of files. For example, you can add files from a CD that is in your CD-ROM drive. You can add MP3 files. Note that if you add MP3 files, they will be converted to the CD-DA format before they are recorded to the CD. Also keep in mind that MP3, which is a compact way to store audio files, uses what's called a lossy compression scheme. That is, if you convert a file from a CD or WAV file to an MP3 file, and then back again, you won't get the equivalent file. MP3 compresses the audio file and you actually lose some quality.

So if at all possible, start out with a CD or WAV file. This way the resulting CD you create will have the best quality sound.

Adding Text to Audio CDs

If you'll look back at Figure 6.4, you'll see that all the filenames of the audio files are what will appear in the Audio Layout Pane. I sometimes shorten names, and don't even capitalize song titles the way I should. I'm lazy, what can I say? However, if your CD burner supports adding text to the CD to allow your player to show you information about songs, then you can add this text during this layout phase.

To find out if your CD burner supports this function, simply select the drive in the Windows Explorer Pane and then, from the Tools menu select CD Drive Properties. From the properties sheets that appear, select the Write tab, shown in Figure 6.6.

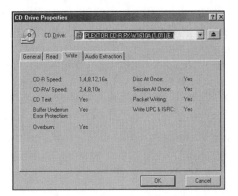

Figure 6.6

Use the CD Drive Properties selection from the Tools menu to see if your CD burner supports adding text to the CD.

As you can see, this set of properties pages can tell you a lot about your CD burner. The important thing here is that where it says CD Text: The data says Yes. That means you can not only record your audio tracks to the CD-R disc, but you can also enter the actual names of the songs, along with other data, and when you play the CD on a CD player that supports this feature, you'll see the song titles displayed.

Adding Text for CD Tracks

To add the CD Text for each track, simply right-click on the track in the Audio Track Layout pane and select Track Properties. Then, from the properties pages that appear, select CD Text. You can see in Figure 6.7 that you can fill in information about the track, starting with the title of the song.

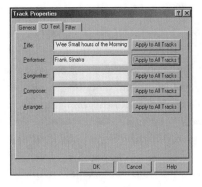

Figure 6.7

Enter the title of the song for the track in the first field in this dialog box.

You'll notice that you can also enter information for the following:

➤ Performer

➤ Songwriter

➤ Composer

➤ Arranger

While the first field, the song's title, may not apply to all the tracks on the CD you are creating, some of the others might. For example, I'm creating a compilation CD of songs by Frank Sinatra, so I can enter his name as the Performer and click the button next to this field labeled Apply to All Tracks. This way I don't have to enter the information again. When you right-click on the next track, for example, you'll see Frank's name again under Performer, if you selected the option to apply this text to all tracks. What a time-saver!

Or if you are making a CD of songs by different performers, simply edit the appropriate information for each track. Since I don't care to see listed such things as the songwriter, composer or arranger (I told you I was lazy), I'm leaving these fields blank!

Don't Get Burned

To expand upon a point that was made in the book's introduction there's a small discussion about the fact that some music companies have already experimented with, and used, and will probably continue to use as the technology develops, different schemes to make it impossible for you to use your computer's CD-ROM drive to copy or extract tracks from a CD. Yet the fair use clause in the copyright laws (at least in the United States) allow you to make backup copies for your own use.

These new copy-protection schemes depend on the fact that your CD-ROM drive on your computer is better at detecting errors than a typical audio CD player. So if you encounter this phenomenon, then I can offer one suggestion: Get Easy CD Creator. Use Spin Doctor. Plug a normal audio CD player into your computer's audio card and record the CD or tracks of the CD using Spin Doctor to create the WAV files (or MP3 if that's your preference) and then you can use them with CD-Maker to create your own compilations. Note again that neither the authors of this book, nor the legal department at Alpha Books is suggesting you make illegal copies of copyrighted music. I'm just suggesting a work-around for these stupid techniques that music companies are using, in my opinion, to circumvent the copyright laws, which allow you to make copies of something you already own!

Creating WAV Files from CDs

If you wonder where I got all these WAV files, it's simple. I extracted them from CDs that I own. Using CD-Maker, this is a simple process. You simply stick the CD in your

CD-ROM drive and right-click on the track that shows up. They'll be labeled something like Track01.cda, where the .cda extension means it's a CD-DA file (the format used to write audio tracks on a CD). You can simply right-click on one of these tracks and, from the menu that appears, select either Play (if you are not sure what track you're selecting) or Convert Audio Format.

For extraction, select the second option. In Figure 6.8, you can see that a dialog box will open, allowing you to choose the location in which you want to save the file. The default name will be the text "Track" followed by the track number on the CD. You can edit this to give the file a more meaningful name. One thing to keep in mind is that when naming a file, you can't always give it the same name as the actual song itself. This is because Windows doesn't like it if you use all the characters available in its available set for naming. Some characters, like the slash marks and others are reserved and have meanings for operating system commands. This is why I saved most of my WAV files with names close to, but not exactly the same as, the song titles. Just pick something that will help you remember the original song title and click the Save button.

Figure 6.8

You can extract an audio file from a CD into a WAV or MP3 format.

Oh, but before you save, notice also in Figure 6.8 that you can use the drop-down menu labeled Save As Type to select the type of file to save. You can select to save the song in either a WAV or MP3 format. Remember that the best quality is achieved by using the WAV format. It's just about the same as the CD-DA format with the bits ordered in a different manner. An MP3 file is a compressed version of the audio file.

However, if you have a portable MP3 player, you can find this feature of CD-Maker an ideal way to extract audio tracks from CDs and download them to your player. If you have an MP3 player that will read CDs that have MP3 files on them, then you can literally record hours of music on a single CD using MP3 format.

However, since we're creating a compilation CD of songs that were extracted from a CD, I'd prefer to keep the quality and re-record using the CD-DA format.

Using Filters on WAV Files

Sometimes you can get WAV files from sources other than CDs. For example, there are many programs, both commercial and some available on the Internet, that allow you to record songs from your old vinyl collection. Need I mention Spin Doctor, which has almost a whole chapter all to itself in this book? However, if you create a WAV file from a source that isn't of the same quality as those made from a CD, you can use CD-Maker's filters to try to improve the quality.

Simply right-click on an audio track in the Audio Track Layout pane and select Filter. In Figure 6.9 you can see that the Track Properties page appears again, but this time the Filter tab is selected.

Figure 6.9

You can use the Filter tab of a track's properties to remove noise, clicks, and pops.

While this technology isn't spectacular, it can result in some improvement. There are other programs you can buy that cost a lot more than Easy CD Creator or NTI CD-Maker that can help to improve the audio quality of audio files from older sources. However, these filters are free, so if you are using a WAV file that came from a non-CD source, these filter choices can help to improve the finished product. I suggest that you experiment to see if it works for you. Note that the Preview button will play the track, using your filter choices, so you can decide before you record!

Playing an Audio Track

If you are selecting from a large number of tracks, it may be that you made an error when you extracted a track and gave it a filename. Don't you just hate it when you give a CD to someone to listen to (just to listen to since giving them the CD would be against the law!), and the wrong song plays when they get to a certain track? Well, after you've composed your audio CD layout, you can check each song before you record. You guessed it, just right-click and select Play.

Editing the Audio CD Layout

After playing around with your audio layout, you might decide that you want to change the order of the audio tracks. This is a simple process. First, you can use the same drag-and-drop method you used to create the layout in the first place. Just place your cursor on the audio track in the layout pane and drag it to a different location.

Yet as with most applications, there's still another method you can use. Simply right-click on a track and select the Track Properties menu selection again. In Figure 6.10 you can see the General tab.

Figure 6.10

Use the General tab and simply change the track number to move an audio track to a new location.

All you have to do is select a different number for the Track Number field and the track will be moved to that position. All other tracks under it (or above it) will be renumbered. I still think the drag-and-drop method is easier, because you can see your results immediately in the Audio Track Layout pane. However, to each his own!

Saving the CD Layout

You know, I've told you I'm lazy, so sometimes I don't finish a job the same day I start it. This is especially true when it comes to creating my own CDs. So rather than just leave the computer turned on and hope there's no storm tonight that might kill my power supply, I can save the layout I've created so far and recall it later when I want to record the CD.

To save a layout, simply click on the File menu and select Save. A dialog box appears that you can use to decide where to store the layout file and give the layout file a name, as shown in Figure 6.11.

Figure 6.11

You can save the layout at anytime and recall it later for editing or for creating a CD.

Note that the .cdm file extension is used for layout files. The layout file itself *doesn't include the actual audio tracks,* just pointers to them. So if you move files about later before you recall this layout file, then you'll have problems!

Burn the Audio CD!

To actually create the CD, you can either work from the layout you've got on screen, or use the File/Open command to look for a saved CD layout. When you open a CD layout that you've saved, it will bring back the same display as when you last worked on it.

But eventually you've got to burn that CD or you'll never be able to play it! Don't worry—CD-R blanks are cheap today. You can always bring back the layout and change it and re-record another CD if you don't like what you initially created!

To burn the CD, you use the same process explained in detail in Chapter 4, by clicking on the Step 2 button or that big button on the top row with the red dot on it. Either way, you'll get the same recording dialog box, shown in Figure 6.12.

Figure 6.12

It's time to burn that CD!

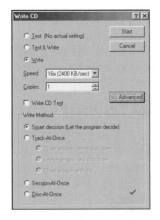

Notice again that I've chosen the radio button labeled *Smart decision (Let the program decide)* and there is a blue checkmark next to *Disc-At-Once.* This will record the entire CD, all tracks you've added to the layout, and close the CD so that it is playable on a regular CD player. Click the Start button when you're ready to record!

Again, the first thing the program will do is write the table of contents for the CD. Then it will start writing each track to the CD. You can watch the Recording in Progress dialog box, shown in Figure 6.13, to determine how long it's going to take to write your CD. You should also watch the Cache field to make sure that data is being supplied to the CD burner fast enough for the write speed you've chosen.

When finished recording your layout to the CD burner, you'll get a notification dialog box and the newly created CD will be ejected from the burner. Now it's time to turn to Chapter 15, "Using NTI JewelCase Maker," so you can create a label and jewel case inserts for this new CD you've created!

Figure 6.13

Watch that cache buffer! Stop working on other applications if your cache buffer is staying less than half-full.

Cross Reference

Before you decide on making labels or jewel case inserts for your CDs I suggest you also read Chapter 13, "What Do I Need to Make Great Labels and Inserts?" You don't have to pay for the most expensive labels, and you'll also find a great way to cut down on the cost of making the jewel case inserts (you know, the front and back covers that list the song titles). There is a cheaper way to create them using simple stuff you can get at a local office supply store at about a tenth of the cost of the pre–scored variety you'll have to buy from those label/insert vendors!

Creating Data CDs

There isn't much difference between creating an audio CD and a data CD. Well, there is that important difference that both use different formats when they write the CD. But the *selection process* is similar. You select files (or folders) from your computer disks that you want to burn to a CD and then you start the recording process. The same dialog box is used when you start the burning process, and we'll get into that a little more.

However, there is one thing to consider. Burning audio CDs is done so you can derive pleasure from the CDs you create. If you want to selectively store files from your computer on a CD, then it's most likely possible that the data CDs are more important than your audio CDs. For example, so long as you own the original CDs or other sources from which you created an audio CD, you can always recreate the CD, if you saved the layout. And if you didn't you can always recreate the layout and start from scratch.

But if you are recording a data CD, it's usually because you have some important information, be it word processing documents or database files, that you want permanent copies of for archival storage. So when you think about it, creating a data CD is more important than creating an audio CD. And because of this I highly recommend that you make two copies of important data, and then store them in different locations! For one thing, you never know what will happen to a copy of data you make.

A good systems manager always has an off-site copy backup of current data. If you have information that is important to you, then create one copy to keep locally and one to store safely somewhere else, such as a bank safety deposit box.

Create the Data CD Layout

Start the NTI CD-Maker 2000 Professional application using the same method you used to create an audio CD. However, from the menu shown *way* back in Figure 6.1, select Data CD from the buttons you see there.

The application will still present you with a window that is similar to the one shown for the audio CDs, but you'll be dealing with computer data files and folders.

Between Tracks

Actually, you can use the CD–Maker Data CD function to copy audio files, such as MP3 and WAV files to a CD using the same process you follow when creating an audio CD. The difference, however, is that you'll be creating a data CD, not an audio CD. In Appendix C, "The Colorful Books of CD Standards," you can explore the various formats that have been designed for CDs. When you create an audio CD, you are creating one that is vastly different than one used for data storage. However, keep in mind that you can always select audio tracks when creating a data CD. But also remember that you won't be able to stick the CD in an audio CD player to hear the tracks. Instead, you'll be preserving those WAV or MP3 files so you can restore them to your computer later and *then* you can use them to create an audio CD! WAV and MP3 files on a computer hard disk are, after all, no different than any other data file on your computer's hard disk.

In Figure 6.14 you can see an example of the window that CD-Maker opens when you select to create a data CD. There is a pane labeled Windows Explorer, which you can use to navigate through the hard disks, partitions, and CD-ROM drives on your computer. You can then drag from the Windows Explorer pane an entire folder to the Data Track Layout pane (at the bottom of the window) or you can drag individual files from the pane next to the Windows Explorer pane. To see individual files, just double click on a drive letter in the Windows Explorer pane or click once on the plus sign (+) that is positioned right before it. The contents of the folder will appear in the pane on the right side.

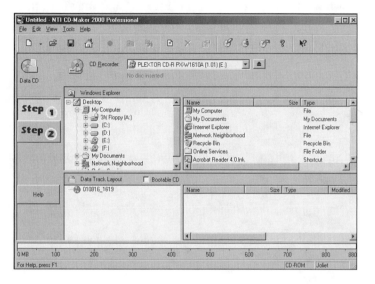

Figure 6.14

The appearance of the window used to create a data CD looks similar to the one used to create an audio CD.

Between Tracks

If you chose the Audio CD or some other button from the CD-Maker menu by mistake, don't worry. Just click on the itty-bitty, down-arrow button shown in Figure 6.14 that's on the far left of the button bar—right next to the one with the appearance of a dog-eared page. This is a standard way of choosing from within CD-Maker the kind of CD you want to create. When you click on that down-arrow, a menu will appear and you can simply select Data CD. As a matter of fact, this is a handy feature to use if you frequently change from making one kind of CD to another, so you don't have to close the application and reopen it using another button from the main menu. Just choose your type of CD here and the program will adjust its parameters accordingly.

Using the Explorer View (Drag and Drop)

Just as when you create an audio CD, you can drag folders or files from the top panes of the CD-Maker window to the Data Track Layout portion at the bottom. Just place your cursor on the folder or file you want copied to the data CD and drag it to the bottom pane.

In Figure 6.15 you can see that I've dragged several folders that I want to burn to a CD.

Figure 6.15

You can drag files and folders from the top panes of this window to the Data Track Layout pane at the bottom to add them to the CD you wish to burn.

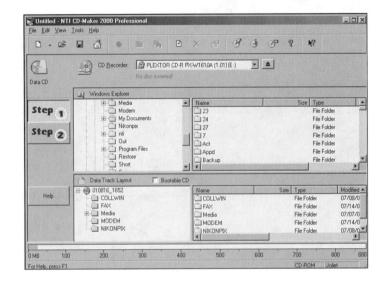

Notice at the bottom of this window you can see that there's a bar graph that shows you how much space (in MB) that you've allocated to the layout. Remember that you can now choose from 650 to 800 MB recordable discs, depending on your drive and its capabilities. Don't exceed the number of megabytes you can write to a single CD. Watch that bar graph at the bottom of the window!

You can also see that in Figure 6.15 at the top of the screen there's a field labeled CD Recorder. Notice in this figure that underneath the drive I've chosen, there's a warning text saying, "No disc inserted!" This is CD-Maker's way of telling you that you still need to insert a blank CD-R disc before it can burn your data to CD! This text stands out as it's displayed in a nice red color!

Using the Add Files Method to Select Files for the CD Layout

If you don't like drag-and-drop, there are two other methods you can use to add items to your Data Track Layout pane. The first is to use the Add button, which is on the button bar under the menu bar. This button also looks like a dog-eared page, but appears with a plus sign (+) inside the button. Just click this button and you'll get the Add folder and file dialog box, as shown in Figure 6.16. You can select files or folders in the standard way you do in most Windows programs and, after highlighting the folder or file, click the Add button.

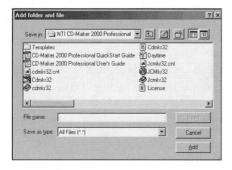

Figure 6.16

The standard Add folder and file dialog box allows you to select individual folders or files to add to the Data Track Layout pane.

If you really are an idiot (I know you're not a *dummy* or you wouldn't have bought this book ...), and beyond the comprehension of dragging and dropping, or using the button bar, then you are not yet beyond hope. There's still another method you can use to add files to the layout.

1. Click once on the Edit menu. (It's at the top of the window!)

2. When a menu appears, click on Add.

3. You'll get the same dialog box shown in Figure 6.17. Use this dialog box to find the files or folders you want to burn to the CD and for each one you select, click the Add button. The files or folders you select will be added to the Data Track Layout pane.

When you're finished selecting data files to burn to a CD, you have two choices:

1. Burn the CD so you can make your backup copy now.

2. Save the Data Track Layout.

If you regularly use the CD burner to make copies of the same application data files, then choose the second option. You can later recall the layout and burn a new CD that copies the same files, though they have been changed with updated data since you created the layout! I call this method the cheap man's backup, since recordable CDs are now so inexpensive (less than 20¢ each when bought in bulk) that you can afford to use the same layout and record your important data files every few days, or as often as your business or personal requirements dictate.

Between Tracks

If you like my idea of a "cheap man's backup," then you might also want to consider using a CD-RW disc—one you can erase and re-record to. Keep several of these in rotation so you can always go back to more than just one backup. However, by simply calling up a layout that has the application data files already selected, all you have to do then is insert the disc and start to burn!

However, before you save the layout, you may want to reorder some of the files or folders, or even rename them, as they will appear on the CD you burn. So let's discuss editing the layout!

Editing the Data CD Layout

Keep in mind that once you've dragged (or otherwise added) files to the Data Track Layout pane, you can edit the contents of that pane and it doesn't affect in the least bit the order of the actual data files on your hard disk. CD-Maker keeps track of where the source files are located. Here you'll just learn how to reorder, or add/delete items that you've placed in the layout pane.

It's Drag-and-Drop Time Again, with a Twist

First, just as you did with an audio CD you can drag and drop in the layout pane. One hint to give you, if you're planning on doing this, is to enlarge the pane. Put your cursor on the bar that separates the layout pane from the upper panes that represent your computer, hold down the mouse button and move the bar up. This will give you more room in the layout pane for moving things around and you won't have to use the scroll bar. As you can see in Figure 6.17, I've moved the bar up significantly, so I can see all the items that I added to the layout pane.

As you can see in this figure, I can now more easily see all my data at once, which makes editing much easier.

To actually edit the layout, you can use the regular drag-and-drop method. However, this method does have its limitations in CD-Maker. If you drag a folder and place it on top of another folder in the left pane (referred to in the documents as the Resource Tree), then that folder won't jump into that space in the tree, but will instead become a subfolder under the folder you place it next to. Perhaps this is something that NTI will address in the future.

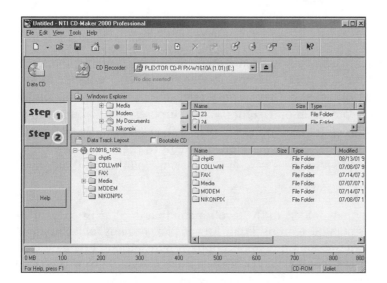

Figure 6.17

You can resize the panes that make up the window by dragging the bars that separate them.

You Can Rename Folders in the Layout Pane

You can rename any folder by right-clicking on the folder and simply selecting Rename from the menu that appears. The folder will then have a square box drawn around it (a standard Windows technique) and you can simply use the keyboard to enter a new name for the folder. This won't change the contents of the folder, but will simply give it a new name. This can be handy, for example, if you are saving application data file folders.

Suppose you have a folder labeled Receipts. You can drag it to the Data Track Layout pane and right-click, select Rename, and then name it something like "Receipts for June." This way when you look at your backup CDs you can more easily identify the data that's stored in the folder.

You Can Delete Files or Folders If You Change Your Mind!

To delete a folder or a file, right-click and select Delete from the menu. Or, highlight the file or folder by clicking on it once and click the big black "X" button on the button bar at the top of the window. You'll get a dialog box to ask you to confirm the deletion, just in case you've picked the wrong file or folder to delete!

Create New, Meaningful Folder Names in the Layout Pane

Want to move things around in the layout and put them in a different folder that doesn't exist on your computer's hard disk? Simply right-click in the layout pane and select New Folder. You'll see a New Folder entry in the pane along with a box drawn around it so you can use your keyboard to enter the new folder name. You can then do one of two things:

➤ Add items to the folder from other files and folders you've already placed into the layout pane.

➤ Add items to the new folder by selecting them from the Windows Explorer panes at the top of the CD-Maker window. To give you another example of how this might be useful, suppose you have several applications that produce similar files and you want to put them on CD for backup purposes, but you don't want to have a lot of folders cluttering up the CD you're about to burn. Just create a new folder in the layout pane and then drag the items to the new folder. You can drag (or use the Add button, as described earlier) to add files and folders to your new folder.

As you can see by creating new folders in the layout pane that don't exist on your computer's hard disks, it's possible to consolidate lots of files into less folders that have more meaningful names. Sometimes applications you install don't name their respective folders with names that you can easily recognize. Using the New Folder option you can create folders on the CD that you can recognize more easily.

Saving the Data CD Layout

If you are going to use the layout you've just created so you can use it again, then you'll need to save it. Just as you did for an audio CD, simply select Save or Save As from the File menu found at the top of the CD-Maker menu bar. The standard Windows Save As dialog box will pop up and allow you to choose both the location where you want to save the layout file, as well as give it a meaningful name. Again, layout files use .cdm as a file extension, so don't change that part or CD-Maker won't recognize it when you try to open it next time.

Between Tracks

I suggest that if you are using CD-Maker to make backups of important data on a frequent basis, you create a folder on your hard disk to hold just these layout files. That way you won't have to go searching for the layout file when you decide to use it again. Also, though you should have realized this by now, it wouldn't hurt to make the folder you store these layout files in as one of the folders that you regularly burn to your backup CD!

You can save the layout you've just created and use it now or at a later time. You don't have to actually burn the CD right after you make the layout file. You can use the File menu and select Open from the menu to open a layout file when you get ready to burn the CD. And since you just learned how to edit a layout file, you can continue to use these files in the future, making edits to them and resaving them as your applications or other needs change.

Burn That CD!

Burning the data CD is just as simple as burning an audio CD, it just produces a different kind of CD! The same dialog box is used. When you've decided you're ready to create the CD, insert a blank CD-R or CD-RW disc in the CD burner and click that big red dot on the button bar, or select the Step Two button on the left side of the window.

Now, if you'll look back to Figures 6.15 through 6.17, you'll notice that at the top of the window where there's a field titled "CD Recorder" it lists my Plextor CD burner. However, underneath this is the text "No disc inserted!" Don't worry. Go ahead and click on the Big Red Dot or click on the Step 2 button. In Figure 6.18 you can see that CD-Maker will remind you just how lazy you are and ask you to insert a blank CD-R (or CD-RW) disc.

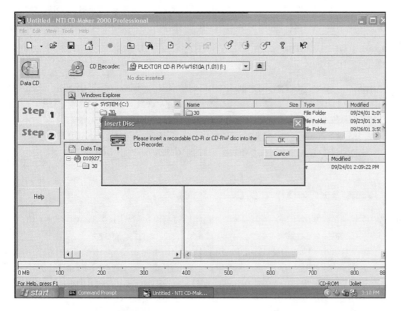

Figure 6.18

If you forgot to put a blank CD-R disc in the CD-Recorder, CD-Maker will remind you.

Just put the blank CD into the drive and the Write CD dialog box will pop up. In Figure 6.19 I've gone ahead and selected the Advanced button so you can see all the choices you can make when creating a CD.

Figure 6.19

The Write CD dialog box again pops up and allows you to select the method used to burn the CD.

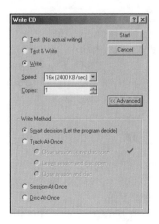

Notice here, however, that the checkmark isn't next to the Disk-At-Once radio button this time. Instead, it's next to the Close Session, Leave Disk Open button. You can read about recording different sessions on a CD in other chapters of this book—check the index! But the gist of the matter is that you can record more than one "session" on a CD if you don't have enough data to fill the whole CD. This way, you can use a CD several times (like for multiple backups), and close the CD when you are finished. CD-Maker provides a method to select which session you want to use when you need to get to the data at a later date.

Note that if you choose any option that says to close the disc, then you won't be able to write any additional data to the CD.

Once you click the OK button, the Recording In Progress dialog box will appear showing you the status of writing your CD, just as it did for audio CDs. And when the process is finished, you'll get another dialog box asking you to click on OK or Jewel Case. For most data CDs I don't create a jewel case, I just write on them with a felt-tip marker. It's your choice! For now, just click OK and leave the disc as it is.

How to Add Another Session to a Data CD

Remember that I told you that if you don't have enough data to fill up an entire disc to go ahead and write the data, close the session, but leave the disc open? Well, I didn't actually say that, but it was the method that CD-Maker wanted you to use. When you've created another layout (or if you are using the same layout at a later time to record the data again since it has changed), just click the Record button again or the Step 2 button and you'll see the dialog box shown in Figure 6.20.

Figure 6.20

You can add multiple sessions to a single CD before closing the CD.

The recording progress proceeds as usual, but you now have a CD with more than one session on it. No problem! NTI has provided a mechanism you can use to select the session you want to look at, but first you must close the CD.

Closing a MultiSession Data CD

When you've finished adding sessions to a data CD, you need to close the CD before you can access the data you've stored on it. This is a simple process. When you record your last session on the CD, don't take the default recommendation that you leave the disc in an open state. Instead, select the radio button on the Write CD dialog box (with the Advanced button selected) and choose the radio button labeled Track-At-Once. Then, in the radio buttons that now become visible under that selection, select the Close Session and Disc radio button labeled, which you can see in Figure 6.21.

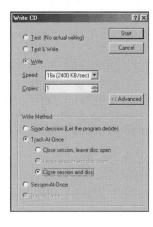

Figure 6.21

When you're ready to close the disc, choose these selections in the Write CD dialog box while you're writing the last session.

Again, like other recordings, the last session will be written, but this time the CD will be closed. Once the last session on the CD is closed, the CD can be read by ordinary CD-ROM drives. However, they'll typically see only the last session, but you'll learn in the next section about how to get to the data stored in the other sessions!

How to Read Data from a Session on a Multisession CD

To use a multisession CD you'll find that if you just stick it in your CD-ROM drive only the last session that you've recorded will be available. You can use Windows Explorer (or other application programs) to read the data in this last session. It will appear to be the entire CD to the operating system. So, if you've been using a multisession CD to record "successive" copies of data files in a backup scenario, then you may need to just look at the last session, which would be your last backup of these files.

However, those other sessions are still on the CD-R and you can still access them. Just fire up NTI CD-Maker and from the main graphical menu that you saw back in Figure

6.1, select the button labeled Session Explorer. It will take a few seconds for the application to read the session data and table of contents data from the CD you've created, and then you'll see the sessions you've created, as in Figure 6.22. Note that here we have three sessions, and the Session Explorer can be used to make any of these sessions available to the operating system so that you don't have to use the CD for just the last session that was recorded.

Figure 6.22

The Session Explorer can allow you to activate a particular session for data recovery.

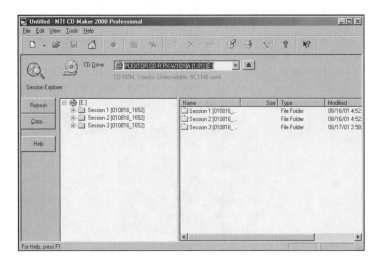

If you want to further look at the properties of this data CD, select, again from the Tools Menu, the entry Disc Info & Tools menu selection. You'll notice in Figure 6.23 that the Disc Info section of this dialog box tells you that the Disc Status field says that the disc is "Unrecordable" (because it has been closed). So that's it for this CD-R. It has been closed and any regular CD-ROM drive on your computer should be able to read the last session.

Figure 6.23

You can view the status of a CD-R disc by using the Disc Info & Tools option from the Tools menu.

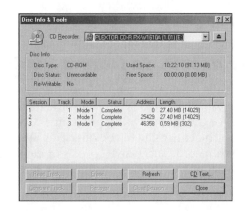

To actually get at the files in the other sessions, however, you'll have to use CD-Maker's Session Explorer and copy the files back to your hard disk or some other media (such as a Zip drive). You can't activate a session like you can with Easy CD Creator. Instead, simply use the left pane shown in Figure 6.22, and use it like you would Windows Explorer. You can double-click on a folder to see its contents if you just want to copy one file from the session. Or, you can copy an entire folder and all its subfolders and files to a location elsewhere on your computer.

To copy, select the session that contains the data you want to retrieve files from. Double-click on a session or click once on the plus sign in the left pane to expose the contents of each session. In Figure 6.24, you can see I've chosen Session 2 and you can see the folders contained in that session.

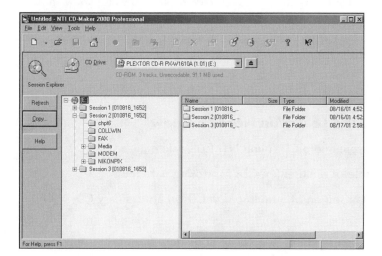

Figure 6.24

Select the session you want to copy files or folders from.

If you only want to get one file or a few files, double-click on any of the folders displayed under the session. Otherwise, to copy a file or a folder to another location so you can make it available to applications, right-click on the file or folder and select Copy from the menu. A dialog box will pop up that allows you to choose the destination to which you want to copy the files. Once you've selected the destination, click the OK button and the files will be copied from the session to the destination folder you've chosen.

In this chapter you learned that creating a customized CD, whether it be composed of audio tracks or data files and folders, is an easy task when using NTI's CD-Maker. The capability to use multiple sessions for a data CD even makes this utility more useful.

Between Tracks

You can also select the file or folder by clicking on it once to highlight it and clicking on the large Copy button on the left side of the CD-Maker Session Explorer window. Or you can highlight the file or folder and select Copy from the File menu. In either case, you'll get the same dialog box that allows you to choose the destination to which you want to copy the files.

The Least You Need to Know

➤ You can create custom audio CDs using NTI CD-Maker.

➤ You can create single or multisession CDs for storing data files.

➤ You can read the last session of a multisession CD on an ordinary CD-ROM drive.

➤ You can use CD-Maker's Session Selector to copy data from other sessions on a multisession CD.

➤ You can convert WAV and MP3 files to different formats using NTI CD-Maker.

➤ You can enhance audio tracks when creating an audio CD by using filters provided with CD-Maker.

Chapter 7

Your Very Own Recording Studio: Using Easy CD Creator SoundStream

In This Chapter

➤ Use SoundStream to record music to your hard disk from CD or any analog source (like LPs or audio cassettes) by connecting through your sound card

➤ Build a Media Library from MP3 and WMA audio files

➤ Record from virtually any source to a CD-R disc, with even more controls than the main Easy CD Creator program offers

➤ Use sound cleaning tools to clean up pops and scratches and those other annoying sound problems found on older recording mediums

If the audio features of Easy CD Creator don't get you everything you need, Roxio's CD-burning software suite has something else that probably will: SoundStream. SoundStream, which is essentially a new version of the CD Spin Doctor from previous versions of the Easy CD Creator suite, allows you to go beyond the capabilities of Easy CD Creator. In this chapter, we'll walk through the process of making a simple copy of a song using SoundStream. We'll also discuss some of the options you can use, such as recording files from a variety of sources to files on your hard drive. This, among other things, allows you to clean up audio to remove hissing, pops, and scratches.

What Is SoundStream?

SoundStream might sound like something that's caused by someone playing loud music on a jet, but in this case we're talking about a great program that comes with

Easy CD Creator 5 Platinum. In previous chapters, we've looked at using the Easy CD Creator application to duplicate CDs and to create audio and data CDs using the main Easy CD Creator application. The SoundStream application expands your recording abilities by letting you choose almost anything you can plug into the soundcard in the back of your computer as the input source for your music. For example, you can use SoundStream to create CDs from records (45s, 78s, EPs, and LPs), cassette tapes, radio signals, microphones, and even your TV or VCR.

After you've recorded the audio tracks you want, you can apply options that allow you to clean up some of the background noise inherent with older recordings such as records. Other options enable you to add special effects to the sounds you record. When you are ready to burn a CD, you can do it directly from the source, or you can create WAV, MP3 or WMA (Windows Media Audio) files on your hard disk that you can experiment with, using the clean up and sound effects tools, before sending them to a shiny new CD.

Between Tracks

Those of you who own Creative Labs Live 5.1 Platinum (or another sound card using the LiveDrive) will appreciate SoundStream greatly, because it finally gives you an opportunity to put all those cool drive-bay mounted inputs to work!

A Word About Phonographs

One thing that I particularly like about SoundStream is that it allows me to continue to listen to the many records I bought either as I was growing up or from yard sales and flea markets over the past few years. This way, I can make a CD copy of these fragile LPs so that they don't have to be subjected to an eventual, slow death when I play them over and over again.

To transfer the audio from old phonograph records you have lying around, you, obviously, must have a phonograph player. Although that might seem redundant, keep in mind that finding a good phonograph player in the new millennium might require the assistance of an archaeologist on par with Indiana Jones. You can look around in yard sales and such, but I caution you to beware of that source. You're likely to get a unit that either doesn't work, or that has a needle in such bad condition that the end results won't be worth the effort or cost.

Don't Get Burned

Playing vinyl records on a banged up phonograph, particularly one with a badly worn needle, can further degrade the only copy you own of a particular record. For this reason, backing up your LPs on CD becomes a valuable alternative.

Although you aren't likely to find phonograph players at the local discount retailers or even some of the supposedly totally audio/video concept stores, you will find them here and there. While the few totally new players that can be found might not be cheap, believe me when I say that it is worth the cost. Shelling out a little over a $100 is a worthy expense if you are going to use the device to transfer music from vinyl to CDs that might never be re-mastered.

And, if you like the results you get using SoundStream, you might start frequenting yard sales a little more often to look for some long-out-of-print titles and discover music you once thought lost.

When purchasing a phonograph player, however, there is one important factor to consider. In the "olden" days of component stereo systems, you bought a receiver/amplifier, speakers, tape deck, and phonograph as separate items. The phonograph plugged into the receiver using a special port that directed its sound through a pre-amplifier. If you use this kind of phonograph with your sound card, there's no pre-amp, so you'll either have to buy one—check Radio Shack, they'll know what you're talking about—or buy a new phonograph that has audio/video outputs, which means that it has its own pre-amp built into its guts.

Between Tracks

If you're stuck trying to plug a preampless phonograph player into your soundcard, there's another way to get around the problem than buying a new "amp'd" phonograph player. If you can connect your current player to a component stereo system that has a headphone jack, you can connect your sound card to the receiver using a headphone cable that has the appropriate plugs at both ends. You might lose a touch of sound quality, but it's cheaper than buying a new phonograph player!

Creating a CD as Easy as 1, 2, 3 ... and 4

Because using SoundStream to create CDs from other music CDs or MP3 files is not much different from doing so in Easy CD Creator, this section focuses on using SoundStream to burn a CD from audio CD tracks, the Media Library or folders on your hard disk. After that, we look at creating WAV, MP3 or WMA files on your hard disk that can be further modified before recording them to a CD.

Starting up the SoundStream application is simple. Just double-click the Easy CD Creator desktop icon, pass your mouse over Make a Music CD, and then click SoundStream from the options in the middle of the window (see Figure 7.1). You can also get SoundStream working for you by using the Start menu. Click Start, Programs, Roxio Easy CD Creator 5, Applications, and then, finally, SoundStream.

Click here
Easy CD Creator 5 platinum
Select a Project
SoundStream
The easiest way to create compilations of your favorite music from MP3, CDs, LPs and more.
make a music CD
musicCD project
Create professional music CDs using advanced features and save your record list between burns.
make a data CD
mp3CD project
Create an MP3 CD with over one hundred MP3 songs and enjoy hours of music on your computer or MP3 CD player.
make a photo or video CD
CD copier
web-checkup
CD label creator
help
roxio

Figure 7.1

Using the Roxio Project Selector to open SoundStream.

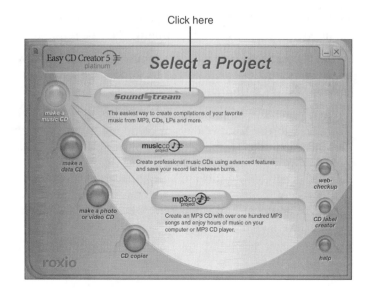

This starts SoundStream, bringing up an application window that looks very different from Easy CD Creator (see Figure 7.2).

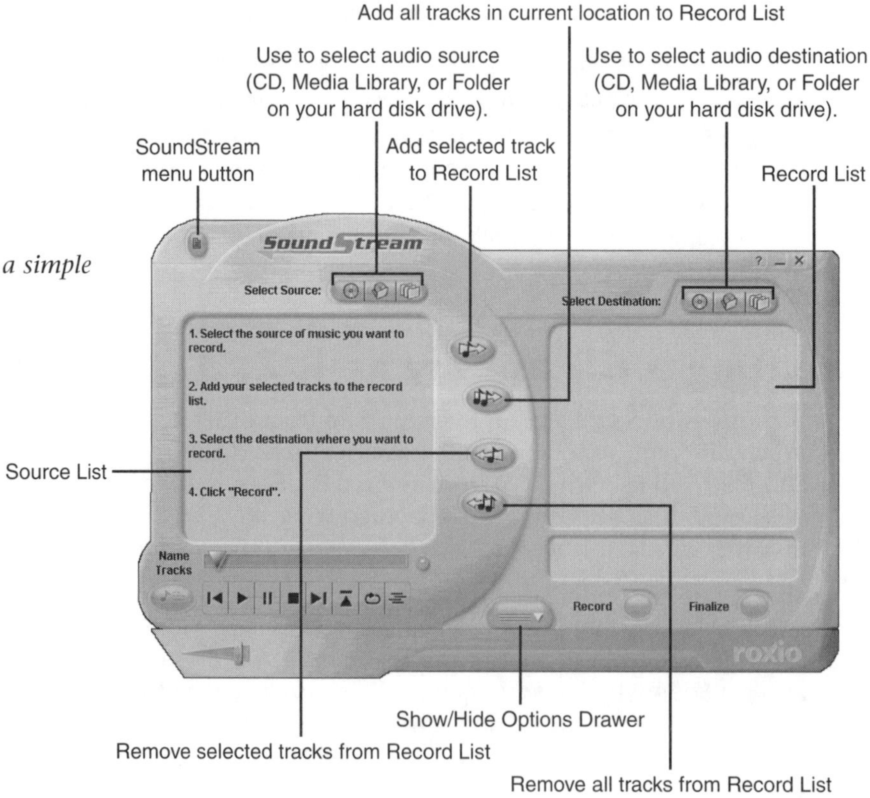

Add all tracks in current location to Record List
Use to select audio source (CD, Media Library, or Folder on your hard disk drive).
Use to select audio destination (CD, Media Library, or Folder on your hard disk drive).
SoundStream menu button
Add selected track to Record List
Record List
SoundStream
Select Source:
Select Destination:
1. Select the source of music you want to record.
2. Add your selected tracks to the record list.
3. Select the destination where you want to record.
4. Click "Record".
Source List
Name Tracks
Record
Finalize
roxio
Show/Hide Options Drawer
Remove selected tracks from Record List
Remove all tracks from Record List

Figure 7.2

Creating a CD is a simple four-step process.

As you can see from the text in the Source List, creating a CD with SoundStream can take as little as four steps. In the following sections we'll dissect how to accomplish each of these steps. If you look near the bottom of Figure 7.2, you can also see an Options Drawer button. This lets you use several helpful tools for getting more from your audio. Keep this button in the back of your mind for now; we'll come back to it soon. Before we get to all that though, let's take a look at how to record music into the SoundStream Media Library.

Recording to the Media Library

A new feature in SoundStream with Easy CD Creator 5 is the implementation of a Media Library for storing information about audio files on your computer. I'm beginning to believe that Media Libraries must be the big thing for the new millennium because virtually every audio related PC program, like MusicMatch, Windows Media Player, etc., etc. uses one. Unfortunately, the Media Library included with Sound-Stream is not nearly as user friendly as those assembled in other applications (for reasons I'll explain as we go along).

Before you can get busy adding contents to the Media Library, you need to jump through a couple of preparatory hoops. In SoundStream, click the SoundStream Menu button and choose Properties from the list that appears. This brings up a properties dialog box, from which you should select the Music Library tab (see Figure 7.3).

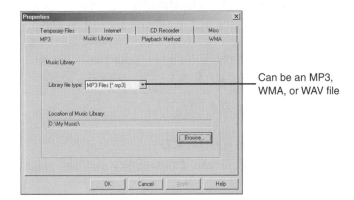

Can be an MP3, WMA, or WAV file

Figure 7.3

The Music Library tab allows you to customize the way in which Sound-Stream stores music on your hard disk.

This is where you select what kind of files you want the Media Library to record audio as and where you want those files stored. You can easily use the default location for storing your audio files, but as you can see from this figure, I've chosen a custom location on my second hard drive. To change the location on your computer, click the Browse button and select a new location. From the Library File Type scroll box select either MP3, WMA, or WAV files.

If you're unsure of which to choose, know that WAV files have the best quality, but are *entirely too big* to be a viable option if you intend to put more than a dozen or so

117

audio tracks into your Media Library. That leaves MP3 and WMA, which really come down to a matter of personal taste. Both are of comparable quality, with WMA files coming out just a touch smaller (per minute of audio) than MP3s. However, for various reasons, including the fact that MP3s are a nonlicensed format, (meaning you don't have to prove to your computer that you own the music when copying it to a portable MP3 player or compilation CD from your computer) I prefer MP3s.

Assuming you didn't choose the WAV file format, there is still one more hoop for you to jump through. For both MP3 and WMA files you need to choose the encoding quality SoundStream will use to create these files. There are individual tabs for both MP3 and WMA files in the Properties dialog box. Click the one appropriate for your use.

Don't Get Burned

If you want a custom location in which to store audio files, make sure that location already exists on your computer. You cannot create new folders from within the Browse For Folder dialog box. If you don't know how to create a folder using My Computer or Windows Explorer, it's probably best that you stick with the default.

Regardless of the tab you chose, you'll see a single scroll box for choosing your MP3 or WMA encoding quality. Regardless of the encoding type, I recommend using the 128kbps, 44kHz, Stereo format. This is on par with CD quality and is the best quality you can use for WMA files. However, if you've got a good ear and are encoding to MP3s, I do know folks who prefer to use a quality setting of 160kbps, 44kHz, Stereo. Once you're satisfied with your selections, click the OK button to close the Properties dialog box.

The first step in making the Media Library useful is actually getting music stored in it. To do this you need to locate a folder on your hard disk with audio files or insert a music CD into your CD-ROM drive that contains music you want to store on your hard disk.

Putting Music in the Media Library from CD

Getting music tracks into the Media Library from CD is no big trial. Just walk through the following steps:

1. Insert a music CD into your CD-ROM drive. SoundStream will immediately recognize that you have inserted the CD.

2. To get track names for an unknown CD click Name Tracks on the Source List side of the SoundStream window. It will take a few moments for SoundStream to connect to the Internet and get the information it needs. Once it's done, you'll see the CD's contents displayed properly (as opposed to, Track 1, Track 2, etc.) in the Source List (see Figure 7.4).

3. Once you have the CD information, you need to create a place on your hard disk to store it. On the Record List, choose the Music Library button. This opens the Save Album As dialog box.

Identified source CD

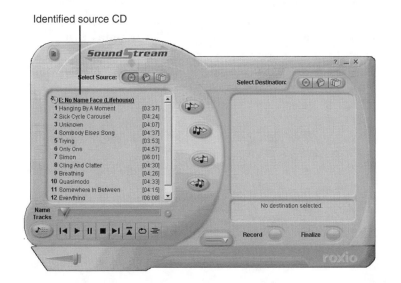

Figure 7.4

A CD that SoundStream has properly identified as Lifehouse, No Name Face, using an online database.

4. Click the New button to bring up the Properties dialog box shown in Figure 7.5 and then enter the album's information (title, artist, and genre). The information you enter here causes folders to be created on your hard drive to store the music in (a folder for the artist with a sub-folder for the CD title).

5. This will add that CD's artist and album titles to the Music Library list on the left side of the Save Album As list. Select the appropriate folder for your CD and click Choose. This sets your destination for the CD files.

6. If you only want certain files off the disc, either select them one at a time and click the Add Selected button or select multiple files by Ctrl-clicking each one before clicking the Add Selected button. To add all the files, click the Add All button.

Between Tracks

If this is the first time you've used SoundStream to put music on your hard drive, it will need to test the audio extraction (or ripping) speed of your source CD drive.

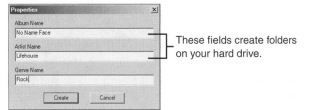

These fields create folders on your hard drive.

Figure 7.5

The Music Library Properties dialog box uses the information you enter to create folders for the CD artist and title on your hard drive.

119

7. Finally, you're ready to begin recording the CD to your hard disk. Click the Record button, bringing up a new recording screen where the Source List used to be, containing yet another record button (as if you didn't mean it the first time) like the one in Figure 7.6. Click this Record button to make all the magic happen (and depending on how many audio tracks you're ripping, be prepared for a lengthy wait).

Once the recording is complete, a small dialog box pops up letting you know. You have but to click OK to send this message box packing.

Figure 7.6

The recording process is monitored where the Source List normally appears.

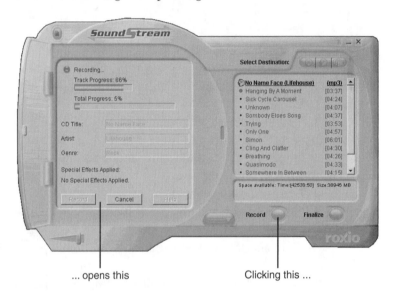

... opens this   Clicking this ...

Putting Music in the Media Library from Music Files Already on Your Hard Disk Drive

If getting files from music CD to the Media Library seems like a tedious process, you might want to just sit back and take a break. Logging existing files on your hard drive into the Media Library, which ought to be an easy task, requires a fair amount of hoop-jumping as well.

Because the Media Library is very specific (and inflexible) about where it wants to store audio files, a folder for the artist and a subfolder for the CD title, it can be a chore getting existing audio files in it without a lot of finagling.

If you've already got a ton of MP3 or WMA files on your hard disk in a filing system with which you're quite happy, but that's not like the one shown here, you may want to consider abandoning your use of the Media Library. However, if you decide Media Library employs a system that is better than yours, use these steps to put your music in the Media Library structure (understanding this will create duplicates of your existing audio files in a new location):

1. In the Source List, click the Select Folder As Source button to bring up the dialog box shown in Figure 7.7.

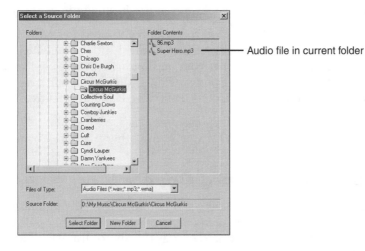

Audio file in current folder

Figure 7.7

The Select a Source Folder dialog box allows you to browse for folders on your hard drive that contain audio files.

2. In the Select a Source Folder dialog box, browse to the location of your existing MP3, WMA or WAV files. When you select a location with valid audio files in it, those files appear in the pane on the right of the dialog box. Once you've got the location you want selected, click Select Folder.

3. The tracks in this folder now appear in the Source List, so it's time to set your destination. Click the Select Media Library as Destination button and follow steps five and six from the previous section to add the destination folder.

4. Now select the tracks you want to add to the Record List and use the Add buttons to get them there.

5. Finally, click the Record button, and then click the second Record button that appears.

SoundStream begins copying the file to its new location, which is a much quicker process than for copying from CD. However, now, you've got a new problem. The file or files you've just copied are taking up space in two different locations on your hard drive. I can only assume you want to keep this new copy, so make sure you use My Computer or Windows Explorer to delete the old location.

Now, if you've got a bunch of MP3 or WMA files on your hard drive that are already organized in the

Don't Get Burned

Should you decide you no longer want to view a CD listing in your Music Library you can delete it from the Save Album As dialog box. Be warned however, that this not only removes the listing from the Media Library, but it also removes the tracks and folders from your hard drive.

style SoundStream likes to use, you might be thinking you're sitting pretty right now. If you've only got music from a couple of CDs, you might be right. But if you're like this author and having tracks from a hundred or so CDs on your hard drive, your smile is going to disappear faster than environmental legislation in the Bush administration.

If you click the Select Media Library as Destination button, all you need to do is click New to bring up the Properties dialog box and enter the CD artist, title and genre information. When you click create, you'll find that your audio tracks are already listed in your library. Simple, right? Now do that for every single CD directory your have on your hard drive. Then report immediately to a doctor to receive carpal tunnel treatment!

Finally, we're ready to start using SoundStream for something other than busy work.

Recording to Folders on Your Hard Drive

Recording files from CD to your hard drive is a very similar process to putting files into the Media Library. The good news is that this is far simpler. Because it's rather pointless to select the Media Library or a folder on your hard disk as the Source list, we'll focus simply on recording from a CD.

1. With a music CD in your CD drive, select the Music CD button for the Source List.

2. In the Record List, click the Select Folder as Destination button. This brings up the dialog box shown in Figure 7.8.

Figure 7.8

This dialog box allows you to select a folder on your hard drive in which to store audio files.

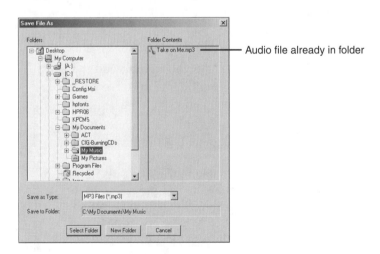

Audio file already in folder

3. Using this Save File As dialog box, choose a location to which you want to store the CD tracks you want recorded (if you plan to store them in folders named after the artist and CD title, just use the Media Library steps from the previous sections).

If you want to put your music files in a folder that doesn't currently exist, get as close as you can in the folder tree to the location you want and click the New Folder button. This adds a sub-folder to the currently selected folder (type in a new name for it).

4. In the Save as Type scroll box, choose to record your music files as WAV, MP3, or WMA. Once you have the folder you want highlighted, click the Select Folder button.

5. Select the files you want recorded to this destination and use the appropriate Add button to add them to the Record List (see Figure 7.9).

Figure 7.9

Music from a CD in this computer's CD-ROM drive has been chosen for storage in this computer's hard drive.

6. Once you're ready, click the Record button once and then click the second Record button that appears where the Source List used to be. This kicks off the recording process just as we described in the section, "Putting Music in the Media Library from CD."

Once the recording process is complete, click OK on the confirmation dialog box and you're good to go!

Recording to CD

For this example, we are going to keep it simple and add source tracks from both a CD and files on your hard drive that can be recorded to a CD-R disc. As with recording to your hard disk or Media Library, you must first select a source using the three buttons above the Source list that I've already described. As when using Easy CD Creator, you can choose select audio tracks from multiple sources. Then select the Select Music CD As Destination button from the equivalent set of Record List buttons.

The list shown in Figure 7.10 has tracks selected from multiple CDs, a folder on my hard drive, and from my SoundStream Media Library bound for a final destination on the blank CD in my CD-RW drive.

Figure 7.10

When recording to a CD, you can select music from multiple sources in your Source List.

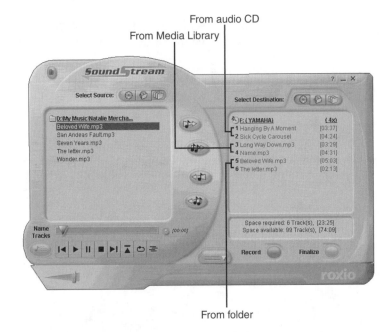

From audio CD

From Media Library

From folder

Before you go looking to hit the Record buttons, there is one more hoop to jump through. Click the SoundStream menu button and select Properties from the list that appears. Click on the CD Recorder tab of this Properties dialog box (see Figure 7.11).

Figure 7.11

The CD Recorder Properties tab let's you ensure that SoundStream has the correct information for your CD-RW drive.

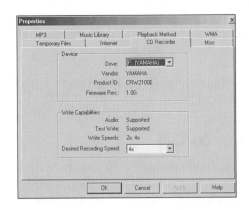

Make sure that your CD-RW drive is selected in the Drive drop-down list and then make sure the Desired Recording Speed drop-down list is also set to a recording speed you're comfortable with (this list will not show a speed that your drive is not physically capable of using). Click OK to close this dialog box.

From here it's a simple matter of clicking Record (again, in two locations as described in the "Putting Music in the Media Library from CD" section of this chapter).

The CD recording process begins. Depending on the speed of your drive and how much music you're recording (up to 74 or 80 minutes, depending on the type of CD-R you're using), this could take anywhere from an hour to five or ten minutes. When the process is complete, click OK in the success dialog box that appears. Assuming you don't intend to add anything more to the disc you've recorded to, click the Finalize button to close the CD.

If you've read Chapter 5, "Drag and Drop with Easy CD Creator," then by now you're probably wondering what there is to differentiate SoundStream from making an audio CD from Easy CD Creator. Believe it or not, there is much more we've yet to discuss. Now that we've gained a fundamental understanding of how SoundStream works, let's take a look at these other advanced features.

Getting the Most from SoundStream with the Options Drawer

SoundStream contains a host of options you can choose from that can be used to obtain music from a wider variety of sources and modify the quality of sound you've recorded. These options can be found by clicking the Show Options Button. This opens up a tray of buttons that you can use to modify and record audio and open applications related to the music content creation and recording process (see Figure 7.12).

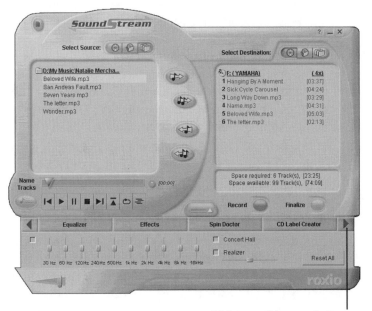

Figure 7.12

The SoundStream Options Drawer gives you access to several audio CD related applications and controls.

Click to scroll for more buttons.

This Options Drawer contains a wealth of controls for you to make use of. These controls include:

➤ Equalizer brings up a graphic equalizer that allows those who aren't tone deaf (like myself) to change the amplitude of selected sound frequencies for an audio track. Unless you already know what all these frequencies are, I recommend you leave these be.

➤ Effect gives you access to three audio quality-related controls: Sound Cleaning Level, Pop Removal Level and the Normalizer. Use the checkboxes associated with each option to enable or disable them.

➤ The Sound Cleaning Level is a tool for removing the hiss if you're recording from an audio tape. Use the slider to control the degree of aggressiveness with which you want SoundStream to attempt to remove the hiss.

➤ If recording from an LP, the Pop Removal Level allows you to attempt to remove the pops that come from playing a scratched vinyl album.

➤ If you're looking to make a compilation CD from several sources, you'll no doubt find that many of those sources were originally recorded at different levels (so some songs play louder than others). Enabling the Normalizer tool causes SoundStream to analyze every track in your Record List for variances in recorded volume level and equalize them.

➤ Spin Doctor in Easy CD Creator 4 was essentially what SoundStream is in Easy CD Creator 5. In Easy CD Creator 5, its focus has moved solely towards recording audio from outside analog sources, such as audio cassettes and LP records. We'll discuss the Spin Doctor in the section, "Using the SoundStream Disc Doctor."

Between Tracks

The Sound Cleaning and Pop Removal sliders are more aggressive when set further to the right and less intrusive (to sound quality) when set to the left.

➤ CD Label Creator predictably opens the CD Label Creator application that we cover in Chapter 14, "Making Killer Labels with Easy CD Creator CD Label Maker."

➤ Sound Editor opens up the Sound Editor application, which you can use to modify WAV files. Sound Editor is covered in Chapter 19, "Roxio's Sound Editor."

➤ Internet Links goes to the Internet and displays a series of links to Roxio's Web site in the Options Drawer (if your connection is not active, SoundStream automatically dials it). None of these links are particularly useful unless there's information you need that only Roxio can provide (like information on product updates).

Other SoundStream Options

If you select the SoundStream Menu button and click Properties, you see a Properties dialog box. We've already dealt with most of the tabs in this dialog box in previous sections, but there are still a few loose ends to tie up. The tabs we have yet to discuss are as follows:

➤ Temporary Files

➤ Internet

➤ Misc

➤ Playback Method

If you click the Temporary Files tab, you'll find a pair of radio buttons. Since Sound-Stream must make use of space on your hard disk temporarily when copying music from CD (or other sources external to your hard drive) to another CD it needs a folder to do that work in. The default selection, Put Temporary Files Where There Is The Most Room should be fine for most users. If you do need to select a custom location, select the second radio button, Put Temporary Files In This Directory. Then click the Browse button to choose that new location.

The Internet tab should look familiar to you if you've made use of the main Easy CD Creator application, as discussed in Chapter 5. The first check box, Force Online Title Lookup, forces SoundStream to look up a CD's information, even if you've already entered it manually. Enable the second check box, Automatically Get Track Titles When CD Inserted, to force SoundStream to automatically check the Internet to obtain disc information for any CD you put in your computer. As discussed in Chapter 5, the Access The Internet Using a Proxy Server check box is only useful for those operating in an office network and can be safely ignored.

The two options available in the Misc tab aren't much to write home about. The first is a button labeled, Reset "Don't Show Me Again." Certain screens in SoundStream occasionally appear to let you know basic information that an experienced user already knows. There is often an option for Don't Show This Screen Again. If you check it, SoundStream will follow that instruction. If you find that you'd like to see screens like this that you've disabled, click this button. Secondly, the check box labeled Display Times For Existing MP3, WMA And WAV Files allows you to show time information for MP3, WMA, and WAV files in the Source or Destination lists.

Finally, the Playback Method tab allows you to choose how to hear audio output on your computer when using SoundStream. The default option, Use WaveOut For Playback is fine for most users. However, if you know that your computer's sound card supports DirectSound, which most current ones do, you can try clicking Use DirectSound For Playback. For the most part the choice made here is about personal taste, and while most users won't notice the difference regardless of which method they choose, it can be worth experimenting with this option.

Once you're done setting options, click OK to close the Properties dialog box.

Using the SoundStream Spin Doctor

As we hinted at way back at the beginning of this chapter, you can use SoundStream to recover aging music collections from decaying analog sources like LPs and audio cassettes. This requires the use of the SoundStream Spin Doctor. To open the Spin Doctor, make sure the SoundStream Options Drawer is open and click the Disc Doctor's button from the list. The screen shown in Figure 7.13 appears.

Figure 7.13

The new face of the CD Spin Doctor is quite different from what users of Easy CD Creator 4 were used to.

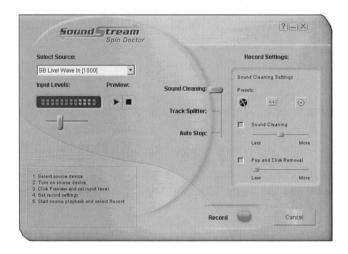

As you can see there are quite a few options listed in this window. However, as this screen indicates, it all boils down to five basic steps.

1. Select a source (like a cassette or record player)

2. Turn the source on

3. Set input levels

4. Set record settings (these are the pop and hiss removal sliders discussed in the options drawer section)

5. Start source playback and select record

Really, this is a bit of a simplification on Roxio's part, but we'll walk you through it, so don't worry.

Selecting a Source

Selecting a source involves making two decisions. One, what the real source of your music will be (like an LP or audio cassette). Two, what input connection on your sound card that will require. The available inputs are listed in Select Source drop-down list. Generally, you'll want an option that indicates an input from your sound card.

Available audio input sources

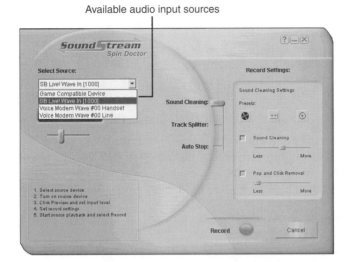

Figure 7.14

To record from an analog source you need to be sure you've selected the right input device in your PC (usually your sound card).

As you can see from the figure, I have a Sound Blaster (SB) Live audio card. Once your source is selected, make sure you've connected it to your PC's sound card and turned its power on. In Figure 7.15, you can see how I've connected my Sony Walkman to my PC using front-mounted ports that come with the Live Platinum 5.1.

Figure 7.15

Connecting an audio cassette player to a PC through the Creative Labs LiveDrive device.

Once connected, ensure that the cassette, LP or whatever audio source you're using is set to the position containing the music you want to capture.

Setting Input Levels

With your audio equipment all set up and rearing to go, you need to make sure you're recording at a level that's not going to blow out your speakers. First, make sure the Input Level slider is set to a position somewhere in the left third of the slider.

Now it's time to preview your audio to ensure that you're hearing what you want to hear. Start playing the music from your source and then hit the Preview Play button. Once the audio begins playing, you should be able to hear it coming out of your computer speakers, and, as shown in Figure 7.16, the Input Level lights should spring to life.

Figure 7.16

Using the Input Level light to judge the recording volume level.

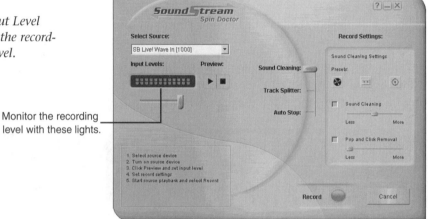

Monitor the recording level with these lights.

Watch the Input Level lights closely. What you want to see while audio is playing is the green lights consistently lit, with occasional spikes into the yellow range. If it gets as far as the red lights once in a while, that's okay, but if you find that you're consistently in the red, lower the Input Level slider (if it's too quiet, slide it further to the right).

Once you're satisfied with the input level, click the Preview Stop button and stop playing your source.

Adjusting Record Settings

Now that you're almost ready to go, it's time to deal with the issue of recording quality. Specifically …

➤ Cleaning up any finger-nails-on-chalkboard type pops or hissing that might be present on your audio source.

➤ Splitting up multiple tracks (after all, vinyl records and audio cassettes don't have easily identifiable divisions between tracks like CDs do).

➤ Setting auto-stop options for controlling when the recording session should end.

Making sure that the Record Settings slider is set to Sound Cleaning, notice that Spin Doctor contains three presets for recording audio sources and the level of cleaning these sources should get. You should feel free to experiment with these sliders manually, but generally speaking, you should just click the Presets For Record, Tape, or CD buttons and leave it at that.

Taking the Record Settings slider down to the option for Track Splitting, you'll see options like the ones in Figure 7.17.

Don't Get Burned

Setting the Split Whenever Silence Is Detected slider too low will cause the Spin Doctor to split tracks too frequently (like between beats in a song). However, setting it too high, will cause it to skip over silences entirely, causing separate tracks to not be split at all.

Don't Get Burned

Don't forget to clean up your source before you use the cleanup options of Spin Doctor. For LPs, use a good record-cleaning kit to make sure the LP is in tiptop condition before you record. If you haven't used the phonograph in a while, make sure the needle is clean and take appropriate action. For tape decks, you can usually use isopropyl alcohol and a cotton swab to clean the tape heads. Doing all this sort of work up front can only help to improve the sound you get recorded to CD.

Although Spin Doctor can perform some cleanup of the sound outputted from your LP, this is done based strictly on the audio signal it gets. For some of its work, Spin Doctor looks for specific patterns in the signal based on the degree you tell Spin Doctor to look for (thus the sliding bars). When it sees these patterns it either eliminates them (as in pops and clicks from scratches) or tones them down (as when it performs a general sound cleanup). Sometimes a particular frequency is toned down or removed—whether it is background noise or part of the intended song, Spin Doctor cannot tell. You should record your audio to a file and experiment with Spin Doctor to find out which settings work best—for each LP from which you're recording!

Figure 7.17

Use Track Splitting options to control how Spin Doctor should split a single analog stream into multiple tracks.

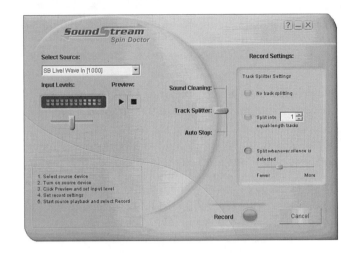

Here you can control if you want Spin Doctor to determine when to split up tracks and, if so, how you want it to do it. To eliminate the option entirely, select No Track Splitting. If you want your audio stream to be broken up into tracks of equal lengths, use the spin-box control to select how many equal lengths you want. Finally, you can have Spin Doctor attempt to split the tracks whenever a certain amount of silence is detected. You'll need to experiment with the slider on this option to find an ideal setting.

If you ratchet the Record Settings slider down one more notch, you get the options shown in Figure 7.18 for Auto Stop settings.

Figure 7.18

Using Auto Stop settings, you can control when Spin Doctor stops recording from an analog device.

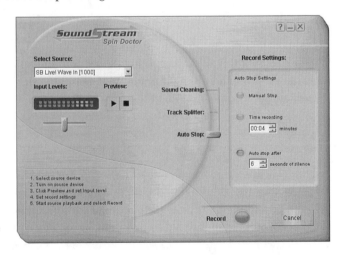

Auto Stop settings allow you to control when recording of analog audio should stop. The best option is probably to stick with the manual stop options and take care of it all yourself. However, if you want to turn over control over this to the Spin Doctor, you can select either Time Recording to record for a set amount of time before stopping, or to Auto-Stop after a specific period of silence. The former option is useful if you're recording a specific track and already know its length. The latter allows you to attempt to break after a break in songs, or by setting for a longer silence gap at the end of a tape or record where there is nothing but silence.

Making It All Digital

Finally, it's time to begin recording. This is probably the easiest part of the whole process. Just get your source to its start point (don't start it yet!) and hit the Record button. This brings up the window shown in Figure 7.19.

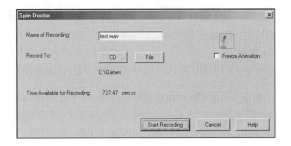

Figure 7.19

Choosing a location to store the analog audio stream and what to call it.

From here you need to select a name for the track being recorded and the recording destination (File or CD). If you select File, you need to choose a folder on your hard drive in which to place the file (you can only record to WAV format). If you select CD (which I don't recommend, you can always record to CD later), make sure a blank disc is in your CD-RW drive before you start. When you're ready, click the Start Recording button and get your audio source playing.

Between Tracks

Usually it's best to record to your hard drive first without using any sound cleaning options. This way you're getting your audio, in its current state, into a digital format on your hard disk. Once it's there you can always experiment with different sound cleaning options or deal with converting it to the MP3 or WMA audio file formats. By recording directly to CD you're pretty much putting all your chips down on the idea that it will be perfect the first time, which probably won't be the case if you're not yet experienced using all these options.

The recording process now begins. While the recording is happening you can only choose to Pause Recording or Stop. Keep an eye on the Time Available For Recording field, as it will let you know if you're running out of storage space on your chosen location for the music. When you're ready to stop, click the Stop button and stop your source from playing. A small SoundStream dialog box pops up, letting you know that your recording was successful. Click OK and go enjoy your new digital music file!

The Least You Need to Know

➤ Use SoundStream instead of Easy CD Creator when you want to build a Media Library or manipulate your audio using options the aforementioned program doesn't have.

➤ If you're just starting out putting music files onto your computer's hard drive, use SoundStream's Media Library to help keep your music more organized.

➤ You can record from almost any kind of analog source—phonograph, cassette player, and microphone—directly to the CD recorder, by way of a temporary file. Or you can record WAV files and edit them before burning them onto CD.

➤ When recording from an analog source, use SoundStream Spin Doctor's cleaning options to do some cleanup work on audio that doesn't play as clearly as it used to. Also, make sure you're starting with a clean source.

➤ If you only want to copy a CD, use Easy CD Copier instead of SoundStream.

Part 4

Eat Your Heart Out, Mr. Spielberg: Creating Video CDs

Video tapes aren't going to last forever. If you have a collection of tapes of popular movies that you bought, you can probably find them now or at a later date on DVD. However, what about all those tapes that you made of the family during holiday times or other special events?

In Part 4 you'll learn how to take digitized video and create CDs that can at least hold up longer than those VHS tapes will. With video capture cards coming down in price rapidly, and with many people now using digital video cameras, putting video to CDs is a great way to preserve your collection until the price of recordable DVDs comes down a little more!

Chapter 8

Pre-Production: What Any Home Video Producer Needs

In This Chapter

➤ What are Video CDs and why should I care?

➤ What is the MPEG standard?

➤ What you need to get started recording video to CD

Ever notice how your older videotapes don't look quite as good as the day they were purchased (or first recorded)? I've been using VHS tape for more than 20 years to store videos I like. One of the problems with videotape, however, is that it suffers from wear and tear and, of course, the ravages of time. The analog format in which the video and audio are recorded on a tape doesn't provide for the complex error correction that can be performed when recording digitally.

Video on CD?

In this chapter we will look not at digital videotape, but at what you'll need to get started in using Roxio Video CD Creator or NTI CD-Maker Video CD and Super VideoCD software to put audio and video onto a recordable CD so that you can view it on your computer or most DVD players. Even though, in this book, we focus on just two applications you can use to create Video CDs (VCDs), it is important to re-member that other options are available; some better, some worse.

Between Tracks

A new feature in Easy CD Creator 5 Platinum is a tool called Video Impression. While it has nothing to do with actually recording video to CD, it can be used to edit your digital video content. Those of us who'd rather be tortured with ten minutes, rather than 20 minutes, of someone's baby videos can appreciate the value of editing out the non-essential parts of a drawn out video. After all, who wouldn't want to see a much shorter cut of the pod race scene in *Star Wars: The Phantom Menace!*

Although your VHS tape might last a few decades, the expected lifetime for recordable CDs is at least 100 years. Barring some major medical breakthroughs, that's long enough for most people! When you use a VCD creation program to make a video CD, there are a few tradeoffs, however. The first is in time, and the second is in quality. A DVD disc can hold an entire movie, along with alternate camera angles and subtitles and so on, but a CD can't provide that kind of capacity. So, if you are planning to put more than about an hour of video on a CD, plan on using two instead.

Secondly, a DVD movie is encoded using an MPEG-2 video standard. Video CDs, however, use MPEG-1 instead. While many differences exist between the two standards, the most important one is in quality. For those wondering what these formats mean, stay tuned as MPEG gets explained in the following sections.

Between Tracks

Even though you can only use MPEG-1 video clips to create a video CD, don't forget that you can still record video in format you want. You can still use the main Easy CD Creator or CD-Maker 2000 programs to copy the actual files to a recordable CD. This way you can still open the files using a suitable program if you want to view them. They won't be usable in a DVD player, but on your computer you should have no problems.

Until DVD recorders become available at a reasonable price (which you can expect to see over the next year or two), and a means is found to legally make copies of DVDs, given their copy protection schemes, I guess you'll have to settle for second best: using CD-R technology.

How Do You Play Video CDs?

The VCD that you can create using VCD creation program follows the standards set forth in the White Book of Standards for CDs. For a quick overview of the White Book, take a look at Appendix C, "The Colorful Books of CD Standards."

Your VCD should play in any DVD player installed in your computer or on an ordinary DVD player connected to your TV set. Note that your mileage might vary, so it's good practice to perform a test before you spend a lot of time and money creating VCDs that might not work. Particularly, if you have an older or cheaper DVD player, you might not be able to use it to play a VCD. You can run into the same kind of problem when trying to play CD-R audio discs on older CD players. Sometimes they just don't work.

The VCD should also work in a CD-I player, if you have one. These are usually used for commercial purposes, so if that's your business, you can use Video CD Creator to make discs.

Arcane CD Speak

The White Book describes the standard format for making a video CD. By creating a standard CD format, various manufacturers can produce players that can use the CDs.

What Is MPEG and Who Are These Motion Picture Experts, Anyway?

The term *MPEG* comes from the standards body that created the MPEG standards: the Motion Picture Experts Group. This body has released several versions of MPEG standards, proving that even the "experts" can't get it right on the first try. For creating a true White Book–compliant VCD, you will need to use MPEG-1. This is an important thing to remember when you decide to buy a video capture device to transfer video-tapes or other recorded material to your computer for the purposes of creating a VCD. If you want to use it with VCD Creator, for example, then you'll need to make sure it can capture in an MPEG-1 standard.

To make matters a little more complicated, variations on the MPEG-1 format exist, specified in levels. The one you'll need to worry about is the one used for a White Book VCD. When you save a file using an editor, look for a "file type" option that specifies a VCD format. For example, one possible option gives you the choice of NTSC VCD 352x240 NTSC (29.97 f/s), which is suitable for a VCD.

Arcane CD Speak

As in the previous paragraph, the key letters to look for are **VCD.** But, for the curious, **NTSC** refers to the type of video signal used to display the image. Ever watched a TV in North America? That signal is NTSC. Many other countries use different signals. The 29.97 number is the number of frames per second for the video clip. A video image is really just a series of still frames shown very quickly to create the illusion of motion. North American television shows 30 of these frames each second. So why does my software say 29.97 instead of 30? Well, if I ever meet the programmers, I'll have to ask.

Regardless of their specifics, there are several video editors available on the market capable of working with MPEG-1 video, and I don't want to make specific recommendations, as personal taste and certainly your budget are significant factors. However, keep in mind that most video capture cards, detailed in the following section, come with additional bonus software that does allow you to edit video.

Buying a Video Capture Device

Before you can worry about recording video using your CD burner, you need to worry about putting video on your PC. Unless you're downloading video from the Internet or recording from a camera attached to your PC, you need a video capture card. Most video cards that I've seen in the stores lately can save a captured video in several formats. If you have a card that doesn't support saving the video file in MPEG-1 format, you're not out of luck yet. If you have a video editing program, like the Video Impression utility included with Easy CD Creator 5 Platinum, then you can probably read in a video file in one format (like AVI) and then save it as MPEG-1. Usually, capture devices include an editing program of some kind, but they're not always the best. However, buying a quality capture board or editing program isn't always cheap, so balance your choice between what you really need and what you can afford!

You have several options when it comes to purchasing a video capture device. You can get an internal card to put inside your computer, or you can buy an external device that hooks up to the back of your computer via a cable, usually of the USB (Universal Serial Bus) or IEEE1394 (Firewire or i.Link) variety. If you're comfortable working with the hardware in your computer, making a purchase and getting it all set up should be no problem. But for those who prefer to just let the magic happen, you'll need the help of that techno-geek friend of yours or the store where you buy the capture board.

Own a Digital Video Camera?

If you have no interest in schilling out money for an expensive capture device, being that even the less expensive ones can set you back over $100, then you might have another option. If you already own a digital video camera equipped with a Firewire connection for transferring video, then you might be in luck. Most digital video cameras, in addition to recording to digital videotapes in the MiniDV or Digital8 format, can receive video from a TV or VCR (though this usually requires special cables included with the camera).

In that case, all you need is a Firewire connection in your computer. While most PCs don't include that connection by default, you can buy a Firewire card much more cheaply than the cost of a video capture device (less than $100). The Adaptec FireConnect 4300 pictured in Figure 8.1, is one of the better cards you can find on the market.

Figure 8.1

The Adaptec FireConnect 4300 makes connecting a digital video camera to your PC for transferring video a simple task.

From here, the process is more time consuming than difficult. If you have video shot with your digital video camera, then all you have to do is hook up your camera to your PC and transfer the video using the software provided with your camera or Firewire card. If you're looking to get your aging videotape collection onto a digital CD medium, be sure to set aside an afternoon.

First, you'll need to connect your camera to an output port on your VCR. How you do this depends on your camera and what cabling was included with it. On my JVC GR-DVL 9800, I received a cable with a headphone-style jack on one end that connected to the camera and standard RCA jacks on the other. These RCA jacks, pictured in Figure 8.2, have the familiar red, white and yellow connectors and, in this case, are connected to the equivalent output connectors on your VCR.

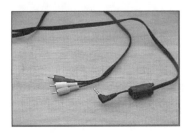

Figure 8.2

This cable connects my digital video camera to a TV or VCR with RCA jacks.

Usually, at this point, you need to make sure your camera is configured to receive, rather than output video. Once set, though, you can start playing a tape or television signal through your VCR, then hit record on your camera. This is just like recording to a normal videocassette, except that now we're dealing with digital videotape.

Once you've recorded the video you want (most digital videotapes won't hold more than an hour's worth of footage), it's time to connect your camera to your computer via a Firewire cable, like the one shown in Figure 8.3.

Figure 8.3

The connector for this Firewire cable, which is already connected to a PC at the other end, plugs into a digital video camera.

Now you have but to use your computer's video capture software (again included with the Firewire card or digital video camera) to capture that video onto your PC. Once that's done you can you use that video however you want, including re-recording it to CD using either the Easy CD Creator 5 Platinum of CD-Maker 2000 software packages!

The Least You Need to Know

➤ If you want to create a video CD, you must have MPEG-1 files. These aren't the best quality video files available today, but they can fit a lot more video onto a lot less space.

➤ A VCD will play in your computer's DVD, on most set-top DVD players, or on specialized VCD players such as the CD-I.

➤ Getting video onto your computer from a videotape or other analog source requires the use of a video capture device or digital video camera.

Chapter 9

Toss Your VCR: Using Video CD Creator to Create Video CDs

In This Chapter

➤ Using the VCD Creator

➤ Creating simple sequence video CDs

➤ Creating video CDs with menus

In the previous chapter, we mentioned two programs you could use to create a video CD. One of them was Video CD Creator, part of Roxio's Easy CD Creator 5 Platinum package. When using the VCD Creator program to make a video CD, keep in mind that this may not be your idea of world-class VCD authoring software. This is not to say it's impossible to use, but for those who haven't done this type of thing before, it can get a little confusing. Just stick with this chapter to steer you past any rocky shoals.

Creating a Video CD

As with the other Roxio programs that are part of the Easy CD Creator 5 Platinum version, you can start up Video CD Creator by double-clicking the Project Selector icon on your PC's desktop or by using the Start menu (click Start, Programs, Roxio Easy CD Creator 5, Applications, Video CD Creator).

Using the Project Selector, you simply select Make a Photo Or Video CD from the first set of buttons that pop up; then, from the second, click Video CD. After you make this selection, the VCD Creator window pops up, and, just as in the Start menu method, the Video CD Creator Wizard appears on the screen (see Figure 9.1).

Between Tracks

When using the Project Selector to open Video CD Creator, you probably noticed an option for a program called Video Impression. This is a tool you can use to capture and edit video. However, as we're firmly focused on the programs that actually let you create CDs, it's a bit outside the scope of this book.

Figure 9.1

The Video CD Creator Wizard can help simplify the process of creating a VCD.

Two ways are available to create Video CDs. You can use the program itself, or you can use this wizard. Although easier, the wizard does limit what you can do with the program, so go ahead and dismiss this wizard dialog box using the Cancel button. This way we can get straight into the VCD Creator program itself, which really isn't that much more difficult to use than by going through the Wizard.

Using the VCD Creator

Even though the Wizard might be an easy method for creating simple VCDs, you might find that using the program directly saves time if you are familiar with it and have a specific goal in mind.

Figure 9.2 shows the VCD Creator program. Here you can see the recognizable File, Edit, and View menus. In addition, menus are available for Video CD and

Between Tracks

To keep the wizard from popping up every time you use Video CD Creator, you can select the check box named Do Not Run Wizard at Startup from the wizard's first dialog box (refer back to Figure 9.1). You can re-enable the Wizard at startup by using the Preferences option in the File menu of the main program.

Playback. Help, as always, is there if you need it. As long as you have this book around, hopefully you won't ever need to use the Help option.

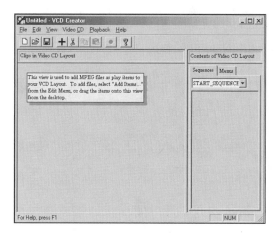

Figure 9.2

Use the VCD Creator program to create the VCD layout and burn the VCD.

The pane on the left side of the program window is titled Clips In Video CD Layout. After you start adding segments of video (clips) to the layout, they show up in this pane. On the right side of the program window, you can see the Contents of Video CD Layout pane, which has two tabs. The first, Sequences, is where the order in which the video clips will play is determined. The second tab, called Menus, enables you to add menus to the CD so the viewer can switch between clips just like song tracks on an audio CD.

Setting Program Preferences

As with many applications, you can set certain options for the program to customize it for your needs. The Preferences option on the File menu brings up the dialog box shown in Figure 9.3. This enables you to make decisions that affect some aspects of how the program works.

This dialog box has two tabs. In Figure 9.3, you can see the General tab and the preferences it enables you to set. These preferences fall under the groupings Startup, New CD Layout, and Show MPEG Information.

You can control the following program Startup options:

➤ **Show Startup Window.** If selected, this just means that the program's logo will be shown when the application is first started up. I know, big yeah! Feel free to disable this one.

➤ **Open Disc Wizard.** This is the check box you select or deselect, depending on whether you want the Wizard to be your main interface when you launch the program. If you're more comfortable with the Wizard, keep this box enabled.

Figure 9.3

The VCD Creator Preferences dialog box gives you control over the program.

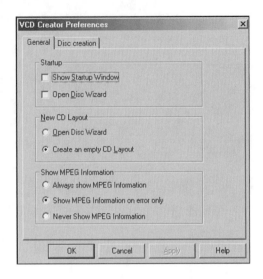

Preferences you can set to control what happens when you select New CD Layout from the File menu are:

➤ **Open Disc Wizard.** If this option is selected, every time you want to create a new CD layout, the Wizard pops up to walk you through it. You won't have to restart the program to get the Wizard running as with the previous option. For this to work, however, you also must select Open Disc Wizard in the Startup selections just discussed.

➤ **Create an Empty CD Layout.** If you select this, instead of the Wizard, the main VCD Creator program becomes the standard method you use to create the video CD.

Under the Show MPEG Information section, you can control when the MPEG information sheet is displayed.

➤ **Always Show MPEG Information.** If you select this, you'll see the MPEG information sheet for all files you choose to add. This includes files that meet the White Book VCD specifications as well as those that contain errors.

➤ **Show MPEG Information on Error Only.** If you get tired of clicking a lot of MPEG information sheets that show good files, selecting this preference causes the program to show the MPEG information sheet only when a bad file crops up.

➤ **Never Show MPEG Information.** If, under no circumstances, do you want to see MPEG file information, this is the option for you. At the very least, though, we'd recommend you choose to show information on error. It's always good to know when you're dealing with files that may not work!

Similar to Easy CD Creator, when VCD burns a disc, it places temporary files on your hard disk to make the process run smoothly. Under the second tab on the VCD Creator Preferences dialog box, you can control the temporary files created by the program. The default, as you can see in Figure 9.4, is to use the Windows TEMP directory, which already exists on Windows systems. However, you can deselect this check box and add other locations.

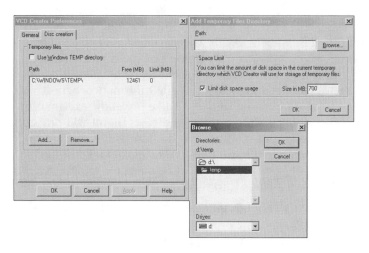

Figure 9.4

You can control the disk locations used for temporary storage.

If you do elect to create other directories (click the Add button) instead of using the default, another dialog box pops up and enables you to enter the path and filename for the temporary file (there is a Browse button here you can click to select the new location). If you want, you can also set a limit as to the amount of space that can be used, just put a checkmark in the Limit Disk Space Usage check box. You can add more temporary locations as needed.

Generally, unless you really understand how to navigate your hard drive, create and move folders, and so on, you are better off leaving these options alone.

Creating the Video CD Layout and Adding Items

Starting with a clean layout—that is, you've just opened the program or you've selected New VCD Layout from the File menu—you can add video clips to the layout you want to create. To add a clip, click the Edit menu and then select Add Item (or click the Add An Item button on the toolbar). This brings up the Add Play Items dialog box, which really looks and operates no differently than

Between Tracks

Files encoded in a compatible MPEG format must either have a .mpg, .mpeg, or .mpv extension.

opening up any other file in Windows. In this case, however, you can only open files that are of the MPEG-1 format.

To select a file for inclusion in the layout, double-click it in this dialog box or highlight it by clicking it once and then clicking the Open button. Continue using the Add Play Items dialog box until you have added all the video clips you want on the VCD.

Each time you add a file using this method, an MPEG Information dialog box appears, telling you whether the clip to be added to the layout meets the MPEG-1 specifications. If VCD Creator has no complaints, this dialog box has a nice, friendly, green check mark at the top. If it gets finicky and doesn't like your files, however, a red X will appear. From there, you need to look to the file information beneath it to find out what it doesn't like. A yellow exclamation point next to an item indicates that it will probably be okay, but is a little off the standard. A big, red X character next to an item indicates that it most likely will not be playable in a DVD player (or a CDI player) if you include it in the layout.

Between Tracks

Common Windows keyboard shortcuts can also be used here. Use Ctrl+X for Cut, Ctrl+C for Copy, and Ctrl+V for Paste.

Click the Add button if the clip is okay and VCD Creator adds it to your layout. If you want to use a clip that does not meet the standards, click the Add Anyway button that takes the place of the Add button. Just don't say we didn't warn you! After you've added the clip, it appears in the Video CD Layout pane as a small box with the clip's file name on it.

Editing or Removing Items from the Layout

Removing an item from the layout is as easy as either highlighting it (clicking it once) and then selecting the scissors icon from the toolbar or selecting Delete from the Edit menu. Either way, the program prompts you before it actually deletes the item from the layout. If you change your mind later, you can always put it back in again. Other options under the Edit menu enable you to cut, copy, and paste items. Sometimes you might want to use the same clip more than once in the layout. One way of doing so is to add it more than once. But, you can save a little time and effort if you use Copy from the Edit menu and then use Paste to insert another copy of the particular clip in the layout. Remember that at this point, we're working with only the layout itself, not the actual files. Thus, editing a layout doesn't have to take a lot of time.

The Playback Menu

If, at the last minute of your production, you want to look at either a single clip or the entire layout (if you have created a sequence for it), you can do so by using the

Playback menu found at the top of the VCD Creator application window. The menu gives you two options. First, you can choose VCD Layout to play the entire video production you've created with your layout. Or, you can take the second option, Selected Clip. This enables you to view any single video clip in the layout. Simply click the clip once to highlight it and then select the second option from the Playback menu.

When you've made your selection, a small window opens to play the clip. Additionally, a set of standard VCR-like controls appears that you can use to control the playback, as you can see in Figure 9.5. If you select to play just one clip, the Play, Pause, and Stop buttons are available. If you choose to play the entire VCD layout, buttons are added so you can skip to the next track or go back to the previous track. If you have defined a menu for the VCD (to be covered soon), the number keys on the controls enable you to jump to the clip for each of the menu's numbered entries.

Note that until you create a playback sequence (as covered in the next section), you won't be able to use the VCD Layout option from this menu.

Figure 9.5

The MPEG Playback dialog box provides the controls you can use to playback a sequence or an entire VCD layout.

Set the Order of Play for the Images—Creating a Playback Sequence

For VCD Creator to make a VCD, you must create a sequence in which the items in the layout will be played. You do this by selecting each clip in the Clips pane (on the left) and adding it to the Contents pane (on the right). You can create two kinds of sequences for your VCD. The first is a simple sequence in which all video clips are played in the order they are found in the particular sequence, from start to finish. The second method involves creating a menu that enables the viewer to select the clip to watch.

Creating a Simple Sequence

The Simple Sequence method plays all video clips in the layout sequence from start to end. For many homemade videos that have been captured and made ready for a VCD, this is an appropriate choice.

To start the process of creating a sequence, click the Sequences tab in the Contents pane and then ensure that Start_Sequence—the default here—is visible in the drop-down menu that shows up on the tab. First, we'll add a clip that will serve as the start sequence that plays when the VCD first runs. When you create menu sequences, this drop-down menu will allow you to switch between them.

Now, to add a clip, simply drag it from the Clips pane back to Contents, in the area underneath Start_Sequence. The item should now appear in this pane.

Continue dragging each clip, being sure to place them in the order you want them in the final playback of the VCD. Use the vertical scrollbar in either pane to get to clips that don't fit in the current view. Figure 9.6 shows the VCD Creator window with clips added to the simple sequence. If you change your mind about the order of the clips, simply use your mouse to drag them around in the Contents pane until you get the order you want.

Figure 9.6

The VCD Creator enables you to specify the order of video clips in a simple sequence.

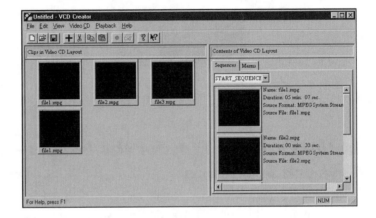

Notice that information about the clips changes when moved between the left and right panes. In the Clips pane, VCD Creator attaches the filename to the clip's icon. In the Contents pane, however, the clip icon is not directly labeled. The filename and additional information about the clip's size, format, and source file (the file on your hard drive that the clip comes from) are listed to the right of the icon. Because a filename won't always match the subject matter of a particular clip, you might want to change its name to something more recognizable using its Properties page.

To get to the Properties page for a clip, simply right-click it and select Properties from the menu that pops up. The first field on the page is called Item Name. Simply type over the existing name in this field and then click the OK button. The clip is now displayed in the Sequences pane with the new name. In the Clips pane, however, notice that the clip is still identified by its filename.

Saving the CD Layout to a File

Now that you've gotten this far, you can create the disc, gear up for creating a menu sequence for the VCD, or save the layout for future use. To save the layout you have created, use the Save or Save As option from the File menu. Using Save As enables you to specify the path and filename for the layout file. Use Save if you have previously saved this layout and are simply updating it.

When you want to open a saved layout, use the Open VCD Layout option from the File menu. You'll have to know where you saved the file, so keeping them all in one place is a good idea. When you open a saved layout, you can make changes to it and save it under the same name or a new name (using Save As).

If you are ready to create a VCD using this simple sequence, jump ahead to the section called "Starting the Recording Process." If you want to learn about creating simple menus for your VCD, stay where you are and we'll talk about that in the next section.

Creating a Menu Sequence for the Viewer to Use

The VCD Creator program enables you to create simple, one-level menus the viewer can use to navigate between the clips on the VCD. The best way to think of these menus is like a chapter list on a DVD movie. On a DVD, this list enables you to advance to various sections of the movie by choosing which part (clip) of the movie you want to watch. Usually, these chapters won't all fit on the same page, so you can use your remote to scroll through to more screens that contain more chapters. Although the method of control might vary based on the type of player you are using, a VCD menu works in much the same way.

Don't Get Burned

Although the comparison to a DVD chapter list makes it easier to understand a VCD menu, they don't work exactly the same. If you select a chapter on a DVD, the movie picks up from that point and plays through to the end. With a VCD, using the menu to play a clip will play only that individual clip. You can, however, group a set of clips under one menu selection if you want.

To some, it might seem like adding a menu is more trouble than it's worth, but adding a simple menu can be a good idea if you have a lot of video clips on the VCD and want them to be easily accessed. After all, you don't want to torture the viewer by making her watch a long string of video clips that she has seen before when a menu can jump right to the important stuff—then again, if it's your in-laws watching, maybe you do.

To create a VCD with a simple menu, you first create a Start_Sequence sequence that will play each time the VCD is first played. Click the Menus tab in the Contents pane (see Figure 9.7).

Figure 9.7

The Menus tab enables you to create a one-level menu structure for your viewers.

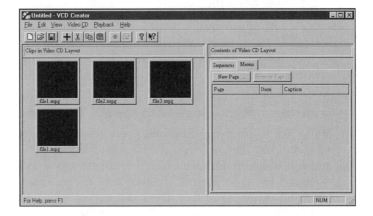

Arcane CD Speak

A page is where you put the menu items a user needs to advance to specific clips on the VCD. If necessary, you can use more than one page to apply to different groups of clips. After you've created a menu page, it appears on the Menus tab. You can right-click and select Properties to get to the Properties page for this menu page. Here, you can select how many times the background menu clip is played and the number of seconds between each play, if any.

As you can see in Figure 9.7, two basic selections can be used: New Page or Remove Page. To start the first page of a menu, click the New Page button. Figure 9.8 shows the first dialog box you can use to select a background for the page. You can choose one of the video clips from your layout or click the Add From File button if you want to choose another MPEG file. This allows you to choose from a file that wasn't added to the Layout pane. Note that choosing a file here will not put it into the Layout pane; it will just include it in the menu you are creating. This clip, video, or still image should show the menu selections to the user, so you need to use a video or photo-editing program to create the file used here.

Figure 9.8

The first dialog box asks you to select a file to be used for the menu background.

When you've made your selection, click the Next button. In Figure 9.9, you can see that the next step for creating a menu page is to enter the number of items that will be in the menu. In this figure we have entered the number 3. This means that we will now have to create three play sequences, one for each selection. When the viewer is using this VCD, he will be able to enter a number (usually using a remote control) to select each menu choice. You can enter up to 99 menu selections, if needed!

After selecting the number of menu items you want, click the Next button.

A dialog box now appears that enables you to see and edit which menu number is attached to which play sequence. If you'll remember, we started out creating the Start_Sequence, which plays when the CD is first started. After you've decided on the number of menu choices you want, you must create a *play sequence* of clips for each menu choice.

Between Tracks

If you create more than one menu page, the viewer can use the left and right arrow keys on the controls of the VCD player to move through menu pages.

Figure 9.9

Enter the number of choices you want on the menu page.

The names of these play sequences are set by default according to sequential order, so menu item 1 defaults to PLAY_SEQUENCE1, item two to PLAY_SEQUENCE2, and so on (see Figure 9.10). In addition to not being particularly descriptive, this will probably bore the reader of the menu. Fortunately, you can change them by clicking the Edit button.

Figure 9.10

You can use the Edit button to change the text associated with a menu selection.

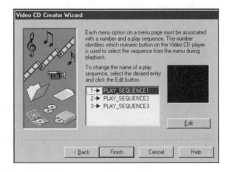

When you are done, click the Finish button. You'll find yourself back in the VCD Creator window. Now, however, you will see your menu page on screen.

Starting the Recording Process

When you're ready to create the VCD using the layout you have compiled, all that's left to do to kick off the recording process is click the button on the toolbar that has a large red dot on it.

However, before you start recording, you can use an option to check the contents of the CD layout to ensure that all the files can still be found. This is a good idea if you are using a saved layout, or one to which you have made a lot of changes. Select Validate Layout from the Video CD menu, and the program performs this quick examination.

If everything checks out okay, you are ready to record. You can either click the red button or select (from the Video CD menu) the option titled Create CD from Layout. Note that in this same menu you can create a disk image of the VCD on your hard disk. This option can be useful when making multiple copies of the same layout.

After you start the recording process, the Record CD Setup dialog box appears. This dialog box is used by most of the Roxio programs to enable you to make some decisions about how the disc is to be recorded. You should take the default for a VCD for most of the items in this box. You can, however, select to make more than one copy of the VCD. If you are just starting to use a CD-RW drive to create a VCD, you might want to use one of the Test options. You can tell the program to test write to the recording drive, or you can tell the program to perform the test and then automatically create the CD if the test is okay. Remember that it takes just as long to test a CD as it does to write to it, so depending on the speed of your CD-RW drive, this can add a lot of time to the creation process. On the other hand, it can also save you from turning a disc into a coaster. If you're pretty sure your recorder won't have any problems writing the disc, just leave the radio button labeled Create CD selected. Finally, you should make sure the program closes the VCD when it's finished.

Click the OK button to start burning the VCD.

If you haven't already inserted a blank recordable CD, VCD Creator prompts you to insert one. When you do, you see the standard Record CD Progress dialog box that shows the progress of the recording session. This dialog box looks and works the same as the one you get when recording CDs using Easy CD Creator.

The recording process runs through the usual recording phases. If you want more details on this process, see Chapter 5, "Drag and Drop with Easy CD Creator." However, the most important thing is for the recording to succeed. When the CD Created Successfully text appears, you'll know that the recording finished without incident.

The Least You Need to Know

➤ If you want to create a video CD, you must have MPEG-1 files. These aren't the best quality video files available today, but they can fit a lot more video onto a lot less space.

➤ VCD Creator has a Clips pane where you choose which video clips to include in your layout and a Contents pane that lets you choose the order in which you want to burn those clips to a VCD.

➤ The VCD Creator program enables you to create menus to make playback easier for your viewers.

Using NTI CD-Maker for Video CDs and Super Video CDs

In This Chapter

➤ What's a VCD?

➤ What's a Super VCD?

➤ How do you create a VCD or Super VCD on a CD-R?

➤ What's the time limit on a VCD?

In the last chapter you learned how to use Easy CD Creator to burn Video CDs. In this chapter, you'll see how this is accomplished using NTI's CD-Maker software. While CD-Maker operates similarly in some of its applications, it doesn't closely match up with Easy CD Creator when it comes to creating Video CDs.

What's the Difference Between a Video CD and a Super Video CD?

If you check out the specifications found in Appendix C, "The Colorful Books of CD Standards," you'll see that the VCD (Video CD) format is defined in the White Book specifications using the format called CD-ROM XA. That is, in idiot's terms, a disc that can hold MPEG-1 video data, yet allow for interactive functions. You'll find that the resolution you get with a regular VCD is about the same as a VCR. Actually, depending on the quality of your video capture card, the computer you're using, and other such factors (need we forget memory?) the quality can actually be a little better or more likely a little worse.

However, VCDs have caught on in some parts of the world where players are specifically made for them. If you use Easy CD Creator or NTI's CD-Maker, you may find that the VCD you create might be playable in your DVD player. It all depends on the DVD. If you can't watch them on your DVD player, then you can always fall back on your computer.

Don't Get Burned

If you are thinking about transferring your family VHS tapes to a VCD for permanent storage, let's stop and think a minute about this. To create a VCD, or a SuperVCD, as you'll learn about in a few paragraphs, you have to capture the video from the VHS recorder onto a digital file on your computer. Most programs that do video capture allow you to actually create very high definition files that preserve most all the video and audio signal. If you're recording from another source, like your cable television box, then you'll probably be able to record MPEG files that are even better than those you can extract from a VHS tape.

So while a VCD might be a fun way to send 30 minutes of VHS fun to a friend, if you truly want to preserve the data, I suggest you record in the highest MPEG format your capture software (and capture card) allow, and save those data files on a CD and wait until better methods come around to create quality audio/video on CDs. As it is, CDs have seen better days! You can now get a DVD recordable drive for under $500 and the recordable disks for under $15.00! If you're a serious video addict, consider waiting one more year and using recordable DVD, which will, I'm certain, be in the next edition of this book!

While you might get up to 80 minutes of audio on a CD-R disc, if you tried the same with a straight video track, you'd get about 2 or 3 minutes. So MPEG-1, which is used for VCDs must be compressed (and thereby lose some of the data contained in the signal) by a factor of up to 200 to 1. That's quite a lot.

In 1995, the VCD 2.0 standard was introduced and allowed for a few more features, such as higher resolution, still pictures, and rewind functions that weren't included in the original VCD White Book specification. SuperVCD is a variation on this that uses either MPEG-1 or MPEG-2 files. When using an MPEG-1 file, SuperVCDs use a higher bit rate. When using MPEG-2 files, it uses a variable bit rate.

But all differences aside, both allow you to do the same thing. Create a CD-R disc you can play in your computer's CD-ROM drive and just maybe your DVD attached to your TV. However, like the sidebar says, just wait until next year when you can record high quality MPEG files to much larger recordable DVD discs! For CD-R VCDs, however, you can expect to get about 20 to 40 minutes of recording time on a single disc. So for such things as movies, you'll have to use an editing program to create smaller files and burn multiple CD-R discs.

But for now …

Creating the Video CD Layout

As you are probably aware by now, NTI's CD-Maker uses a common graphical interface for its many different functions. Creating a VCD or SuperVCD is no different than creating an audio CD. You can drag and drop files into a layout pane, or use the Add Files option (that big button at the top of the screen that looks like a dog-eared page with a plus sign in the middle of it).

Once you create the video layout, you can move files around and then burn the VCD. It's as simple as that.

So What's in a File Format?

To burn your VCD using CD-Maker, you need to use one of the following formats:

➤ MPEG-1, for the MPEG Video CD 2.0 specification for a VCD.

➤ MPEG-2, which must conform to the MPEG-2 (ISO 13818-, 1994) specification.

Here I could refer you to the White Book specifications, but that book would cost you a bunch of money, believe me! However, when you use another program (such as Ulead VideoStudio or MGI's VideoWave software, which are widely available) you will find that they allow you to save in a variety of formats. And believe me, there are a wide variety of formats! It isn't just MPEG-1 or MPEG-2, there are many variations on each of these, depending on bit rate, frames per second, pixel size, and many other factors.

If you're confused, well, so am I. Sometimes I have a difficult time getting a file into the right format before I can create a VCD. However, I can offer you a pointer that may help with any program you use to create a VCD. Go to www.vcdhelper.com and check out the resources you find there. You'll find everything from bit-rate calculators (which can estimate from reading your source how many CD-R discs it will take to record the video) to conversion programs. You'll find at this site links to both commercial products and shareware products. It's a good place to start if you intend to do a lot of VCD productions!

Between Tracks

All video capture cards come with some sort of drivers and software that allows you to view on your computer screen the video that the card is intercepting. Many come also with either full-fledged products, or limited-version products of other company's software that can be used for editing the video you capture. I highly recommend you take advantage of this software! For example, your video capture card software may not allow you to capture the video to a hard disk in a format that CD-Maker will use to create a VCD. In the documentation, NTI even tells you that you may need to purchase some kind of conversion software. Examine the specifications and see if the software that comes with your video capture card (or some other software you download or purchase) will allow you to "save as" in a format that can be used to create a VCD. Both Easy CD Creator and NTI's CD-Maker are very, very picky about the files they can accept for creating VCDs. You'll most likely have to use another program to convert your files first!

Anyway, no matter which method you choose to create the layout (drag and drop or Add File), you can be sure that NTI's CD-Maker will tell you if it doesn't like the file type. It will barf and tell you that the file can't be used. So, before you begin to use Add File or drag and drop to create a VCD layout, check the just-mentioned Web site and make sure you have the correct format, or have converted your file(s) into the correct format first!

Video file formats vary widely in quality, and the amount of data stored. VCDs use a lower quality format (a variation on MPEG-1 standards). If you use a product such as Ulead VideoStudio to capture video files, then you know that even though there are several MPEG specifications (such as MPEG-1 and MPEG-2), there are also sub-variations with each of these! Generally any video capture program will indicate the choice you should make when creating an output file to be used for a VCD. It will be a variation on the MPEG-1 format.

Looking Around the Layout Window

In Figure 10.1, you can see the typical NTI layout window, with the Windows Explorer pane on the left side, which you can use to navigate through your computer's drives to find the one that holds your video files. On the right side of this top part of the window you scroll down to find the individual .mpg files that you'll use for your VCD.

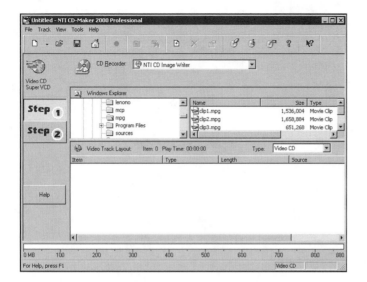

Figure 10.1

This is the standard view you use to create a layout for audio or video CDs.

In the middle of the window, between the upper panes and the lower layout pane, you'll see some information fields. The first is simply text that indicates you're creating a Video Track Layout. If you see something else here, like Audio Track Layout, then perhaps you chose the wrong button on the main menu! If so, look at the top of the window and click on File, then New and then Video CD/Super Video CD. Alternatively, you can click on the small down arrow that's right under the Track menu. This produces the same menu as New, so you can simply select Video CD/ Super Video CD. You should then see Video Track Layout in the portion of the window that separates the upper and lower panes.

The next item in this informational section is labeled Play Time, and you can use this to keep track of how long the video CD you create will play. Use this to judge your timing as you are adding files.

The last field in this section is not informational, but instead is a drop down menu called Type. This is where you can select to make a Video CD or a Super Video CD. The selection you make here does two things. First, it tells CD-Maker what kind of VCD you want to make! Second, it causes CD-Maker to test each file that you try to add to the layout to be sure it meets the MPEG-1 or MPEG-2 specifications so that it can be used in the VCD you are about to record. If the file doesn't meet the specifications, it may be rejected entirely (and you'll get a message that looks similar to the one in Figure 10.2), or if it almost passes, you may get a message like the one shown in Figure 10.3, saying that it might work, but there are no guarantees!

At the bottom of the screen is the layout pane, and as you add video files to the layout you'll see the type, length and source columns to help you keep track of the clips you add. To add a clip, you can use either the regular Add File method or the drag-and-drop method.

Figure 10.2

CD-Maker tells you straight out that this file won't work, so it doesn't let you add it to the layout pane.

Figure 10.3

This is just a warning showing you what is wrong with the file. If you proceed you may or may not get a VCD, or you may end up with a coaster!

Using Add File

If you're not certain where the files are, then I suggest you use the Add File method. Click on the Track menu and select Add, or use the button bar underneath the menu bar and select the dog-eared page that has the plus sign on it. In Figure 10.4, you can see the standard Windows Open dialog box that allows you to browse and select files from different drives and folders.

Once you've located an .mpeg file using the Add File method, simply click the Open button to add the file to the layout portion of the VCD window. Your selections will show up in the layout pane in the order you select them. Don't worry, you can use editing techniques later to reorder the film clip sequences if you want!

Figure 10.4

You can browse the computer to locate the video files you want to record.

Using the Explorer to Drag and Drop

For those who are accustomed to Windows operating systems, the drag-and-drop method is probably the easiest method to use. While Add File lets you browse the computer's disk subsystem (and any network file shares you are connected to) drag and drop is much simpler if you're used to using Windows operating systems. You can use the Windows Explorer pane on the right side of the top of the Window to quickly change from one disk drive or directory to another. The left pane next to this can be used to locate files so you can drag them to the layout pane.

Editing the Video CD Layout

You can use the drag-and-drop method in the Video Track Layout pane to move files around to change the order in which they will play. Just drag a file from one place in the layout to another. You can also use another method to move clips around. Right-click on any file in the Video Track Layout pane and select Track Properties. As you can see in Figure 10.5, the properties sheet has a field labeled Item Number. Change this to a different value and it will move to that position in the layout pane.

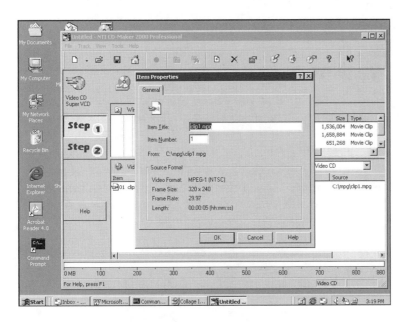

Figure 10.5

You can change the value in the Item Number field to change the position of a file in the layout pane.

If you find you no longer want to use a particular clip, you can select Delete from the menu that shows up when you right-click on the item in the layout pane. Note that this just deletes the file from the layout pane, and doesn't delete the actual source file on your computer's hard disk!

Between Tracks

If you don't like the right-click method for playing or deleting items in the Video Layout Pane, just click once on the file in the layout pane and then select one of those options from the Track menu.

Playing Video Clips

If you are working with a lot of clips, sometimes it can be difficult to remember just exactly what's in each file, especially if you are as bad at naming files as I am. Heck, what does "clip1.mpg," or "clip2.mpg" tell me? Yet, when I'm in a hurry I usually name things that way. So, if you want to see the clip, simply right-click on it (either in the layout pane or in the Explorer pane) and select Play. Windows Media Player (or your default player) will pop up and play the clip for you.

By using the preview option you can make a final check on each clip before you add it, or you can preview items in the layout pane as a last minute sanity check to be sure you've gotten your video clips all in the right order.

Adding Video CD Layout Properties

You can view the properties of each file that you add to the Video Layout Pane, as you saw earlier in this chapter. However, you can also edit properties for the VCD as a whole. This information will be burned to the VCD and can be used by some playback devices, so it's a good idea to fill it in.

To get to the properties pages for the VCD, you can use File/CD Layout Properties, or you can right-click on anywhere in the Video Track Layout pane and select the same thing. In Figure 10.6, you can see the first tab, which allows you to define a number of fields.

Figure 10.6

The Album tab is the first tab of the CD Layout properties pages.

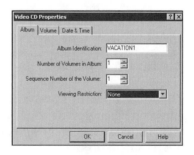

The fields you can fill in here are as follows:

➤ **Album Identification.** Use any text you want here to identify the VCD.

➤ **Number of Volumes in Album.** If you are going to need more than one CD-R disc to record all of your clips, number each one so you'll know the order in which they should be played back. Use this field to indicate the number of volumes in the entire set.

➤ **Sequence Number of the Volume.** This is the order in a multi-volume set that tells where this VCD belongs.

➤ **Viewing Restrictions.** This is a drop down menu that allows you to select from None, or Category 1, Category 2, Category 3. Some VCD players will allow you to restrict, for example, children from viewing certain categories.

Click on the Volume tab and you'll see another set of fun fields to play with (just when you thought this was an easy thing to do!). These fields are defined by the ISO 9660 standard to describe the volume. You don't have to fill in all of the fields, however. In Figure 10.7, you can see what this tab looks like.

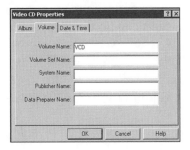

Figure 10.7

The Volume tab lets you add more information to the VCD.

The fields you can fill in here are as follows:

➤ **Volume Name.** This is a name for the volume and it is recommended by the standards that this field be included. So stick something here! You can use alphabetic or numeric characters.

➤ **Volume Set Name.** If you are creating a set of disks that will be part of the same volume set, use this optional field, and make sure each disc has the same value here. You can't have a different Volume Set Name for each volume in the same set. It must be the same for each disc that is part of the same volume set.

➤ **System Name.** You can use this optional field to indicate the operating system the VCD can be used with. For a VCD, you should probably just leave this blank. Remember that the ISO 9660 standards apply to several kinds of CD formats, not just VCDs.

➤ **Publisher Name.** If you are producing VCDs for business purposes, you might want to use this optional field to indicate the creator of the VCD.

➤ **Data Preparer Name.** Again, if you are a business, and want to identify someone (or something, any text will do), you can use this optional field.

The last tab, shown in Figure 10.8, allows you to enter the date and time values for when the VCD was created and modified, and also provides for a field called Expiration and one called Effective.

Figure 10.8

The Date & Time fields are found on this tab.

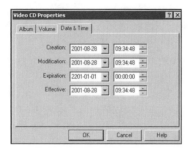

The Expiration date is just a field you can use to indicate when the information contained on the burned CD can be considered to be no longer useful, or obsolete. In a business environment, this may be useful. The Effective field can be used to specify the date and time of day through which the volume can be used. These last two fields you can ignore, since most players don't enforce them.

When you're finished entering information into the Video CD Properties pages, just click OK.

Saving the Video Layout

When you've finished playing around with the files you want to burn to a VCD, then you should save the layout. Even if you don't intend to create more than one copy of the VCD, saving the layout is a good idea for a few reasons. First, if the burning process doesn't succeed, you can reopen the layout and try to locate the problem. Perhaps you added a particular file that didn't quite meet the necessary specifications. Remove it, resave the layout and try again. Second, with the power crunch that appears to be going on in this country today, you never know when Mr. Electric Company is going to zap your neighborhood! If you've saved a layout and your power gets blown away during the burn, you can always wait around for a few hours, and when the power is restored, continue and burn your VCD!

Creating the Video CD

You can create the VCD just like you do audio or data CDs. Once your layout is as you want it, click that big red dot on the button bar, or select the Step 2 button on the left side of the main window. The standard dialog box that CD-Maker uses to burn CDs will pop up. In Figure 10.9, you can see an example of this dialog box with the Advanced button selected.

Figure 10.9

It's time to burn that VCD!

Notice that there is a checkmark next to the Disc-At-Once field in the Write Method part of this dialog box. This is because I've chosen the radio button labeled Smart decision (Let the program decide). CD-Maker knows it's making a VCD, and that you won't be adding additional sessions. You can use the Smart decision radio button, or click the Disc-At-Once button, either way the VCD will be created and then you an play it back on your VCD player, some DVD players, and your PC.

Test Before Writing the CD

At the top of the dialog box shown in Figure 10.9, you can see that you can ask the program to do a test before it actually starts to record information to the CD-R disc. This testing will determine if your computer's hardware can keep up with the CD burner for the data you've selected. If you've used the Test (no actual writing) or the Test & Write radio buttons before, then you might want to just skip testing and use the Write radio button to burn the VCD. However, if you've gotten a lot of coasters, I recommend the Test & Write button!

Burn the CD

Once you've made your choices of how to write (or test and then write), click the Start button to begin the burn. As you can see in Figure 10.10, the program will display a dialog box that tells you what it's doing, from recording the table of contents for the VCD to actually writing the tracks.

Figure 10.10

CD-Maker will show you the progress it makes as it burns your VCD.

When it's finished, click the OK button and you're done. Be sure to check out the VCD both on your computer and on your DVD player, if you own one. The VCD should be playable using the CD burner that created it in the first place. If you're lucky, you've got a DVD player that understands VCDs. If you're luckier, you've got a DVD player that also understands MP3 files, but that's another story altogether.

The Least You Need to Know

➤ You must start off with video files that are in a format that CD-Maker can use. You can't use .avi files or just any old video format.

➤ You can only fit so much video and audio onto a VCD. You're not going to get a two-hour movie on one CD-R!

➤ Adding, deleting, and editing the layout for a VCD with CD-Maker are just about the same as making a data or audio CD. Drag and drop, or use Add File.

Part 5

Limitless Real Estate for Your Data: Using a CD Recorder Like a Hard Disk

Using CD-R or CD-RW discs usually brings to mind making a copy or a custom CD, as you learned in previous parts. However, both Easy CD Creator and NTI CD-Maker come with utilities that enable you to use a feature called packet writing. What it all boils down to is that you can use your CD-RW discs (and in some cases your CD-R discs) like a hard drive. Drag and drop or use the copy command—just like you would on a hard drive.

The chapters in Part 5 teach you to use DirectCD and FileCD for just this purpose. If you use a CD-RW disc with these programs, it's like having an extra hard disk on board. And with a CD-RW disc you can delete files, as you can on a hard disc.

Chapter 11

Dial Direct with Easy CD Creator DirectCD

In This Chapter

➤ What is packet writing?

➤ Using read/write discs (CD-RW) or write-once discs (CD-R)

➤ Formatting the disc

➤ Using a DirectCD formatted disc

In earlier chapters, we talked about writing tracks and sessions, and the limitations that exist on what you can write to a recordable CD. Using packet-writing software, the rules can be bent a little. Instead of having to write an entire track at once, you can use the recordable disc much like an ordinary hard disk. The DirectCD program from Roxio takes advantage of this feature and can be very useful.

Packet writing enables small amounts of data to be written to the CD simultaneously. Instead of a whole track of data, small chunks can be written. This takes up a little more space on the disc, but the convenience it provides to the user makes up for this. Using a CD-RW or CD-R disc as if it were a hard disk means you can use your everyday Windows applications and utilities to write to the disc. So when using Microsoft Word, for example, you can use the Save or Save As option to save your latest masterpiece directly to a CD.

CD-R, CD-RW, DirectCD, and You

As you probably already know, two main types of recordable CDs exist: CD-R discs, which are write-once, and CD-RW discs, which allow you to write, erase, and write again. You can use both of these kinds of recordable CDs with DirectCD. The difference between them is cost: CD-RW discs are much more expensive than write-once technology. Their cost is justified, however, if you need a disc that can be updated frequently.

Between Tracks

Another advantage of using the RW discs is that if a problem occurs during recording to the disc, you can always erase it and start over. With a CD-R disc, if the write fails for any reason, the disc is toast.

Both types of discs enable you to update or modify data on the disc. However, the CD-RW drive can erase RW data that's no longer needed. The CD-R disc simply marks as deleted the blocks of data that are changed and writes new blocks of data instead. Of course, because the "deleted" material is technically still on the disc, if you use CD-R discs with DirectCD, you'll eventually run out of space if you modify the information too much.

Using DirectCD from Roxio

By default, when you install Easy CD Creator 5 Platinum, Easy CD Creator sets Windows to load DirectCD automatically whenever you turn on your computer. However, should you need to bring up DirectCD manually, click on Start, Programs, Roxio Easy CD Creator 5, Applications and then DirectCD Format Utility. Either way, you'll know DirectCD is functioning from the small icon that looks like a drive with a CD on it present in your System Tray (see Figure 11.1).

Figure 11.1

The DirectCD system tray icon gives you quick access to DirectCD options.

DirectCD icon

For DirectCD to work properly the recordable or rewritable disc in the drive must be formatted to match its requirements. If the disc in your drive has not been set up when you launch DirectCD, you must tell DirectCD to format it for you. If you have already formatted the CD-RW disc in your hard drive, you can simply start using your disc just as if it were a floppy or hard disk installed in your computer.

Formatting a Disc Before Its First Use

To format the disc, double-click the DirectCD icon (again from your computer's system tray) to bring up the main DirectCD interface window. Click the Format button in the middle of this window. Figure 11.2 shows the Format dialog box. There are a few options you must select here in order to proceed.

Using this dialog box, you can give the disc a label (name) that makes it easy to distinguish from others you create. Use up to 11 characters in the label, but make it something meaningful that you'll recognize later. You also can use the only check box found on this dialog box to enable compression on the disc. Compressing information makes it take up less space on a disc, but it also requires you to be running DirectCD to read the disc. Don't use this option if you plan to read the disc on another computer that doesn't have DirectCD installed.

Figure 11.2

The Roxio Format CD dialog box allows you to set up a blank CD for use with DirectCD.

Finally, you may have a choice in terms of which format type you want to use to format the disc. Full Format, which is required if formatting the disc for the first time, or Quick Format, which is a much faster format process. Quick Format requires that this disc has already, at some point, been formatted as a DirectCD disc (in effect it's just for quickly erasing a DirectCD formatted CD).

When ready, click the Start Format button. DirectCD pops up with a dialog box informing you of how long it will take to format the disc. For a full format, expect it to take between 25 and 45 minutes (so be sure you're ready to begin this process). When you do click the OK button to continue, you'll see the screen shown in Figure 11.3.

During the progress of the format, this dialog box enables you to see the elapsed time, allowing you to come up with a reasonable guess as to when the disc format will be complete. When the formatting process has completed successfully, this dialog box disappears, leaving you with the main DirectCD interface (see Figure 11.4).

Click OK to start using the disc.

If you look at the CD Info pane in the DirectCD window, you'll see that you lost a little real estate during the process. Because the DirectCD program has to use up some of the space on your disc so that it can use the disc like a hard drive, your CD doesn't have as much free space as it did before the format. In my case, a 650MB CD (the normal 74-minute disc) was left with 529MB of space after the format. While that is a fairly large chunk of space, it's the price you pay for the convenience of not needing Easy CD Creator and all that data layout stuff to write to your CDs!

Between Tracks

If the Format CD dialog box shows that your recordable or rewritable CD is not ready even though you've already inserted it into your CD-RW drive, try reselecting your drive in the dialog box. DirectCD isn't always smart enough to detect when a CD has been placed in the drive and you need to give it a little jump start.

Figure 11.3

Measuring the progress of a DirectCD format operation.

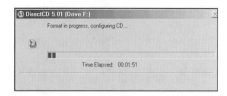

Figure 11.4

The CD Info pane shows that the disc in the CD-RW drive has been properly formatted to work with DirectCD.

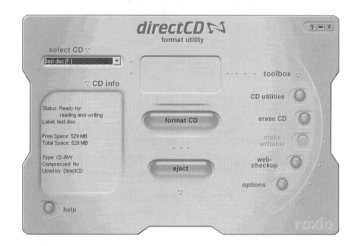

Now, if you look at the DirectCD window you'll notice there are a few buttons we've yet to discuss.

DirectCD Options

The options available in version 5 of DirectCD are much simpler than what you had to choose from when using it with Easy CD Creator 4. Rather than having to sort through several tabs of information, very little of which you need, in this version you have but to click the Option button (see Figure 11.5).

Leading off this Options dialog box are a series of three check boxes. These boxes are:

➤ **Show the CD Ready Notification.** Selecting this check box causes a prompt to inform you when a DirectCD disc (a disc that DirectCD has already formatted) has been inserted in the drive.

➤ **Show the Ejected CD Notification.** Selecting this causes a message to be displayed when you eject a disc.

➤ **Show Icon in System Tray.** This option controls whether or not the icon shown in Figure 11.1 appears in your system tray. Disabling this icon does not disable DirectCD, so I'd advise against doing so. However, if you've got a system tray full of icons that you don't want to see, this is one way to get rid of one of them.

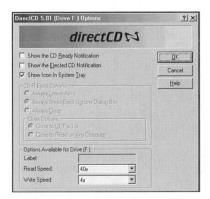

Figure 11.5

The DirectCD Options dialog box contains all the controls you need to determine how the DirectCD program works and set it accordingly.

Of these three options, the only one I would recommend leaving enabled is the Show Icon In System Tray check box. If you insert or eject a DirectCD Ready disc from your CD-RW drive, do you really need an annoying message telling you so?

The middle section of the DirectCD Options dialog box is usually going to be disabled. This is a good thing, since these have to do with how DirectCD preps the disc so it can be viewed on other computers. Generally, the defaults options are best, since they allow you to choose when you eject the disc whether or not to close it for viewing on other computers.

Finally, at the bottom of this dialog box is a section that lets you select the read and write speeds for this disc. The values available in these drop-down menus depend on the capabilities of your CD-RW drive, so you cannot actually choose an incorrect setting. However, you will probably do best to take whatever the default values are for these and adjust them later, based on your experience. For example, most likely you will be able to set the read speed much higher than the write speed. This is because reading data is a much simpler process for the drive than writing or erasing it.

Don't Get Burned

If you have problems writing to the disc, try selecting a slower write speed of 1× and increasing it incrementally until you get up to a speed you can reliably use. If you don't get a good disc write at 1×, something is probably wrong with your disc or the drive you are using.

Ejecting or Erasing the Disc and Fixing Problems

In addition to the Format CD and Options buttons, the DirectCD window has several other controls.

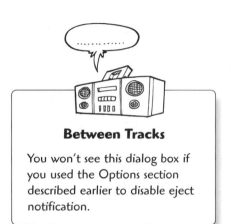

Between Tracks

You won't see this dialog box if you used the Options section described earlier to disable eject notification.

When you want to eject a DirectCD CD, you can use the eject button on the CD drive or the button on this window. In either case, a dialog box pops up after the disc has been physically ejected. The information displayed tells you that you can now use the disc on other CD-RW drives, and on CD-ROM drives if they have the Roxio UDF Reader software installed. Click the OK button to dismiss this dialog box.

If you're having problems writing data to your DirectCD disc, you might want to consider letting DirectCD take a crack at fixing them. Clicking the CD Utilities button will display the DirectCD Utilities dialog box, as shown in Figure 11.6.

Figure 11.6

Using the DirectCD Utlities dialog box you can attempt to scan a disc for problems or undelete lost information.

The first button on this dialog box, ScanDisc, tells DirectCD to look for and repair any problems on a CD-RW disc. A confirmation dialog box then pops up. Unless you're having second thoughts, click the Scan button. Once the scan has been successfully completed, you'll see a dialog box like the one shown in Figure 11.7.

Finally, if you're using a CD-RW disc and no longer want to use it as a DirectCD disc, you can use the Erase CD button to remove all data and formatting from the disc (make sure you don't need any data currently on it). Click this button to get this process underway. When you do, a small dialog box will appear with the information that the erase process will take one to two minutes to complete. If you're sure you want to erase the disc, click OK.

Once the process is done, a dialog box letting you know the CD is now blank appears. Just click OK to send this dialog box packing.

Figure 11.7

This disc had no problems on it that need fixing.

Using the DirectCD Disc

Once formatted, you can treat the DirectCD disc just like it is a hard drive on your system. You can save files to it, copy files to it, or use other commands from application programs. In Figure 11.8, you can see that a disc I formatted and named "storage1" is in my CD-RW CD drive.

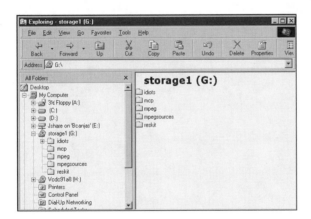

Figure 11.8

The G: drive contains a disc labeled "storage1," which is accessible through most Windows applications, such as Windows Explorer.

As you can see, I've already written some files and folders to this disc. If you are using CD-R media, remember that, even though you can mark a file or folder as deleted, that doesn't free up any disc space because as the data is not actually removed from the disc. So, if you are going to use CD-R discs under DirectCD, it's better to use them to copy only data that you do not need to modify or delete. A good example of this is copying report files to the CD-R disc for long-term storage.

Given that I devoted a lot of pages in Chapter 5, "Drag and Drop with Easy CD Creator," to showing you how to make a data CD, you might wonder why you would want to use DirectCD and have to go through all that formatting mumbo-jumbo. The truth is that, depending on your needs, you might not want to. However, don't underestimate the convenience of having the ability to add data to a disc from ordinary Windows programs.

The Least You Need to Know

➤ You can use DirectCD with CD-R or CD-RW discs.

➤ DirectCD has to format a disc before it can use it.

➤ Once formatted, the CD acts just like a hard disk when used in the RW drive.

➤ You can continue to add, modify, and delete files on a CD-RW disc, but you cannot delete (or at least recover space) from a CD-R disc.

Chapter 12

Using NTI FileCD

In This Chapter

➤ Learn how to format a CD-RW disc using FileCD

➤ Find out how to copy files to a CD-RW disc

➤ Learn how to erase (reformat) a CD-RW disc and use it again

➤ Learn how to delete or rename files on a CD-RW disc

➤ Change the language the FileCD program uses

Just like Easy CD Creator, NTI CD-Maker has a packet writing application that allows you to use a CD-RW disc as if it were just about the same thing as a regular hard disk. You'll learn in this chapter how to use FileCD to copy data files to a CD-RW disc one file or folder at a time. Using this technique you can write files to the recordable CD as you need to, rather than waiting until you have a large number of files to burn.

Using NTI FileCD

When you use the installation CD for NTI CD Maker, you'll notice that there's a separate selection to install FileCD. Just click on that menu option and follow the usual dialog boxes to select a directory, and FileCD will be installed on your computer. Once you've done this, you'll find that there are two ways to start the program.

First, you can use Start/Programs/NTI CD-Maker 2000 Professional/FileCD. You can also use the icon placed on the desktop, if you chose that selection during the installation process.

Setting FileCD Options

In Figure 12.1 you can see the FileCD main window with the Disc menu options selection showing.

Figure 12.1

You can use the Disc menu to format a disc or to set options for FileCD.

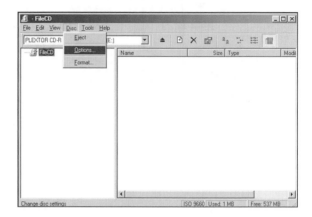

In Figure 12.2 you can see the Options dialog box. It's quite simple. You can choose between the two formats that FileCD supports. These are …

➤ **ISO 9660.** This is an almost universal disc format and can be read by most operating systems without the need to load additional drivers or have the FileCD program installed. This is the standard CD-ROM file system that was developed in 1988 to create a format that was compatible across multiple platforms, such as PCs and Macintosh computers. This is the method I suggest you use when you format your CD-RW discs!

➤ **UDF.** This stands for Universal Disk Format. This is the format used for both CD-ROM and DVD discs. When used with a program like FileCD, a method of recording called packet writing is used to make more efficient use of the space on the disc.

Figure 12.2

Use the Options dialog box to set the default type of file system to use.

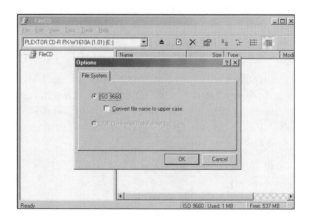

180

Between Tracks

In Figure 12.2 the UDF radio button is grayed-out, meaning you can't select it at this time. This is because I've already inserted a disc into the CD burner that has been formatted using the ISO 9660 standard. If you want to use the UDF format, make sure that there is no disk in your CD-RW drive and both selections will be available. After you've chosen a default format, you can insert the CD-RW disc into the drive.

In this options dialog box, you can set the default that you want FileCD to use when it formats a disc. Note the check box labeled Convert Filename to Upper Case that's right under the ISO 9660 selection. When the ISO 9660 specification was first established, upper case filenames were part of the standard. Selecting this check box will make sure your CD is compatible with older CD-ROM drives that are ISO 9660 compatible, but just not up to the latest standard which does support both upper- and lowercase filenames. If you select this check box, then when you copy files to the disk, any lowercase (or mixed-case) filenames will be converted to uppercase.

You might try using both methods to see which suits your needs. If you want to write to a CD-RW disc using FileCD and expect it to be readable on a CD-ROM drive elsewhere, you should probably use the ISO 9660 standard. While it is an older standard, it is more widely implemented today. Note also that you can download from many Web sites a driver that you can load on a PC to enable it to read UDF discs. Newer drives (in the past three to five years) will support a function called MultiRead. If you have an old PC that's been humming away for years that has an older CD-ROM drive, then you won't be able to read CD-RW discs in that drive! As cheap as CD-ROM drives are, however, that should not be a problem. Just spend a few bucks (less than $50 in most cases) and replace the CD-ROM drive!

How to Format a FileCD Disc

FileCD is a utility that can be used to treat a CD-RW disc as if it were just a big floppy disk. That is, instead of having to create a layout using the CD-Maker application, you can simply use Windows Explorer to copy files to a CD-RW disc. However, in order to use a rewritable CD, you first have to format the darn thing using the FileCD program.

Formatting a New CD-RW Disc

You can format a blank disc by inserting it into the CD burner and selecting Format from the menu shown back in Figure 12.1. In Figure 12.3, you can see that the default file system is selected (ISO 9660 Format) in the Format disc dialog box. You can fill in text in the label field (which can be up to 11 characters). When formatting a new CD-RW disc you must choose the radio button labeled Full (format and write CD file system structures to the disc).

Figure 12.3

*Use the Format disc dia-
log box to format the
CD-RW disc before its
first use.*

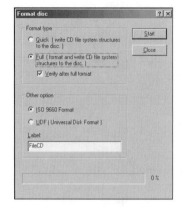

I also recommend you use the check box in Figure 12.3 labeled Verify after full format. This adds just a few minutes to the formatting time, and verifies that the CD drive can read through all the file system structures that were created during the formatting process.

When you're ready, click the Start button. The dialog box shown in Figure 12.4 will pop up to warn you that your action will destroy any data on the disc, so be sure you've got the correct disc in your CD burner before you click the Yes button to continue!

Figure 12.4

*FileCD will warn you one
last time before it formats
the disc.*

During the formatting process you'll see the progress that the program is making. At the bottom of the Format disc dialog box a bar graph will slowly make its way across the screen, while the Time Elapsed field will tell you how long the format is taking. At the right side of the bar graph you'll see a number telling you the percentage of the formatting progress so you can judge how much longer the process will take. You can see this in Figure 12.5.

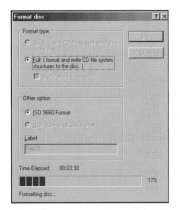

Figure 12.5

You can watch the progress of the formatting and estimate how much longer it will take by looking at the bottom of the Format disc dialog box.

When the formatting is complete, the text under the bar graph will change from Formatting Disc … to Verifying Disc … if you chose the Verify option. This won't take long, so just be patient! It's a good idea to use the verify option the first time you format a disc to check to see that no errors were made when writing file structure information to the disc.

Finally, the text under the bar graph will change to Initializing File System …, which will take another minute or two, and then you are done. A small popup dialog box will let you know that the process is complete, and all you have to do to start using the disc is to click the OK button and then close the Format Disc dialog box.

Reformatting a CD-RW Disc

While you can easily delete files from a CD-RW disc using File CD, it's quicker to just reformat the disc using the Quick (write CD file system structures to the disc) radio button in the Format Disc dialog box. This just resets the file system structures so that any data on the disc can't be accessed. If you want to be sure that all of the data are erased, then you should use the full format option again. The quick format option doesn't take nearly as much time, so unless the disc contains confidential information, choose the quick-format method and then click on the Start button. Again, you'll see the progress being made by looking at the bottom of the dialog box.

It's also possible to reformat a CD-RW disc that was originally formatted and written to by another program (such as Easy CD Creator). When you insert a disc of this sort in the CD burner and FileCD is running, you'll see a dialog box like the one shown in Figure 12.6 pop up to let you know you've inserted this kind of disc.

Figure 12.6

You can reformat a CD-RW disc that was originally formatted using some other application.

183

If you inserted the disc by mistake, click the No button and remove it! If you stuck it in the burner because you want to use it with File CD, then click the Yes button, and the regular Format Disc dialog box will appear. Use the full format option to format the disc.

Adding Files to a FileCD Disc

You can use programs like Windows Explorer to copy files to the CD-RW disc once it's been formatted. However, it's not as flexible as the DirectCD program that Easy CD Creator provides. There are two methods you can use to add files (and folders) to a CD-RW disc using File CD.

1. Drag the file or folder from Windows Explorer to the windowpane of the FileCD application. You can't drag items in Windows Explorer to other folders in Windows Explorer. You must drag them to the FileCD program window.

2. An easier method is to right-click on a file or folder in Windows Explorer and then select the option Send To FileCD. If you send a large folder of information, a dialog box will pop up and show you the progress as the files are copied.

Keep in mind that CD-RW drives are a lot slower than a computer's hard drive, so when copying a lot of data, such as a folder that contains a large number of files or possibly several large files, you won't get as fast a response as you do when copying from one hard disk to another.

Once you've sent files to the CD-RW disc, FileCD will tell you that in order for these files to be visible to other programs (such as Windows Explorer, or another application), you must open and close the CD tray to cause the operating system to refresh it's information about the disc. Click the Yes button to this dialog box and the files are ready for use by other applications.

Most any application you use should be able to read a file on the CD-RW disc. You can even use the MS-DOS Command Prompt to view or copy the files from the CD-RW disc to another disk.

Just keep in mind that in order to write to the disc, you must use one of the two methods previously described. For example, you can open a file on a CD-RW disc that uses FileCD, but you can't write the file back to the disc. You can write it to another location and then use the above methods to copy it back to the CD-RW disc.

Other FileCD Options

FileCD is a good program to use for staging a disc that you want to later burn to a CD-R disc. It is also a good way to copy files to a disc you want to take to another computer to read. You can always reuse the CD-RW disc, so it's a good way to carry files between work and home computers, especially since many data files and large applications used on today's computers won't fit on a single disk anymore.

There are a few other things you can do with FileCD that may be helpful. For example, in the FileCD window you can right-click on a file or folder and use the Delete or Rename menu options. Delete, of course, will delete the file from the disk. Rename gives you the capability of giving the file or folder a new name.

And if you want, you can change the language that FileCD uses. Simply click on Start/Programs/NTI CD-Maker 2000 Professional/FileCD/GUI Language Selector.

File CD will then allow you to choose from the following languages, but the change won't take effect until you restart FileCD. Indeed, you should close FileCD if it is running before you invoke the Language Selector program.

You choose the language from a drop-down menu. Once you've selected the language you want to use, click OK.

The Least You Need to Know

➤ FileCD can let you use a CD-RW disc like a regular disk drive.

➤ You must format a CD-RW disc before it can be used.

➤ You can reformat a disc to quickly erase its contents.

➤ You can choose among a variety of languages to use with the program.

Part 6

Picasso Was Overrated: Creating Great-Looking CD Labels and Jewel Case Inserts

There's an old saying in the consulting industry: Appearance is everything. The same goes for your CDs. Both Easy CD Creator and NTI CD-Maker come with applications that enable you to create fantastic CD labels and jewel case inserts. You can buy blank jewel case boxes at most all electronics stores now, so you might as well dress them up a bit!

The chapters in Part 6 will first offer some advice about labels and inserts, then teach you how to use the programs to create the labels and inserts.

Chapter 13

What Do I Need to Make Great Labels and Inserts?

In This Chapter

➤ A quick look at several kinds of labels and inserts

➤ Do-it-yourself inserts!

➤ Do's and don'ts of making CD labels

The CD labels and jewel case inserts that come with most recordable discs are pretty plain and usually littered with manufacturer logos. As you'll find in this chapter, there's no need to subject your CD burns to such inartistic treatment. Roxio Easy CD Creator 5 Platinum and NTI CD-Maker 2000 come with utilities that allow you to print CD labels and jewel case inserts. Using these programs and the appropriate paper stock or pre-cut labels, you can print out customized disc labels and jewel case inserts to suit whatever project you have on your plate.

So Many Programs, So Many Labels

When any new device is created for use with a PC, you can be sure that a new market will open up for other products to support the new device. The recordable CD drive is no exception. Indeed, several companies have jumped in to provide supplies for you to use with your CD-RW drive.

The most obvious example is the blank, recordable CD itself. These are made by many manufacturers, and their usefulness on your system will depend on myriad factors, such as your drive model and your particular media. However, we've already discussed recordable media in Chapter 2, "The Machine Behind the Curtain: How CDs and Recordable CDs Work."

The other "expendables" you should think about are paper jewel case inserts and label stock. You can pick up these labels at any office supply store and most consumer electronics stores as well (like Best Buy and CompUSA). Some of the major brands include Farrow's Neato, Memorex, Stomper, and Avery. There are also new brand names and varieties coming into the market even as this book is being produced. The big advantage in using these products is that they generally include mechanisms for cleanly putting a label on a CD. The adhesive "glue" that all but permanently affixes a CD label to a CD is some serious stuff. If you don't line it up properly when attaching it to the CD, there's no swinging around for a second landing attempt. The applicator mechanisms that come with certain CD label kits allow you to easily affix CD labels correctly each and every time.

Depending on your budget, the number of labels you want to make, and whether or not you need an applicator mechanism, the cost of these packages can get pretty significant. There is another option, though, and we'll quickly dig into that before starting moving on to the next two chapters, which deal with actually creating the labels in the aforementioned programs. Why put the stock before the program? Because CD Label Creator and JewelCase Maker both support just about any label/insert type you might want to use.

Cross Reference

For information about using the CD Label Creator in Easy CD Creator 5 Platinum, check out Chapter 14, "Making Killer Labels with Easy CD Creator CD Label Creator." For the scoop on releasing your artistic talents in NTI CD-Maker 2000's JewelCase Maker, see Chapter 15, "Using NTI JewelCase Maker."

Between Tracks

Many, if not most, of the major CD label products come with their own software, which you can use to print your custom labels. The usefulness of this software depends on the package, but generally, CD Label Creator or JewelCase Maker are still your best options.

Card Stock and Jewel Case Inserts

Before you start worrying about which card stock or inserts to buy, it's important to understand the lingo used to describe each part of a CD label or insert. It may be basic, but these terms are used on most CD label packages to describe how many of each label or insert it contains. You do want to know what you're buying, right?

Basically, what you're dealing with are labels, which attach to the actual compact disk, and inserts, which go into a CD's jewel case. The label is, obviously, simple enough to grasp. But the inserts are broken down into a couple subcategories, as follows:

➤ **The U-card.** Forms the bottom and spine of the jewel case.

➤ **Front/Inside Cover.** These are pretty self explanatory. Hopefully, these are part of the same insert sheet. However, as described in the previous section some labeling kits only provide inserts that fill the role of the Front cover.

Figure 13.1 illustrates each of these, along with the orientation for applying a CD label, for the more visual folks among us.

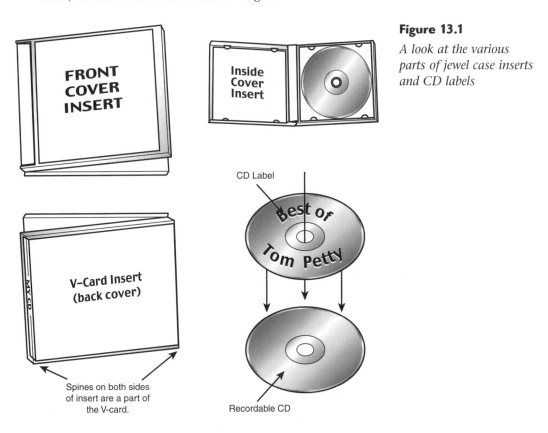

Figure 13.1

A look at the various parts of jewel case inserts and CD labels

For those who don't want to get soaked paying for expensive brand-name inserts, you can use your CD label software to print to *card stock*, which can be found at any office supply store. It's usually near the stationery section. This kind of stock has many uses, but if you can find it in the 50 to 65 lb range, you've got about the same thing as what comes in the expensive packages CD label vendors try to sell you. Most card stock also comes in colors. If you are using a black-and-white printer instead of a color ink jet, this can spice up your inserts. Heck, color stock is useful even if you have a color printer because it could save you a ton of ink! After all, why soak white paper stock in red ink if you can just buy red paper to begin with?

Besides cost, the trouble with most label and insert packages is that they don't come with enough jewel case inserts to match the number of CD disc labels you get with them. Who knows why they do this. I blame it on that secret society, led by Colonel Sanders and Big Foot, that runs the world. On top of that, some products only print to one side of the front jewel case insert. This is a drag when compared to brands like Stomper, which design their jewel case inserts so that you can print the front and inside covers on the same sheet of paper (see Figure 13.2).

Figure 13.2

Pre-scored inserts for a jewel case's front cover are generally found in two varieties. Printing these two inserts on the same sheet (and folding it in half) makes the insert thicker and much less likely to just slide out of the jewel case like the flatter, one-sided inserts often do.

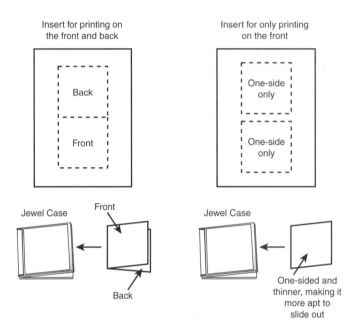

Although you might not have any issues with spending a few extra dollars on brand-name labels, just remember that the only difference between card stock and prepackaged inserts is that card stock doesn't have the pre-scored lines that make taking it apart after you print it an easy job. Of course, recent studies suggest that a special pair of cutting instruments, called scissors, could actually serve this purpose!

CD Label Do's and Don'ts

There are a few things you must keep in mind about CD labels and inserts. First, the label side of the CD-R disc is actually closer to the data layer of the disc than the data layer is to the bottom of the disc. The other side, where the disc is read, has a protective layer about a millimeter of distance between the surface and the data layer.

Because no such protection is on the label side where you are going to be sticking CD labels, you have to be very careful after you place the label. First, under no circumstances should you try to remove a label after you've stuck it onto a CD-R disc. You can damage the reflective surface and render the CD unusable.

Second, if you print with an ink jet printer, remember that water causes the printing to run. Don't leave CD-R discs with ink jet–printed labels lying around on the coffee table or anywhere else it might get wet!

Also keep in mind that jewel cases are not exactly indestructible. Inserting a U-Card requires that you first pry up the plastic portion of the CD case that holds the CD in place. Although it's a simple process, it is very easy to snap off the pegs that hold it in place. This, of course, pretty much hoses any further use of the case. I find the easiest way to avoid this is by opening the jewel case and laying it on a flat surface. Then, use your fingernails to pry up the center portion of the holder that is located where the front and back sides of the jewel case join.

When printing to precut inserts, it's also a good idea to print to a regular sheet of paper first. If you place the test page back to back with the labels page, you can make sure that the printer is printing inside the labels and not slipping off the edge. If it is off a bit, you'll need to use your CD label creation software to adjust how paper aligns with the printer.

Finally, if you use a ballpoint pen to write on the label surface, whether it is directly onto the CD's label surface or onto a sticky label that you've attached, do so very carefully. Because the reflective surface is such a short distance away, it doesn't take much pressure to push the ink into the data layer (destroying the disc). If you press hard enough, you can actually see whatever you write all the way through the other side of the CD. To be safe, use a water-based, felt-tip pen instead. You can usually find them sold next to CD bundles in retail stores.

Don't Get Burned

If you are using an ink jet or other similar printer technology, you should probably give the label or inserts a little time to dry so you don't smear the ink when applying them. I recommend at least a half hour.

Between Tracks

You don't need to label everything, do you? Remember that you can always use a felt-tip pen (with water-based ink, not oil-based) to write a brief description on the label side of a recordable disc. And, of course, most blank CD-Rs come with jewel case labels you can write on, as well.

The Least You Need to Know

➤ You can use pre-made labels, generic print stock, or even plain paper to create custom labels for your CD.

➤ Certain jewel case inserts only provide for the case's front cover, but not the inside front cover.

➤ Be careful when attaching a label to a CD. Because of the powerful adhesive, you'll only get one chance. Use a CD applicator mechanism to ensure proper alignment every time.

Making Killer Labels with Easy CD Creator CD Label Creator

In This Chapter

➤ Using CD Label Creator for audio CDs

➤ Using CD Label Creator for data and other CDs

➤ Get more out of your text in CD Label Creator

➤ Use categories to link text fields and save yourself from repeatedly typing the same information

➤ Use graphics to add pictures and backgrounds to your CD labels and covers

After you've got your labels or paper stock, as discussed in Chapter 13, "What Do I Need to Make Great Labels and Inserts?" all you need is an easy way to print the right information on them. Enter Roxio's CD Label Creator. This program is an excellent one that does just about everything the other programs, which come with some brand-name labels, do. For most purposes I think you'll grow to like Roxio's CD Label Creator for its ease of use. It also has a huge advantage over some other programs I've looked at in that it can automatically look up and insert artist, title, and song names onto your labels using the layout you used to create the disc. That can save you a lot of typing!

In this chapter, we're going to look at how to use CD Label Creator to make both basic and more advanced labels and inserts for use with audio and data CDs. CD Label Creator has several easy methods for inputting track, artist and even data folder information, so once we've got the basics down, we'll look at other methods you can use

Between Tracks

After you successfully burn a new CD from Easy CD Creator, you can jump directly to the CD Label Creator. The Success dialog box that appears when the burn is done contains a button labeled CD Label Creator. If you click this button, you go directly from creating the CD to making the jewel box case and label for it.

to manipulate text, link data fields together and even add pictures and backgrounds to your CD labels and jewel case inserts. While these features won't make your CDs burn faster or more reliably, they do allow you to give them a more professional look, or at least a snazzier one.

Using Roxio's CD Label Creator for Audio CDs

You can start up the CD Label Creator the same way you start up most other Roxio applications, through either the Project Selector or the Start menu. For the latter, click Start, Programs, Roxio Easy CD Creator 5, Applications, and finally, click CD Label Creator. If you'd rather use the Project Selector, double-click its desktop icon, hover your mouse-pointer over the CD Label Creator button, and then select the second CD Label Creator that appears in the middle of the window (see Figure 14.1).

Figure 14.1

Selecting CD Label Creator from the Project Selector takes you to Easy CD Creator's very useful application for making CD inserts and labels.

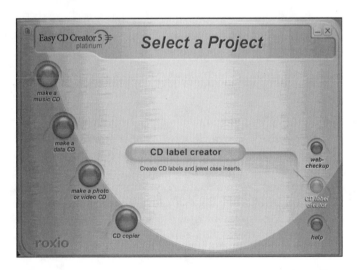

Once you select one of these options, you're brought to the main CD Label Creator screen shown in Figure 14.2.

A close look at the screen shows that it's not going to be a difficult program to operate. There is the usual menu at the top, starting with File and including standard menus, such as Edit and Help. Under this is a toolbar that can speed up many tasks. To the far left is a Page bar, which allows you to select which part of the CD label or jewel case insert you want to see.

Page bar   Drawing space

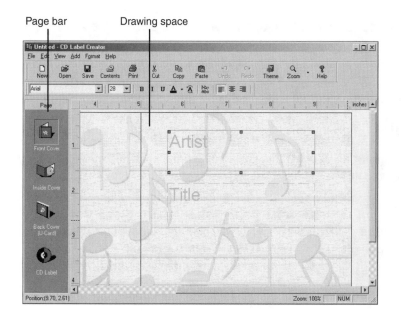

Figure 14.2

The main window of the CD Label Creator is modest, but it hides a wealth of tools for creating terrific labels and inserts.

Most of the window, however, is taken by the drawing space where you can construct the printouts that can be used to line the back and front of a jewel case. Using this program, you can also print a label that can be applied, by one of several popular applicators, to the CD. Assuming that the Front Cover icon on the left of the window is selected, this drawing space shows an editing field outline in which you can insert the name of the artist of the CD. The field under it enables you to enter the title for the CD. Off to the left side of this front cover is an area that can be used to add song tracks. Ignore that one for now, as we'll look at it in just a minute.

Veterans of Easy CD Creator Deluxe 4.0 might remember a pesky little creature that looked like a dot with a face that would appear near the bottom of, the then, Jewel Case Creator window (was actually a wizard). In a perfect world, this demon-spawn of Clippy (of Microsoft Office fame) would have provided users with valuable help information when needed. In practice, he just took up valuable screen real estate. Mercifully, Roxio has put this annoying little spell-meister to the sword so you won't have to waste valuable mouse clicks exorcising his scrawny butt from your screen.

So now that we have opened the program and offered a basic understanding of the interface, let's get to the real work of making some inserts for your audio CDs.

Cross Reference

This section focuses on using CD Label Creator to make audio CDs. Even though the process is very similar for data CDs, you can get data CD specifics by setting your sights on the section called "Using Roxio's CD Label Creator for Data CDs," later in this chapter.

197

Adding CD Information and Contents Automatically!

The best place to get started in making audio CD labels and inserts is to automatically have CD Label Creator add some tracks to your inserts. Since this requires a virtual palette for the program to work from, you'll need to make sure you've inserted an audio CD into your CD-ROM or CD-RW drive. CD Creator can get CD information in one of three ways:

➤ If you have an Internet connection and are making a label for a commercial music CD (or a duplicate of one), you can download the CD's information using the same online database described in Chapter 5, "Drag and Drop with Easy CD Creator."

➤ If you have downloaded the information for this particular CD previously (even if it was from within the main Easy CD Creator program), CD Label Maker has that data stored on your PC and can recall it upon command.

➤ Finally, if your CD has it's track, artist or title information encoded on it (including compilation CDs created with Easy CD Creator), CD Label Maker can read that information straight off your CD.

Between Tracks

Unlike Easy CD Creator, in which you must enable your automatic Internet connection for audio CD data downloads, if CD Label Creator wants to access the Internet, it will. By default, it doesn't ask you first, it just dials away (unless you're already connected, in which case it starts looking for the CD information).

If you want to have better control over this process, select the Edit menu and choose Preferences. The dialog box that appears contains several tabs; choose the one for Internet. The three check boxes here should look familiar to you if you've read Chapter 5. To prevent CD Label Creator from going to the Internet at all, make sure each check box is cleared (although this would defeat the purpose). To make sure CD Label Creator asks you nicely before dialing an Internet connection, make sure the first two check boxes are enabled (Enable Audio CD Information Download and Prompt Me Before Attempting Internet Download).

If you don't know what information is required of the Access The Internet Using a Proxy Server check box, then you really don't need to worry about it at all. Just leave the box disabled.

You don't actually have to choose between these methods. CD Label Creator automatically goes with the simplest option. To let the program work its magic, click the Add menu and then select CD Contents. If you have not downloaded the disc's information yet, you'll next see a dialog box telling you that a music service is being contacted on the Internet to get the album information. This, of course, is why you need that Internet connection. Regardless of whether the information is coming from the Web or is already stored on your hard drive, it should take just a few moments to complete the process.

Once CD Label Creator has the information it needs, it fills up your inserts and CD label views with that data. The CD I'm using for this example was identified properly as *August and Everything After* by the Counting Crows. By default you should already be in a view that shows the CD insert's front cover. If you're not, go ahead and press the Front Cover button to display it. Because CD Label Creator uses that nice folded cover technique I mentioned in Chapter 13, it puts information about each song title and its length on the inside cover. Clicking the Inside Cover button on the window's left toolbar brings up this information (see Figure 14.3).

Inside Cover button

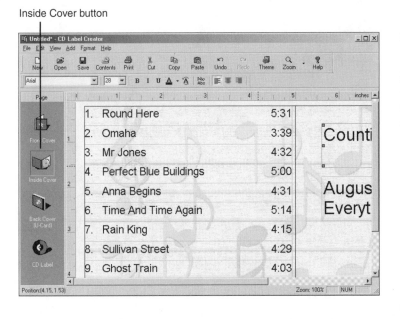

Figure 14.3

The inside portion of the folded cover jewel case cover lists each track, along with its total length.

Now, if only doing your taxes could be that easy! All you had to do was click Add and then CD Contents, and instantly you've got yourself a jewel box cover.

If you click the icon labeled Back Cover, you'll find it looks similar to the inside cover (see Figure 14.4). Indeed, they are similar in that they both list the song titles and the play times. This back cover, which is also called the U-card, has a subtle difference. On each side of the cover you'll see text written in a vertical mode. This portion of the printed card will be folded so that when you insert it into the back of the CD jewel case, it will show the song titles on the rear of the case, and the album artist and title on both spines.

Figure 14.4

The U-card is where information for the back and sides of the jewel case comes from.

U-Card button

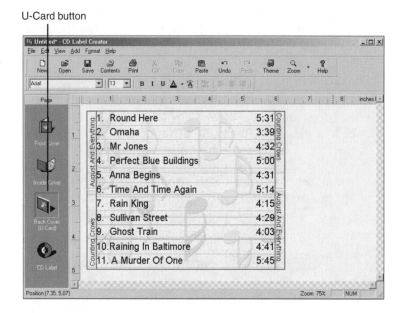

The final button on this toolbar is for the CD label itself. As you can see in Figure 14.5, CD Label Creator places the album artist and title on the CD label.

Don't Get Burned

If you want CD Label Creator to be able to identify compilation CDs you may have created with Easy CD Creator, then it's important to make sure you've identified the individual tracks before having burned the CD (and then chosen to Write CD Text on the Record CD Setup dialog box; refer to Chapter 5).

This is necessary because, after all, any compilation CD you create won't be listed in the Internet database! (Unless you're able to exert some considerable influence over the folks who maintain it.)

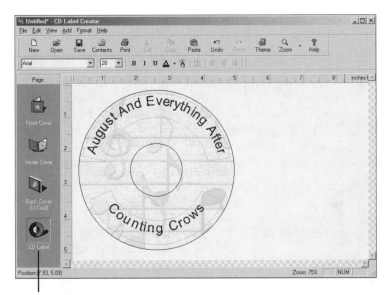

CD Label button

Entering Information the Hard Way: By Hand!

Unfortunately, it's not always possible to create all the components of the jewel case with just a few clicks. It can be a little more difficult if you're using an unidentified compilation CD or if the album is not found in the Internet database (a rare occurrence). I've personally tried a wide variety of CDs and have yet to have one that wasn't found, but as many of us found out in high school chemistry, nothing is an exact science (a discovery for which I am still paying off the bill). If you do run into this problem, you'll have to enter the information manually.

The good news about typing in information yourself is that once you're done, you can save the label information, just like you saved Easy CD Creator layouts. This way, if you need to print a new copy or modify the inserts in some way, you can open it back up whenever you need to. To save the layout, just click the File menu and choose Save As. From here, you can give the layout file a name, clicking OK to save it on your hard disk.

Arcane CD Speak

Handles are little boxes that appear in each corner and halfway between each side of a selected field.

Entering the Title and Artist

As you saw in Figure 14.2, CD Label Creator has two boxes, called *fields*, that appear by default on the jewel case insert's front cover. You can use these fields to enter information about the CD title and recording artist or group. You can select one of these fields by clicking it. After it's selected, the border around the field turns dark and several *handles* appear around it, which you can see in Figure 14.6.

Figure 14.6

You can manually enter the information for the jewel case cover by typing it into the available fields.

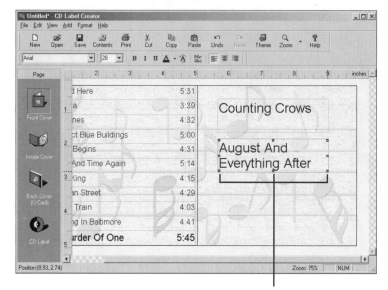

Handles appear on a selected field

When you position your cursor over a handle, it turns into a double-arrow symbol. You can then press and hold down the mouse button while you drag that particular handle to change the size of the field. The handle you click determines the direction in which you can move when resizing (horizontal, vertical, or diagonal).

Similar to a painting on a wall, you also can move a field to a different location on the cover. Just place your cursor inside the field, and then click and hold. It turns into cross hairs, enabling you to drag the field to any part of the cover.

Obviously, you aren't going to jump through all these hoops if all you want to do is give these fields appropriate names. To add text to a field, just double-click it. This opens the selected field for editing via your keyboard.

Because the field is highlighted automatically, all you have to do is start typing in the artist's name. As soon as the first key is pressed, the word "Artist" disappears, replaced by whatever you're typing. You can change both fields as often as you want.

One nice feature about using the built-in templates CD Label Creator supplies is that certain fields are linked. For example, the CD title appears on the front cover, the edges of the U-card, and the CD label. Obviously, having to enter the same information for each field is a waste of your time. However, because CD Label Creator links these fields together, what you type in one automatically appears in the others, too.

Adding the Titles of Each Track

Adding the artist and title were easy—they were short and didn't take much time! The next thing you have to do is the most tedious part.

Entering in each song title, in order, and, if you want, adding the play times for each song can take a bit of time if you have a lot of tracks or type using the time-honored "hunt and peck" method. To add this information, click the Inside Cover icon on the left side of the CD Label Creator window to bring up that view. The view, like the rear end of a horse, isn't much. Because each track gets its own field and, at this point, CD Label Creator doesn't have a clue how many tracks are on your CD, the Inside Cover (and Back Cover) is blank.

To start entering the track titles, click the Add menu at the top of the window and then select Track. In Figure 14.7, you can see that a new dialog box, titled Add New Track, appears. Here you can enter the track number (which always defaults to the next new track number), the track title, and the time, which refers to the total length of the track. That, of course, means minutes and seconds, so don't be a wonk and enter, "An Eternity," as the time for the Guns 'N' Roses song, "November Rain."

Between Tracks

Keep in mind that if you don't care to know the length of a track, you don't have to enter anything for the duration. If you've put together a compilation from various CDs, you can even use this field to enter other information, such as an artist's name.

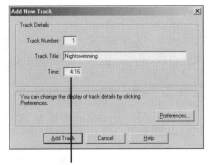

Despite the field name,
you can enter any text,
including the artist/group name, here.

Figure 14.7

The Add New Track dialog box enables you to enter information for each track on the CD.

Note the Preferences button in Figure 14.7. This brings up the Preferences dialog box, which has several tabs that can help give you more control over your label designing experience. This is the same Preferences dialog box that pops up when you select Preferences from the main program's Edit menu. For now, don't worry about this feature. We will discuss the preferences you can set for the program in the following sections.

Entering information in this window is no different than any other generic Windows dialog box. You can move between the fields with a click from your mouse or use the Tab key to jump through them all in order. You can give the track names any title you want, but generally speaking, naming a track Celine Dion's "My Heart Will Go On" when it's actually Poison's "Unskinny Bop," is only good for practical jokes.

Between Tracks

If you're working with a compilation CD with various artists, you probably care a lot more about knowing a track's artist than it's play duration. The Time field may imply that it's geared toward numbers, but you can enter text as well. CD Label Creator won't know the difference between your entering "5:23" or, "Tracy Chapman," for the track *Cold Feet*.

Don't Get Burned

Before you even think about starting the printing process, make sure you have the correct kind of paper or label stock in the printer first! For more information on label stock, check out Chapter 13, "What Do I Need to Make Great Labels and Inserts?"

When you've entered all the information you need for the first track, click the Add Track button and the track information appears on the main program window. The Insert New Track dialog box does remain on the screen, though, incrementing the track number by one; you can continue to add tracks until you are done, in which case, click the Done button (replaces the Cancel button after you add your first track). Take note when entering track information that CD Label Creator sizes the text you enter according to the number of tracks you use. This helps ensure that everything fits on the label appropriately.

Printing the Jewel Case Inserts and CD Label

After you've used the CD Contents or the manual-entry method to finish your CD covers or label, you can print the results. If you thought adding the titles and artist information was easy with Add/Add CD Contents, printing is just about as easy.

To get started, click the Print icon on the toolbar or select Print from the File menu. The Print dialog box pops up to enable you to make some changes before you print. In addition to selecting the printer (if you have more than one), there are some other options on this dialog box, shown in Figure 14.8, that you also need to pay close attention to.

The most important button on this dialog box is the Page Setup button. This opens the Page Setup dialog box where you can select the kind of stock you are printing with (see Figure 14.9). There are three tabs on this dialog box for each type of label or insert you can print: Front/Inside, Back (U-Card) and CD Label. If you are using labels from one of the firms mentioned earlier in Chapter 13 or from one of the myriad others, this is where you make sure CD Label Creator knows it.

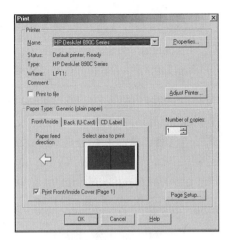

Figure 14.8

The Print dialog box gives you many options.

Use the tabs to select the part of the CD label/insert with which you want to work.

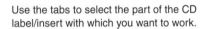

Figure 14.9

The Page Setup dialog box enables you to select the kind of label or jewel case insert stock you are printing.

Clicking the drop-down box labeled Current Paper Type brings up the list of paper options you can choose from. CD Label Creator supports the majority of the big names and, if you go with my preferred method and use generic card stock, includes a generic output option.

After choosing the type of paper you're using for each of the labels, click the OK button on the Print dialog box to return to the print window.

Finally, you need to select which of the label types you want to print. Near the bottom of the Print window (shown in Figure 14.9), is a dialog area with three tabs (again, for each of the label types). Each of these tabs has a check box on it that enables you to select the labels you want to print. If you want to print just the front and inside covers, you can. If you want to print all the covers, but not the CD label, you can. If you want to become the leader of the free world … you're reading the wrong book.

After you've selected what to print and what you plan to print it on, you're finally ready to put an end to the insanity and print! Click the OK button at the bottom of the window and await the results.

205

Using Roxio's CD Label Creator for Data CDs

Using CD Label Creator to make data CD labels isn't much different from making them for audio discs. The only key difference is that instead of working with track times, artists and song titles, you're working with folders and their file contents.

Between Tracks

If your current theme is designed for audio, when you add contents from a data CD, CD Label Creator asks you if you would like to switch to a data-oriented theme. Unless you've got other plans, choose Yes and select one from the list that appears.

Adding the CD Contents

Adding the contents of a data CD to the jewel case inserts of a CD can be an ominous task! It's not likely that you're going to store just two or three files (unless you're creating artwork with high graphics resolutions or working for NASA). Instead, you're likely to store a large number of files, and probably folders, on any CD-R you record.

To add a data CD's contents to your inserts, click Add, CD Contents. If you have chosen a data theme (as explained in the next section), the program attempts to fill in the contents of the CD, as you can see in Figure 14.10, by simply listing the files and folder in the main directory on the disc (until it runs out of room).

Figure 14.10

The CD Label Creator starts a list of the folders and files it finds on your disc if you click Add and then CD Contents.

Files or documents · · · · · CD title

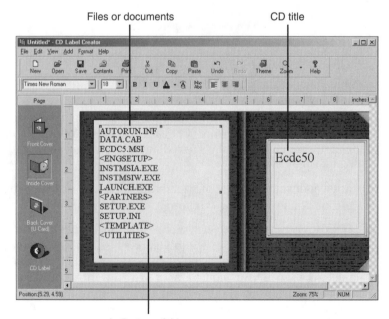

Indicates a folder

Obviously, using the Add Contents method won't be useful to you unless you have a very small number of files (that also have very descriptive names). Also, if you don't need to list the files or folders, you can do away with a U-card for this CD and just print the CD label and the front card piece. For that, all you need is a descriptive title. Choose Front Cover from the left toolbar; you see just a single field, similar to the one in Figure 14.11.

Since CD Label Creator inserts a label that was assigned to the disc when it was written, if anything, it will probably look rather bizarre, like a codename or locker combination, which isn't particularly useful. Changing this field, as I have done in Figure 14.11, is no different than changing the title of an audio CD. If you double-click inside the field, the existing name becomes highlighted. Enter a useful new name, press Enter, and that's all she wrote.

Between Tracks

If your data CD is part of a periodic backup of important information on your computer, you should include a date as part of the disc title.

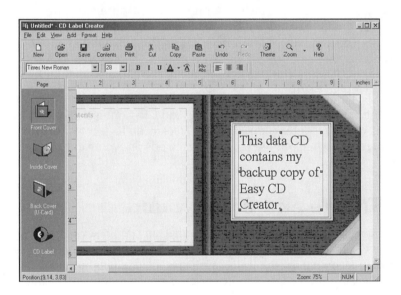

Figure 14.11

The front view of a data CD shows only one field in which to place information.

Should you run out of room entering the name or description for your disc, remember that you can resize the field by clicking it once to select it and then clicking and holding one of the handles to stretch or shrink it as necessary.

Editing Text on Jewel Case Inserts for Data CDs

As you saw in Figure 14.11, only one large field, by default, is on the front of the CD cover. When you choose CD Contents from the Add menu, the inside insert and the

Cross Reference

To get more information on the controls for adding tracks, see the section, "Adding the Titles of Each Track," earlier in this chapter.

U-card insert automatically get a listing of the directories and files on the CD, space permitting. Only a single field, however, is used for this listing. This differs from the track listing produced for audio CDs. In that case, each track becomes a separate field you can edit. Here, you have only one field.

You can easily edit this field any time you want. To replace the existing text, just double-click the field; the text in the field turns blue. You can press the Delete key to delete the text and then enter your own. Remember, in addition to using the handles to resize a field, you can move the entire field around on the page by placing your cursor inside it, holding down the left mouse button, and dragging it.

Using Add Tracks for the Data CD Cover

Oddly enough, you can also use the Add Tracks option from the Add menu when using a data CD jewel case theme. Because we covered using the Add Tracks process earlier in this chapter, we won't go over it again here. Using this capability, you can add a numbered list of items that describe the purpose of the CD, or even a list of the major programs or data files. Because the disc doesn't really contain any audio tracks, you can just leave the time field blank.

There is one pitfall to this method: It is exclusive to the Add CD Contents method. If you've already used the Add CD Contents option, Add Track is no longer available. This rule also works in reverse. After you use the Add Track option, you can no longer click Add CD Contents.

Choosing Your Theme and Background

Up to this point, we've covered how to get the CD information onto the various pieces that make up the CD insert and CD label. One thing we've completely ignored is the background art that accompanies the jewel case parts. For those who find CD Label Creator's default background for labels to be about as pretty to look at as Linda Blair in *The Exorcist,* there is good news. These "background" elements can be changed to much more appealing options with just a few mouse clicks. In the following sections, we look at themes, backgrounds and how to incorporate your own artwork into the cover.

Themes

With CD Label Creator, you get a small selection of *themes*. In the examples shown so far in this chapter, the musical notes background, meant for audio CDs, is called the

Music (audio) theme. CD Label Creator comes with dozens of themes, both for audio and data CDs. We won't cover them all here, but instead just tell you how to change them. For those who regularly visit the Internet—and who doesn't nowadays—visit Roxio's site at www.roxio.com for frequent updates that enable you to download new themes.

Arcane CD Speak

Many Windows users are already familiar with the concept of Themes, which let you customize the appearance and responsiveness of the user interface. In the case of Easy CD Creator a Theme involves giving your inserts and labels a special look. Easy CD Creator 5 includes a couple dozen themes ranging from Rock and Roll to Autumn.

When you click the Format menu in CD Label Creator and then select Change Theme, it brings up the Change Theme dialog box shown in Figure 14.12. You can see the current theme displayed, for the folded front cover/inside card, the U-card, and the CD label. You can also see titles of other themes to choose from (many of these themes are geared only for audio or data CDs and are labeled as such using parentheses). If you make a lot of copies, you might want to vary the themes a bit, so that all your CDs don't look alike! Unfortunately, the theme titles in the left window pane don't give you one clue about what they actually look like. Clicking one of these titles, however, enables you to use the right pane to view the various themes. To change a theme, just click it and then click OK.

Between Tracks

Because clicking OK with a theme selected changes your labels to that theme, be sure that it's the theme you want. If you're only browsing the themes for the moment and don't want to change, click Cancel instead.

Notice that a small check box is also near the bottom of this window called Set As Default Theme. If this box is checked when you click OK, any new labels you create will start out using the current theme.

Each theme is marked
as a data or audio theme.

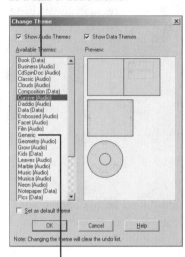

Figure 14.12

You can change the theme for the jewel case art by selecting Format/Change Theme.

Generic can be used for both
data and audio CD labels.

Backgrounds

This is similar to changing themes, but instead, you can vary the background by selecting a picture or color. To open the Backgrounds dialog box, click the Format menu and select Change Background. If you click Select a Color from the box that comes up, you will see the familiar (to regular Windows users) dialog box that enables you to select a background color. Note that you'll need a color printer, such as an inkjet, for this to work properly. If it's only black and white, this selection is about as useful to you as a bowling ball in a game of Ping-Pong.

Don't Get Burned

Choosing a background color overrides whatever theme you are using. Therefore don't choose a color like Blue and expect to be able to see the Radio theme you selected earlier.

If you decide to change the background color, just click that color and then click OK. When choosing a background color, it's important to keep in mind the color of the text for your CD. Even the best eyes aren't going to pick up black text on a black background! We'll discuss changing text colors later in this chapter.

Let's Talk About Preferences

A subject that fits neatly between this information about how to create basic CD inserts and labels for CDs and the next section that talks about taking your

210

label designs to the next level is the Preferences dialog box that enables you to control certain aspects of how the CD Label Creator program works. To bring up the Preferences dialog box, select Preferences from the Edit menu in CD Label Creator. Figure 14.13 shows this dialog box and the tabs you can use.

Figure 14.13

The Preferences dialog box contains tabs that let you control some aspects of the program.

Under the first tab, named Front/Inside, there are two pairs of options. The first set consists of the Front/Inside Options, where you can select from two check boxes. The first, Print Front/Inside Cut and Fold Lines, tells CD Label Creator to print a thin set of lines along areas of the front and inside jewel case inserts for where to cut and fold the inserts. The second, Print Front/Inside Outline, prints a visible border around the inserts.

The second pair of options is found under the Track Details section of the dialog box. Here you can control how much information about a track is printed on the inside cover. Specifically, you can disable the display and printing of track numbers and track durations (information not everyone finds necessary). I have two check boxes selected. The first simply tells the program to pop up one of those reminder boxes when your cursor falls on an object, such as when you pass over a field you can edit and the text "Double-click to edit" appears. These reminders can be very useful if you don't use the program frequently. The second option is how you turn on or off that little CD guide guy who appeared at the beginning of this chapter. If you truly need to be guided, step-by-step, through some tasks, leave this check box selected so he will appear when you first start up the program.

Even if you turn off this little guy, you can still invoke him because you'll find on the toolbar a mini-picture of him labeled CD Guide.

Between Tracks

The information on the Front/Inside tab is identical to the options found on the Back (U-Card) tab except, of course, the options on this tab control information for the jewel case U-Card, instead of the Front/Inside inserts.

211

The CD Label Tab

The information contained on the CD Label tab is very similar to what's found on the tabs controlling the various jewel case inserts. However, in addition to giving you control over cut and fold lines, solid borders and the display of track numbers and times, this dialog box let's you control whether to put tracks on the CD label (rather than just the artist/group and CD title). If you enable this check box, you can also choose to show track information in one or two columns.

The Assistance, Internet, and Units Tabs

The tabs described in this section are all very basic. First of all, the Assistance tab lets you get some basic extra help from CD Label Creator. With this option enabled, any time you hover your mouse pointer over an object that requires you to double-click it to make edits, CD Label Creator causes a small pop-up message indicating just that.

The Internet tab is where you can control the download of information about a CD from an Internet source. We discussed this tab in the section for creating audio CD labels.

Finally, the Units tab enables you to specify the method used for measurement in CD jewel case layout. You can select inches or centimeters.

Between Tracks

Although you can do a lot in terms of creating your own fields, don't forget that predefined fields still have their advantages. Their biggest asset is that they can be linked so that, for example, when you fill in the artist's name on the front jewel case cover, it is automatically filled in on the U–card and CD label as well.

Taking It to the Next Level: Advanced Ways to Edit Your CD Labels and Inserts

Now that we've dealt with the basic ways to create labels and inserts using CD Label Creator it's time to take things up a notch. If you don't care for the default text styles you're forced to use, want to input your own background pictures, or want to learn how to use links to relate different fields together, this is the section for you.

Other Ways to Play with Text

To kick off this graduate program in CD Label Creator, we'll deal with some of the ways you can manipulate text to give your CD labels a better look. In the first place, you don't have to stick with the fields that are predefined for each template. In true Jesse Ventura style, you can create your own independent fields and edit them as you see fit.

The most basic aspect of adding your own flavor to a jewel case layout is to add your own new text fields. For the purposes of this example, I'm going to make it easy to add text by starting out with a blank format. That is, instead of using one of the pre-defined themes that already contains text fields and graphics material, I have selected the theme called Generic from the Format, Change Theme menu. This gives you a clean slate with which to work.

Working with a generic theme leaves you with only a few basic fields that you can easily remove by selecting them and hitting the Delete key. This allows the true artists among you to work free from the interference of CD Label Creator's handholding. Of course, that means you need to create some new fields yourself. To add a simple text field, just click the Add menu and then Text. In Figure 14.14, you can see that the text field shows up in the center of the layout, with the words, "New Text," in the field.

You can make the text box larger or smaller by using the handles that appear as small boxes on each side of the field when you click it. To place your own poetic prose in this field, just double-click it and type whatever strikes your fancy.

Between Tracks

In addition to double-clicking, you can also put a field into editing mode by right-clicking the field and selecting Edit Text.

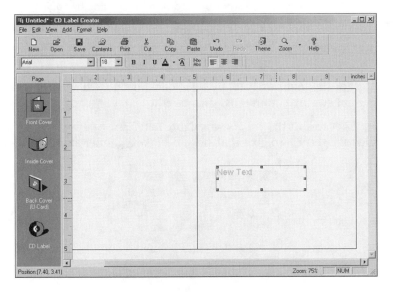

Figure 14.14

Add text fields manually to give yourself more control over a jewel case insert's contents.

You can choose to create several text fields on any part of the jewel case inserts or the CD label. For example, you could make one large text box that could be used to enter both the artist and title of a music CD. Or if creating a data CD, you could use the large box to enter a title and a paragraph explaining the contents of the disc.

Changing Text Field Properties

You can change many things about the text that appears on your CD jewel case or label. After you've double-clicked a field to put it into editing mode, you can use the drop-down menus on your toolbar to change the *font* or *point size*. If you use a word processor such as Microsoft Word or Notepad, you're probably used to working with this stuff.

Arcane CD Speak

Points and **fonts** are printer's terms that define the kind of character you'll see on the printed copy—or in today's terms, on the computer screen. A font is a typeface that has a distinctive style or look. The point size, which is measured in $1/72$ of an inch, represents the size of the characters as they appear on the screen or printed page. Increasing the point size increases the size of the font.

You can change properties for the text box itself by right-clicking the text field. A small menu pops up with the usual editing commands, such as edit text, cut, copy, and delete.

Other options, which we'll get to shortly, are also available here. The one we're interested in right now is called Properties, so give it a click and take a gander at Figure 14.15.

Figure 14.15

The Properties sheet for the text box enables you to specify a wide range of options for the field.

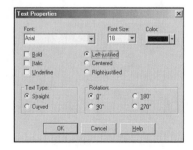

The dialog box that pops up enables you to modify both the font and point size for the text, along with other attributes for the text box itself:

➤ **Color.** This option uses a drop-down menu to enable you to select the color for the text you'll enter into the text box.

➤ **Text Style.** You can select the check boxes labeled Bold, Italic, and Underline to change the style of the text.

➤ **Positioning.** You can select the check boxes labeled Left-justified, Centered, and Right-justified to position your text in the box.

➤ **Text Type.** This option gives you two radio buttons that determine whether the text will be displayed in a straight line or in a curved format. Select Straight or Curved for this option. Straight text is the ordinary text you usually type on a page. Curved text makes the text box curve so that it can, for example, conform to the shape of a CD label. Figure 14.16 shows you a text box that started out as a rectangle and then was changed to have the curved attribute.

➤ **Rotation.** You can rotate your text box by using the radio buttons for 0, 90, 180, and 270 degrees.

When you've finished making your selections, just click the OK button. Of course, you can also click Cancel if you change your mind.

In Figure 14.16, you can see that a curved text box fits around the CD label perfectly. Just because it's a curved text box doesn't mean that you can't continue to do the other things with it that you can do to an ordinary text box. Figure 14.16 also shows that you can still grab the handles to resize the box and it will still keep its curved shape. When you double-click to edit a curved text box, however, another straight text box appears to make your typing easier. When you've finished adding or modifying the text, press Enter and the text you've edited will appear in the curved box.

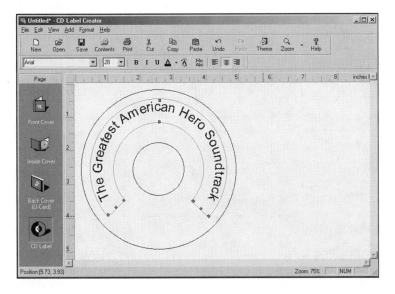

Figure 14.16

A curved text box is ideal for a CD label.

Although the uses of the features discussed here might seem limited compared to an application like Microsoft PowerPoint, those who want to design elaborate jewel case covers can be a bit more creative with these options.

Linking Text Fields

When you used a predefined theme to start your jewel case layout, you probably noticed that some fields were linked to others. For example, if you enter the artist's name on the front cover, it also appears on the CD label. This is because these two fields are members of the same category. All fields in the same category contain the same text. Even though themed labels select the categories for you, that doesn't mean you can't set them yourself, too. If you have information that needs to be repeated in several places, you can just create the appropriate fields and then place them in the same category.

Between Tracks

You should keep in mind that, generally speaking, categories in CD Label Creator really don't mean anything in terms of what kind of text or numbers you can enter in them. Even though you can't create your own categories, if you want to use a category not shown in the list, just select any one and use it however you see fit.

To get to the category option, highlight a text box (so that the sizing handles show up) and then give it the mighty right-click treatment. From the menu that appears, select Category. In Figure 14.17, you can see the many categories available.

Several categories are available to choose from. Although not shown, because it is scrolled out of view, you can also select None so that the text box can stand alone. Just click the category type with which you want the field to be associated and click OK. After you repeat this process, using the same category type, for other fields in your layout, you will find that changing the text in one changes it for all.

Figure 14.17

You can assign a category to each field. This links the fields to make text entry much easier.

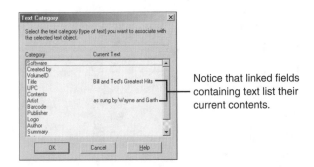

Notice that linked fields containing text list their current contents.

Just remember, if you have linked text boxes in your layout that are of varying sizes, such as a CD title on the front insert with it repeated on the spine of the jewel box, you must size the text for each one appropriately. You don't want to waste a precious jewel case label because you're trying to squeeze in a 24-point font on the spine that only holds an 8-point font!

Adding Background Graphics

One of the niftier CD Label Creator features discussed in this chapter was for adding themes to your jewel case. Although the program has a number of themes—for both data and audio CDs—that you can use, you can also toss them aside like used garbage and add your own.

For those who haven't worked much with graphics files, the various formats and types can seem a little overwhelming. With CD Label Creator, you have to worry about only two because they are the only ones the program supports: *bitmap* (files with a .bmp extension) and *JPEGs* (files with either a .jpg or .jpeg file extension). If you have a graphics file in one of these formats, then you can import that picture into your jewel case layout and make minor edits to it.

Two methods can be used for importing a graphics file into CD Label Creator. First, you can import the picture itself into a field and then size and position it somewhere in the layout, as you would a text field. Second, you can select the graphics file to be the background for your jewel case and label. In either case, you must make sure you know where the file is stored on your hard disk. Usually, it's best to use one folder, such as My Documents or My Pictures, to store these files. There is an advantage to using the first method in that you can add more than one picture. As always, you can still add text no matter what graphics you're using.

To import one or more pictures (not as a background), first select the view, such as Front Cover, U-Card, or Label, and then do the following:

1. Click the Add menu and select Picture.

2. A dialog box appears enabling you to locate the picture file. When you find the correct file to insert, double-click the filename or highlight it by clicking once, and then click the Open button.

3. The picture then appears on the layout. You can move the picture around to place it where you want it by holding down the left mouse button inside the picture field and dragging it to a new location. The picture file, similar to text boxes, also has handles you can use to resize it.

Figure 14.18 shows an example of a picture that has been imported to the front cover.

Between Tracks

If talk of graphic file formats only serves to make you dizzy, don't worry! If you're not sure if the application will support it, just try it and see. The worst you'll get is CD Label Creator complaining that it can't read it.

Figure 14.18

You can add pictures in addition to text for your jewel case layout. Don't expect them to look as good inside the CD Label Creator interface as they will when you print the label or insert.

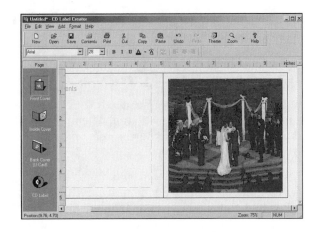

To add a background picture, which can be used to cover the whole front cover, back insert, or label, use the following steps instead:

1. Click the Format menu.

2. Click Change Background.

3. The Change Background dialog box that appears enables you to select a background color or a picture. Note the other options available in this dialog box allowing you to choose where the background is located. It can be placed on any part of the jewel case insert or CD label, and can even be spanned across the front cover and inside cover. Click Select a Picture.

4. A standard Open dialog box appears from which you can locate the directory and file that contains the picture you want to use. When you've made your selection, click the Open button.

Arcane CD Speak

The term **thumbnail** is often used in graphics programs to refer to a miniature representation of a graphics file that can be previewed much more easily and quickly.

5. You should now find yourself back in the Change Background dialog box. However, for the views you've selected, you'll see *thumbnails* of the picture you selected.

6. You can continue and select a different background picture for each of the major components of the jewel case and label. You do not have to use the same picture for each part of the package.

7. Click OK when you are satisfied with the picture(s) you've selected. The background picture(s) will now be displayed when you select those views in the main program (see Figure 14.19).

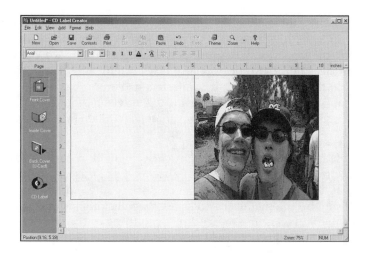

Figure 14.19

You can add pictures to be the background of part or all of the jewel case and label printout.

After you've added one or more background pictures, you can still add text boxes, circles, and squares to continue composing your jewel case and CD label artwork.

Adding Circles and Squares

If adding text and pictures isn't enough for you, you can also add circles or squares to the layout in the same manner you do the background figure. Just click the Add menu and select Square or Circle. For each circle or square you include, you can select certain properties for it. These shapes are manipulated in the same way you would manipulate a normal text field. However, a few options unique just to shapes are available, which you can find using the shape's Properties page (see Figure 14.20). Like any other object on the CD Label Creator layout, just right-click the shape and choose Properties from the menu that appears.

Figure 14.20

You can change the fill, line, and color properties for a circle or square.

The options here are pretty self-explanatory. For both circles and squares, you can select the background color and a variety of patterns that can be used inside the boundaries of the circle or square. You also can vary the color and width of the lines that draw the object or change the pattern lines. All these options have drop-down lists that enable you to select whichever one suits your needs.

219

Now, when you want to put this all together, an important thing to remember is that each of the items we've worked with, whether they be text boxes, circles, or squares, can be moved around from foreground to background—top to bottom or vice versa. Because CD Label Creator places new fields on top, any text I might have had in the same place as the shape would now be hidden. If computers had any common sense, they would understand that hidden text isn't of much use. But let's face it: for all that computers can do, they're really still pretty dumb. Fortunately, CD Label Creator lets you set things straight.

To change the order of these kinds of objects, just right-click the field in question and select either To Top or To Bottom from the menu that appears. Even though To Top works great if you can see at least part of a hidden object, if it's totally hidden there's nothing you can click to bring up the menu. Instead, just keep clicking away on the objects and fields hiding what you want to see, sending everything to the bottom, and eventually your missing item will pop to the top!

Close the Case (Jewel That Is)

While Jewel Case Creator doesn't afford you the kind of power you'd find in a high profile, even higher-priced, graphics application, it's an ideal utility for quickly and easily creating attractive CD labels and inserts. This is especially true if you're making a gift of a CD for a relative or significant other who doesn't know how easy it is. For you guys in the audience, you should pay particular attention. This sort of thing can break up the tedium of endless bouquets of flowers for every time you staple the family cat to the floor while laying carpet!

The Least You Need to Know

➤ Although it's not terribly powerful, using Roxio's CD Label Creator is an easy way to quickly create audio or data CD labels and inserts.

➤ You can use CD Label Creator's Add Contents option to automatically try to identify the names and lengths of tracks on your CD. If that doesn't work, you can use the Add Track option to enter them manually.

➤ When creating text fields, CD Label Creator enables you to customize the type of font, its size, and its orientation on the CD and jewel case layouts.

➤ You can link text fields by associating them with one of several available categories.

➤ CD Label Creator can do a lot more than just add song titles to your layout. It also includes basic graphical capabilities that enable you to insert your own pictures, backgrounds, and shapes.

Chapter 15

Using NTI JewelCase Maker

In This Chapter

➤ Learn how to create an audio CD label set

➤ Find out how to edit or add text and graphic objects to the layout

➤ Experiment with changing the format of text that appears in the layout

➤ Learn how to set up the page format for the brand of labels or paper stock you use

➤ Print CD inserts and labels!

As you learned in the last few chapters, it's one thing to burn CDs; it's another to make them look presentable. If you want to spice up your CD or keep track of what is on a CD, you can use NTI JewelCase Maker. In this chapter you'll learn how to use this utility, which works almost like Easy CD Creator's label-making program, with a few differences.

Create a Label Set

When you use NTI CD-Maker to create or copy a CD, the last dialog box that is displayed will ask you to click the OK button or to click a button called JewelCase Maker. If you choose this second option, the JewelCase Maker application will pop up and you can go ahead and create a label for the new CD, as well as jewel case inserts. If you want to start the program at another time, simply bring up the NTI CD-Maker menu by double-clicking on the Desktop icon. When the main menu pops up, click on the Tools menu and select JewelCase Maker from the menu. Or, if you are one of those who don't like icons on your Desktop, use Start/Programs/NTI CD-Maker 2000 Professional/JewelCase Maker. In Figure 15.1 you can see the main window for the JewelCase Maker program that you will use to create your labels and jewel case inserts.

Figure 15.1

The main window for JewelCase Maker gives you a blank page to begin with.

Between Tracks

NTI CD-Maker JewelCase Maker has several pre-defined templates you can use other than the one for an audio CD. This template is used only as an example in this chapter. The concepts for using the other templates are the same, however, so no matter which you choose, you can still use the feature described in this chapter to create and print labels and CD inserts.

If you are familiar with Easy CD Creator's program for creating jewel case inserts and labels, this screen will look almost identical! On the left side of the window are buttons that allow you to choose the insert you want to work with, as well as a button for the label. However, before you start to edit, use the File menu and select New to bring up the Open Template menu. You'll see here a number of pre-defined formats you can use to create your label and inserts (Figure 15.2). For this example, let's select Music CD and click the OK button.

In Figure 15.3, you can see the template used to create a music CD. I've selected the front insert. It has two pages, and can be folded much like the front cover insert you create using Easy CD Creator. The main difference, however, is that there is only one format. What you see is what you get, in Figure 15.3, unless you decide to create your own customized graphics and text.

222

Figure 15.2

You can choose from a variety of pre-defined formats when starting to create a new label set.

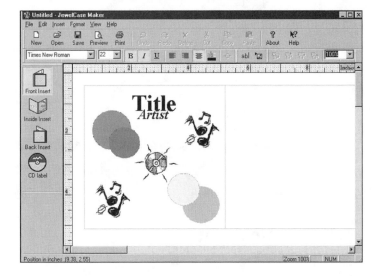

Figure 15.3

The Music CD format allows you to edit the objects that you see in this display.

For example, if you want to go ahead and use the graphics that are shown in this display, just change the Title and Artist fields. To edit a field, simply double-click on the field, and an editing box will pop up allowing you to change the text. In Figure 15.4, you can see that I've double-clicked on the Title text and I've entered my own text.

To exit the editing box, just click elsewhere on the window outside the editing box, and the text will appear on the label. One small problem you may run into here, though, is that while the editing box may disappear and the text will then show up on the label, you may find it difficult to edit the next field, called Artist. Why? Well, click once on the Title field, and you'll see a box drawn around it, showing you the dimensions of the label insert that it covers. If you entered a long title, the box covers the Artist field (as you can see in Figure 15.5); if you try to double-click on Artist, you'll get the Title field back instead!

Figure 15.4

Double-click on the text fields to add your own text.

Figure 15.5

Click once on a field to see which portion of the insert it covers.

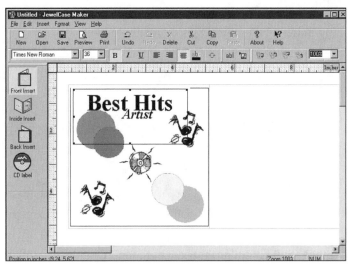

The simple thing to do in this case is use the sizing handles you can see in Figure 15.5, to make the Title field smaller. The sizing handles are those black squares that appear halfway between the edges on each side of the editing box when you click on it a single time. In Figure 15.6, you can see that I used the sizing handle on the bottom of the dialog box to move the frame that surrounds it so that the Artist field is now exposed. To use a sizing handle, just click on it, hold down your left mouse button, and drag the portion of the field you want to move until it's where you want it to be.

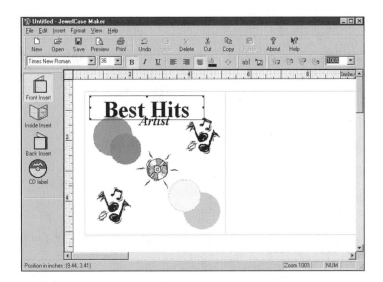

Figure 15.6

You can use the sizing handles to change the portion of the insert that a field covers, and thus expose other fields that may lie beneath.

Editing Graphics Objects

So far you've seen how the text objects are handled in JewelCase Maker. You might have noticed in the previous figures that there are also graphics objects that make up this front cover. Graphics are handled in a different way than text objects in JewelCase Maker. For example, you can add graphic objects from files you've created using other programs, and you can use the default graphics editor for the type of graphics object you want to work with. In the standard template shown in the previous figures, the cover is a bitmap image, so if you want to edit it while still in the JewelCase Creator program, just use one of the following methods:

➤ Double-click somewhere outside the text boxes, but within the graphics area. This will bring up the default editor for bitmap images, which is usually Microsoft Paint. You'll still be in JewelCase Maker, but all the Microsoft Paint tools and options will be available for you to use to make changes to the graphics of the label insert. When finished editing in place, just click somewhere outside the area you are editing (such as the right side of the front label insert) to return to the regular mode for JewelCase Maker.

➤ You can also use the Edit menu. Click on the object (anywhere outside the text boxes) and from the Edit menu select Edit Bitmap Object. From the submenu that appears, select Edit if you want to edit the object while still in JewelCase Maker. Or select Open and Microsoft Paint (or the graphics program appropriate for the file type of the graphics object) will open in a separate window. You can edit the object from there and then exit the graphics program. If you use Microsoft Paint, you'll find that under the File menu there is an Exit & Return option. Click on this and you'll be back into JewelCase Creator, with your edits intact.

Since I didn't like the particular graphics that are the default for the Music CD layout, I used Microsoft Paint to cut the entire graphics section from this layout. Note that when you bring up the graphics editor, the Title and Artist fields do not show up, so you don't have to worry about editing around them. Only the graphics portion of the layout will be available in the editor you use. Since I selected to delete all the graphics in this layout, it's time for me to add a graphic!

Adding Graphics Objects

Inserting a graphics object is as simple as browsing for it. To insert a graphics object:

1. Click on the Insert menu.

2. Select New Object.

3. Place your mouse on the layout where you want the upper-left corner of the graphics object to start.

4. Hold down the left mouse button and drag your mouse to where you want the bottom-right of the graphics object to appear.

5. A dialog box (shown in Figure 15.7) will prompt you for the type of object to insert. You can use the Browse button to locate a graphics file you've already created and then click the OK button.

Figure 15.7

You can insert graphics files you create yourself into the CD layout.

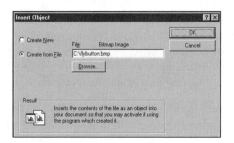

As you can see in Figure 15.8, I used a simple picture of a fly, which is a common theme used throughout this particular artist's work over the past 30 years. To each his own! You can insert multiple graphics objects using the same method described previously. For example, if you are copying a CD (for your own use only!) you might find an example of the CD or record cover on the Internet. You can save that picture as a graphics file and then use your cursor to resize the graphics portion of the front cover so that the picture you import will look just like the original CD cover. A tip to keep in mind is that the better the resolution and quality of the graphics object you find, the better it will look when you print the finished jewel case inserts.

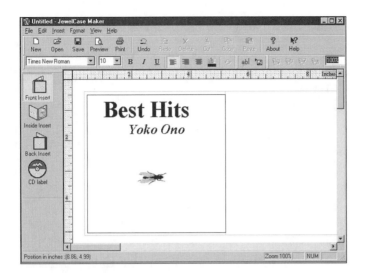

Figure 15.8

You can insert graphics on the CD layout using files from other sources.

Adding Text Fields

While it's usually sufficient to just put graphics and the artist's name and CD title on the cover, you can add text fields also. For example, looking at our front cover, which can be folded in half, you can see that you can place text fields on the right side of this layout to include the song titles. There is a separate button for this to allow you to create a separate insert for this, but by creating this text on this fold-over cover, you'll find that the jewel case insert will be less likely to fall out when you open the jewel case.

To add a text field, use the following steps:

1. Click on the Insert menu and select Text.

2. Place your cursor on the part of the layout that you wish the text to appear on (don't worry about the exact position, because you can move the field later).

3. When you've positioned your cursor on the layout, click once and a text entry box will appear, as shown in Figure 15.9. You can see here that I've used several text boxes to add song titles. At the bottom is a new text box with the default text "New text here." Just place your cursor inside the box and start typing, and your text will replace the "New text here."

4. If you enter text that is longer than the size of the text box, the text box will enlarge as you type to contain the text you enter.

5. When finished creating a new text field, click anywhere outside the text box, and the text will appear on the layout.

Figure 15.9

You can add text fields to the layout by using the Text option from the Insert menu.

Formatting and Editing Text

In the previous example, the text font used was Times Roman, a standard font used by any word processing applications. If you'll notice, at the top of the JewelCase Maker dialog box there is a field you can use to select the font and size of the text. You don't have to use the default.

You can edit the text and change its properties after you've already typed it in. For example, click once on the text field and then try using the Font or Font Size drop-down menus at the top of the window. When you select a different font or size, the text in the text field will change accordingly. You can experiment with different fonts and sizes until you find one you like. To end the formatting, once again, just click outside the text box.

If you want to change the style of the text, just use the buttons at the top of the window. You'll see the B (bold), I (italics), and U (underline) buttons, and you can probably guess what they do! Notice that when you select one of these options, it applies to all text in the text field. You can't make one word bold, the next italic, and so on. You can, however, place multiple text boxes next to each other, and line them up and then apply different styles to each individual text box.

To edit the text in a text field, just double-click on the text field. When the box appears around the field, you can place your cursor anywhere and start typing to add text. You can use the regular Delete and Backspace keys to edit text. In addition, you can hold the left button of your mouse down and drag it over text you wish to replace, and then just enter the replacement text.

Another way to edit the text field, which is simpler if you just want to replace the entire text, is to click on the field once and then from the Edit menu, select Text. All of the text in the field will be highlighted and as soon as you start typing it will replace the text that's already there!

Again, when you're done making edits or formatting changes to a text field, just click anywhere outside the field, and the box will disappear and the text will appear on the layout.

Changing Text Properties

There are a few other things you can do with text that can make your CD inserts and labels look more professional. For example, you can rotate text by specifying the angle:

1. Select the text field by clicking it once (don't double-click!).

2. From the Format menu, select Rotate.

3. Each time you select Rotate, the text field will be rotated by 90 degrees. You can also use the Rotate button on the Toolbar. It looks like two curved lines with arrows pointing to each other.

If you are going to use a color printer for your label inserts (and who doesn't, now that ink jet printers are so cheap?), then you can also change the color of the text. Simply ...

1. Select the text field by clicking it once.

2. Click on the Format menu and select Color. In Figure 15.10, you can see the Color Selection dialog box that appears to allow you to either select a pre-set color or create your own. When you've selected the color, click OK. The text in the field will then change to that color.

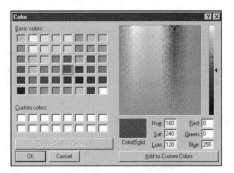

Figure 15.10

Changing the color of text can make your inserts stand out!

It's Moving Time

You can easily move objects around in the layout. This includes both text and graphics objects. This can be useful if objects overlap. For example, if you have added one or more graphics objects to the layout, you certainly want any overlapping text fields to be brought to the top or the front of the layout so that they overlay the graphics. Otherwise, portions of your text could be hidden by the graphics.

Moving objects involves very simple steps. To move an object to the front, click on it once to select the object. Then, from the Format menu, select Order. A submenu will appear that offers you the following selections:

➤ **Bring to front.** This option moves the object to the top or front of the layout so that it overlays all other objects that it may overlap.

➤ **Bring to back.** This option moves the object to the bottom of the object hierarchy so that every other object that overlaps it will cover up the portions of the object where they overlap.

➤ **Move up one.** This moves an object up one position in a multilevel hierarchy.

➤ **Move down one.** This moves an object down one position in a multilevel hierarchy.

This is really a great feature when you are using multiple graphics objects. Experiment to create a collage that will make your CD cover unique. You can also use buttons on the Toolbar for this feature.

Creating the Remainder of the Label Set

Unlike Easy CD Creator, fields in JewelCase Maker are not "linked." That is, if you enter text in the Artist and Title fields in the Front Cover layout and then click the Label button, the text doesn't automatically show up on the label. Instead, you have to use the same methods described in the first part of this chapter if you want to create a good-looking label. In Figure 15.11, you can see the default label used for the Music CD template.

Figure 15.11

This is the default for the Music CD layout for a CD label.

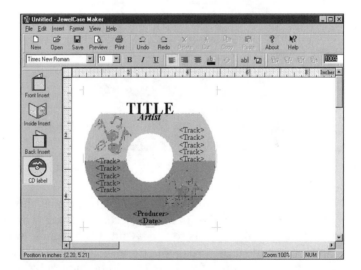

The same goes for the inside insert, which is why I simply created text fields to add the song titles myself. You'll notice on the CD label format in Figure 15.11 that in addition to default fields for the Title and Artist, there are also fields you can use to enter the names for the audio tracks on the CD. Simply double-click on these to enable the text-editing box and insert your text here.

The same goes for the back cover (usually referred to as a U-Card). In Figure 15.12 you can see that it provides default text fields that you can double-click on to enter track titles. In addition, there are fields for the edges of the CD where you normally put the artist and title of the CD.

You can use the same techniques here to change or add to the graphics you want to appear on the back of your CD.

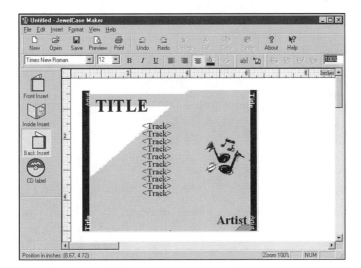

Figure 15.12

The U-Card (or back insert) also requires you to enter the information again.

Saving a Label Set

Once you've created the label set, you can save it if you want to use it again. Or if you get tired having to re-enter the information for the label, U-card, and front cover, then you can save the work you've done so far and reopen the layout some other time to finish your work. It's also a good idea to save your label set every now and then when you're creating it in case you suffer from one of those awful "system lock-ups" or perhaps a jammed printer. You never know when a fussy computer is going to do something that will make you wish you'd saved your work!

To save a label set:

1. Click on the File menu.
2. Select Save As.
3. In the Save As dialog box, select the folder in which you want to store your jewel case layouts, and give a name to this particular layout. Note that the file extension is .jwc. Click the Save button.

231

Opening a Label Set

When you are ready to use, or perhaps edit, or maybe even print a label set, then you can reopen a previously saved layout. The technique is similar to saving a layout—just choose Open from the file menu, locate the .jwc file you created, and click Open. The previously saved contents will then be available in JewelCase Maker so you can edit or print the label set.

Printing Label Sets

Before you print a label set, you need to be sure that the printed page will be set up correctly so that everything prints where it should on the page. This is important for pre-scored inserts and especially for labels, since you need to be very specific about where the printing occurs on the page!

Select the Paper Type First

First select the paper type to use for the label and the CD inserts.

To do this with JewelCase Maker:

1. Click on the File Menu.

2. Select Page Setup.

3. From the dialog box shown in Figure 15.13, select the tab for the page type you want to print. I've chosen the CD Label tab, since this is the one I think is the most important.

4. You can then select the other tabs to choose the appropriate page setup for those parts of the CD inserts. When you're finished, click the OK button.

Figure 15.13

Select the paper (or label) stock you will use for printing.

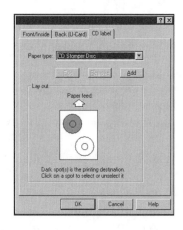

In Figure 15.13, I've selected Stomper, since I have had such good luck with these labels, and they are rather inexpensive when compared to other brands. However, you can use the drop-down menu labeled Paper Type to select another brand if you wish.

After you've selected the page layout, you can go on and print your label and CD inserts.

Check Those Options!

If you are as cheap as I am, you buy, as suggested in a previous chapter, cheap 50- to 65-pound card stock at the local office supply store and use a generic paper type for label stock. You can then use a paper cutter or scissors to cut the jewel case inserts before you use them. If you have lots of money to blow, then go ahead and pay about 10 times the cost to buy pre-scored inserts! However, if you're cheap like I am, then you should use an option to draw lines when printing the inserts so that you know where to cut to make your inserts fit perfectly inside your jewel cases.

Select Options from the Edit menu. As you can see in Figure 15.14, you can select to print outlines around the inserts you print, so you'll know exactly where to cut.

Figure 15.14

Use the Options dialog box to have the program draw lines showing you the boundaries of the jewel case inserts.

Between Tracks

Don't use this feature for labels or pre-scored inserts! For labels, you don't need to know where the boundaries are, since these simply peel off and are already pre-scored. For pre-scored inserts, you'll probably end up spending more time (and wasting more inserts) trying to line up your printer perfectly. And again, since pre-scored inserts (the expensive alternative) don't need these lines to be drawn, they will only distract from the appearance of the output you produce. So for labels or pre-scored inserts, turn off this option!

Print the Label and Inserts

To print a label set, select the button on the left side of the window for the component you want to print, such as the front cover or the label, then click the Print button. The standard Windows print dialog box will pop up. However, don't click OK yet! Note under the section titled Print Range that pages 1 through 4 are selected by default! This will cause all four of the components to print, one after the other! I suggest you click the radio button Pages and select to print from page 1 to page 1, as shown in Figure 15.15. This way you can load the card stock and labels separately to make sure you print the correct items in the right order! For example, if you load the label stock and the card stock for a set and one gets jammed, you may end up with the label printed on card stock, or the other way around! This is why I recommend printing one page at a time.

Figure 15.15

Select the print range to print just the single page.

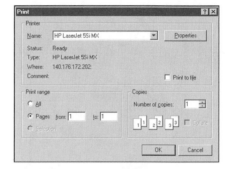

If you manually feed your printer, you can use the 1–4 print range, but I find it easier to print each component one at a time and check the output before continuing. The choice is up to you!

In this chapter you learned the basics of JewelCase Creator. I suggest you experiment with the program options and find out what best suits your purposes. For example, I find that for application installation CDs I usually just print the label, and skip the card stock. I then use the thin jewel cases to store these important CD backups. For audio CDs, where I want to see the artist and title on the edge of the CD, I make the inserts.

The Least You Need to Know

➤ You need to create the separate components of the label set separately. That is, you have to create the front cover and the label, since there are no "linked" fields as in Easy CD Creator's jewel case application.

➤ You can enter text in standard boxes that exist in templates you can use for creating a jewel case set. You can also add text boxes and use formatting options on any of them to make your text look great.

➤ If you don't like the graphics associated with a CD JewelCase Maker template, you can use a graphics editor to change or delete the graphics, and insert your own pictures or other graphic files.

➤ When it comes time to print, the simplest method is to choose to print each component one page at a time.

Part 7

Wait! There's More, So Buy Now: More Fun Software and Utilities!

You're gonna find lots of stuff here. First, you'll learn how to use programs to create photo albums on CDs that you can give to others who can play them even if they don't have the same software you do. You'll also learn about sound editing using tools provided with both Easy CD Creator and NTI CD-Maker. As an added bonus, we'll take you through the ins and outs of MusicMatch Jukebox—the only tool you'll ever need if your CD burning addiction is limited to storing and burning audio!

You'll also find a troubleshooting chapter for some of the more common problems that occur when burning CDs. In the end, this part of the book may prove to be the most valuable to you.

Chapter 16

MusicMatch: Making Your PC the Ultimate Jukebox

In This Chapter

➤ MusicMatch Jukebox is one of the best programs available for those who keep a lot of audio files on their computers

➤ MusicMatch Jukebox has three core components: the Player windows, the Music Library window, and the Recorder Window

➤ Use the Music Library to create a compendium of all your MP3, WMA, and WAV files

➤ In addition to ripping music from CDs, MusicMatch can burn music files back to CDs

Throughout this book, we have used Easy CD Creator 5 Platinum and NTI CD-Maker 2000, which are both great applications, as our examples. Of course, these aren't the only software programs available for creating CDs. In just the last two years, there has been a boom in new software, such as Nero that can accomplish all your data and audio CD recording needs. There are other applications, though, that offer much more specialized services. Because we think it's one of the handiest tools for the digital audiophile, we're going to devote this chapter to the use of MusicMatch Jukebox. For those who live to acquire, sort, and create two tons of specialized CDs for the road, it doesn't get much better than this program (even more so if you prefer to use your PC as a digital jukebox for all of your music).

Introducing MusicMatch Jukebox 6.1

MusicMatch Jukebox is an application you can use to find, create, organize, and play MP3, WAV, and even Windows Media files. You also can play CDs with the Jukebox, record those CDs to your hard drive or, of course, record music on your hard drive to CD.

To begin, MusicMatch Jukebox can work with the following file types:

➤ MP3 files

➤ Windows Media files

➤ Music CDs (CD-DA)

➤ WAV files

➤ Shoutcast

➤ M3U files

Between Tracks

Note that this chapter is based on MusicMatch 6.1. While other versions operate in a nearly identical manner, certain features, along with the overall look of the program, may be different in your version should it be older or more recent.

You don't have to worry about the details of what these formats are. The point is that with this wide assortment of formats, you'll have no problem acquiring audio files from most sources. And several sources exist—including your local CD-ROM, Internet radio, Internet sites, and so on.

The good news is you don't have to do much to get MusicMatch. You can download the latest demo version of MusicMatch Jukebox from the Web at www.musicmatch.com. This demo version doesn't have all the features MusicMatch has to offer enabled, but you can register for and download the full version of this application. Currently you can do so with a year of free updates. If you're willing to fork over the money (about $30), then you can get the lifetime subscription in which all future versions are yours at no extra charge. If you find that you do like using this program, the lifetime subscription is well worth the cost.

Don't Get Burned

One of the key features that is disabled in the demo version of MusicMatch is the ability to burn CDs, so don't expect everything in this chapter to work just as advertised if you're working with the demo.

Getting to Know MusicMatch

After you first launch MusicMatch Jukebox, you see an opening dialog box on top of the regular MusicMatch Jukebox window. It's titled Welcome to MusicMatch Jukebox. Use this if you want to quickly familiarize yourself with the program's features, some of whose explanation is beyond the scope of this chapter.

After you dismiss this screen, you see the main window of the program, as shown in Figure 16.1.

Figure 16.1

The main window for MusicMatch Jukebox enables you to perform many functions.

One important thing to note here is that the screen you see in Figure 16.1 is a compilation of three windows all scrunched together. It might look like one window here, but technically it's not. If you look carefully you can see the divisions between sections. If you want to move all three windows as a single unit, just click and drag on the title bar of the top window. Otherwise, you can click and drag the other two separately by using their respective title bars.

Between Tracks

If you don't see all three windows (Player, Media Library, and Recorder) when opening MusicMatch Jukebox, don't fret. MusicMatch typically opens in the same condition in which you left it and these windows can be opened and closed individually. For this chapter it's best if you use the View menu on the Player window and make sure both the My Library and Recorder options are enabled (a checkmark next to the option indicates as such).

The top window is called the Player. It sports the typical universal audio controls for play, pause, stop, and so on. This is where you get information about the music track currently playing and what tracks are in your Playlist (which we'll cover in a bit). The

Recorder window is the bottom window shown in Figure 16.2. Here you can record music from a CD to your hard drive. Finally, the window stuck in the middle of these two is the Music Library, which is where you organize the music on your hard drive. In addition to using the View menu, you can bring up the Music Library window when it's not on the screen by clicking the My Library button on the Player window.

Controlling the Player Window

The Player window in MusicMatch is more or less the Mission Control center for the entire program. Its main function, of course, is to play music. Let's take a close look at the Player window, as shown in Figure 16.2.

Figure 16.2

The Player window sports a variety of controls over all facets of MusicMatch.

As you can see, to the left of the window there are a series of CD-like controls. These operate pretty much as you'd expect, with buttons for stop, play, skip track, previous track, etc. With the scroll bar to the left of these controls you can set the volume with which MusicMatch plays back music. While this is all pretty straightforward, there are a few other controls here worth calling attention to.

First of all, in the center of the Player controls is a red dot, which is what you'll use to activate or close the Recorder window. Near that is a horizontal slider. When playing, this slider measures a track's progress. To skip ahead or backward in a track just drag the slider around to the approximate point in the song to which you want to listen. Finally there's a series of four buttons beneath the Player controls and current track information. They are:

➤ **My Library.** This button brings up the Music Library, as it was shown in Figure 16.1. Your Music Library contains all the information you could possibly need regarding the audio tracks on your hard drive.

➤ **Radio.** This feature takes you online, allowing you to select from hundreds of Internet-based radio stations. If you work at home or are allowed free Internet reign where you work, this is a handy way to have all the music at your disposal that you can handle.

➤ **Music Guide.** The Music Guide takes you to the Music Match Web site, where you can catch up on their latest news and offerings.

➤ **Now Playing.** The Now Playing guide, depending on the state of your Internet connection, shows information about the currently playing track. If you're offline, it lists out the information it has available about the currently playing track, including title, artist, album and genre. When you're online, it uses the Internet to open a full Web page loaded with information about the artist.

Each of these buttons controls how the Media Library view appears. For the purposes of this book, we're going to stick to the Media Library, as discussed in the next section.

Finally, there's the playlist portion of the Player window. Although you can play individual songs from wherever you find them, MusicMatch Jukebox uses the concept of a playlist to organize audio files into groups. You can create a playlist yourself and use it to hear any grouping of songs you want, in whatever order strikes your fancy. The three buttons along the top of the playlist are:

➤ **File.** The File button sets the playlist to show the most recent active collection of audio tracks on your hard drive that you have selected (so it may be empty if you've not used it before).

➤ **Radio.** Like the Radio button we discussed in the previous section, this opens up a Web page with options for connecting to an Internet radio station. The difference is, this also opens a default station and starts playing right away.

➤ **CD.** If you have a music CD in your CD drive, this button sets the playlist so that it shows the contents of that CD.

Finally, with File selected in the playlist section of the Player window, you'll notice a series of buttons beneath the playlist. Choosing Open, brings up the dialog box shown in Figure 16.3.

Between Tracks

If you have more than one CD drive (can include your CD-ROM or CD-RW), you may need to select the drive containing your music CD. When you click the CD button you'll notice that the series of buttons beneath the playlist change. One of those buttons, labeled Drive, allows you to select from all available CD drives.

Figure 16.3

The Open Music dialog box allows you to select music on your hard drive to listen to.

As you can see, you can open the music you have available based on a variety of criteria. We'll get into the specifics later in this chapter, but for now, know that you can double-click through the options listed here, select individual or groups of tracks, and put them in your playlist.

Getting Used to the Recorder

Now that we've got the Player window sorted out, let's step through the controls available on the Recorder window, which you can see in Figure 16.4.

Figure 16.4

The Recorder window is where you "rip" tracks from a music CD to your hard drive.

As you can see, there are only a handful of controls you have to worry about here. In the small window to the left, you can see information about the CD currently in the drive set for recording. This will display either the CD name and artist, that the current disc is a data CD (like your Microsoft Windows disc) or that the drive is currently empty. We're going to assume that you have a music CD in this drive.

Arcane CD Speak

While the term might sound like it means you're going to be running at mach 5 from a music store with stolen CDs, the term "ripping" actually applies to the process of copying music files from tracks on a CD to files on your hard drive. At this point, I'm convinced it's a record company term used to make you think you're doing something wrong, but know that there is nothing illegal about ripping tracks from CDs you've purchased to your PC.

Beneath the small display window are four buttons:

➤ **Record.** Begins recording selected tracks from CD to your hard disk drive.

➤ **Stop.** Stops a recording in progress after it completes the current track it's ripping from the CD.

➤ **Cancel.** Immediately cancels the recording of a CD to your hard drive.

➤ **Eject.** Ejects the disc currently in the drive.

When a music CD is in the drive you're using to record, you'll see a listing of its tracks in the right side of the window. Accompanying each track is a check box, which you can use to select the tracks you want to record. To make the task of selecting tracks simpler you can use either the All or None buttons above this list to select each track on the CD or none of them (allowing you to add tracks one-by-one). Along with these two buttons is a third button, labeled Refresh. If you've changed discs in your recording drive, you can use this button to refresh the contents that appear in the CD contents list.

Between Tracks

As with listening to a music CD with the Player window, you can rip music tracks using any available CD drive in your computer. To choose from the available drives, go to the Player window and click Options, Recorder, Source, and then the drive that you wish to record from.

Also note from the list in the Source pane that you're not restricted to your CD drives as a source. If you have analog music input through your sound card or you want to record voice through a microphone, you can do so from here as well.

The MusicMatch Music Library

With the possible exception of the Player itself, the Music Library is the core of the MusicMatch program. As you can see in Figure 16.5, this library contains a listing of all the music on your computer.

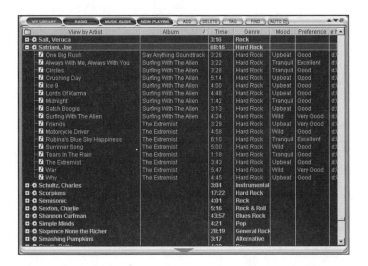

Figure 16.5

The Music Library turns your PC into a digital music jukebox.

Between Tracks

If you compare Figure 16.5 to the Media Library portion of Figure 16.1, you'll see that the buttons for My Library, Radio, Music Guide, and Now Playing have moved between the Player and Music Library windows. If the two windows are connected, these buttons appear on the Player. However, if you pull them apart, as was done when capturing Figure 16.5, the buttons shift to the Music Library window.

The controls on this window appear simple, but they belie a wealth of options that you have at your disposal. First, let's tackle the series of buttons at the top of the window:

➤ **Add.** Clicking this button opens the Add Tracks To Music Library dialog box (see Figure 16.6). With this button you can add tracks to your Music Library that already exist on your hard drive.

Figure 16.6

With this dialog box you can choose audio files on your hard drive to include in your Music Library.

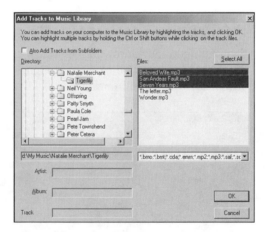

➤ **Delete.** This button removes a track from your Music Library. If you choose this option, the dialog box that appears also has a check box that allows you to remove the track from your hard drive as well.

➤ **Tag.** Audio files, such as MP3s, have a track "Tag" that can store information about the track, including the artist, album and track names, genre and more. Clicking this button allows you to edit a track's tag information.

➤ **Find.** If you start putting every track of every CD you own on your hard disk, you'll find that your Music Library gets pretty big, pretty darn fast. Use this button to search for a specific track in your library.

➤ **AutoDJ.** Can't decide what to listen to? Use the AutoDJ to have MusicMatch create a playlist for you. You can choose the total running time of the playlist and have the AutoDJ filter music using track tag information, including song tempo, preference and genre.

Once you have tracks in your Music Library they appear in the main part of the library's window. As you can see from the previous figure there are several headings that can be used to classify the music. The information for filling these headings comes from the track's tag. Like using Windows Explorer, you can click the + signs on the leftmost listing to expand the tree and see different tracks. By clicking on each of the library headings, you can sort the listing of tracks according to that header's category.

Between Tracks

The leftmost heading in the library is the key by which tracks are sorted. By default, this key is the artist or group. You can change this option by clicking the folder icon on the leftmost heading. This produces a list by which you can view all the tracks in your library; just click the option you want to resort the entire list. Generally, I recommend sticking with the Artist option.

If you're not happy with the default headings MusicMatch has available in the Music Library, you can change them by clicking Options in the Player windows, followed by Music Library and Music Library settings. This produces the dialog box shown in Figure 16.7.

From this window you can enable up to seven columns to be shown in the Music Library using the available check boxes. While enabling all seven possible columns would considerably clutter the Music Library view, having four or five with the information most pertinent to you is quite handy. The column headings you can have visible in the Music Library include the album, artist, genre, preference, mood, situation, tempo, filename, and much more.

Figure 16.7

The Music Library's Settings dialog box allows you to control the Music Library view.

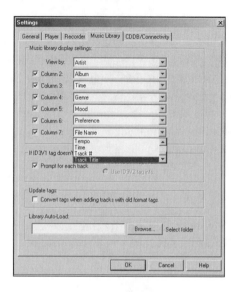

Putting MusicMatch Jukebox to Work

Now that we've gotten familiar with the MusicMatch interface, it's time to start learning how to make all these different features and controls work for you.

In the following sections, we'll take a look at some of the main uses of MusicMatch, including building a playlist, recording CDs to your hard drive and recording a playlist to CD. There are other ways in which you can make use of this program, but these are the most useful, so let's get started.

Acquiring Audio Files from CD

Before you can play any files, you must get them onto your computer in the first place! You can acquire the MP3 and other audio files you need from the Internet by using MusicMatch Jukebox to rip them from a CD, or by using other available software to create these files (we're going to focus on getting them from CD in this section). Technically, you can also acquire music from friends, although most of us know that the legality of that is in dispute in the courts and will probably be for many years as laws are updated to catch up with the fast-paced Internet revolution. Nobody has a problem with you lending a book to a friend to read, but it seems those international music companies don't feel the same way when it comes to music.

Extracting tracks from your CDs is easy using the Recorder window shown back in Figure 16.4. Insert the audio CD and the recorder will identify it (going to the Internet to do so if it has to). If it doesn't, give the Refresh button a click. Using the check boxes that appear with each track, select the individual tracks you want, or use the All button to select them all, if that's your desire. Regardless of whether you are recording two tracks or twenty, click the Record button on the left side of this dialog box when you're ready to start recording these files to your hard disk.

248

The default location the Recorder uses for the files it extracts from your CD is C:\Program Files\MusicMatch\Music. You can change this by clicking Options, Recorder, and Settings in the main player window. The Settings dialog box that pops up gives you the ability to configure many aspects of the Jukebox program.

The options in this dialog box are pretty self-explanatory, and because we're more concerned right now with choosing where to store your music, look to the dialog box's upper-right corner and click the Tracks Directory button. This brings up yet another dialog box, which is shown in Figure 16.8.

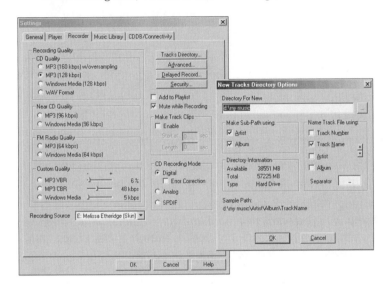

Figure 16.8

You can change the directory the Recorder uses to store newly recorded songs.

In addition to letting you customize where to store music files, this dialog box also enables you to decide how to name the new files. You can change the default directory for new songs by simply highlighting the Directory For New Songs field and entering the path you want. If you want to have MusicMatch Jukebox automatically create subdirectories based on the artist or the album title (or both), under this directory, use the check boxes found in the Make Sub-Path Using section. Using these features, you can decide on a main directory path that is used to store all your music files.

Note that when you use the sub-path options, you see that, at the bottom of this dialog box, the Sample Path field shows you what you've selected.

You can also see in this figure that you can further customize how music files are named and stored on your computer. For example, when you want to record a song from a CD, you can name the song in several ways:

➤ The actual song title (use the Track Name check box)

➤ The artist's name (use the Artist check box)

249

➤ The number of the track as it appears on the CD (use the Track Number check box)

➤ The album name (use the Album check box)

➤ Combinations of the above! (Select more than one check box)

For example, one of my favorite songs is "Right Now" by Van Halen. This song appears on a couple of their CDs. If I wanted to name this song, I might want to use both the Artist and the Album check boxes, so I could look back and determine from where it was obtained. Perhaps you are like me and sometimes buy a CD just for one song. In that case, you might just use the Album check box.

If you do use more than one of these check boxes, MusicMatch Jukebox names the file accordingly and places a separator character between each of your choices when it creates the filename. The Separator check box allows you to select any character you want to separate the names, although a hyphen, underscore, or space generally works the best in practice.

Click OK when you've finished viewing or modifying information in this dialog box.

This brings you back to the Recorder tab in the Settings dialog box. When you're happy with your settings here, click OK again to return to the main MusicMatch window.

When you've selected the tracks you want to record and have made any adjustments you want on the Settings dialog box, just click the Record button to start the actual recording process. As each track is recorded, you'll see a progress bar slowly (or quickly depending on your hardware and patience) start marching toward 100 percent. When it reaches that number, the check mark disappears from the track's check box and the Recorder moves on to the next track. When it's done, you'll find each of the tracks listed in your Music Library.

Generating Playlists

As we've already discussed, the two central themes around which this application runs are your music library and playlists. The library tells MusicMatch which audio files are on your hard disk and where they are located. The playlist is nothing more than a collection of audio files from your library that you want played as a group. This is similar to a collection of tracks from a music CD. The idea of libraries and playlists is a standard feature you'll find in most good media software. Because you can use playlists to burn a disc, they pretty much make you the producer of your own CDs. You can generate playlists in a variety of ways. In the following sections we'll take a look at a couple of those ways.

Creating a Manual Playlist

A manual playlist is one in which you select each song individually. It might be time-consuming, but it does help ensure that you get only the songs you want. You do this by dragging the song from the Music Library window to the Playlist pane in the Player application (or right-click the track and choose Add Track(s) To Playlist. After you've selected all the songs you want for a particular playlist, just click the Save button in the Playlist pane. The Save Playlist dialog box pops up and enables you to give a name to the Playlist so you'll be able to retrieve it at a later time.

To open a Playlist after you've created it, just click Open. Then, in the Open Music dialog box, click the Playlists button and select the list you want to open.

You can delete songs from any playlist by simply clicking the song in the list and pressing the Delete key on your computer. If you want to re-order the playlist, simply click the song in it and drag it to a new location in the list. To make this change permanent, be sure you use the Save button. This opens up a Save dialog box in which you can give the list a new name or save over the old one. If you choose the latter, MusicMatch Jukebox lets you know you're about to overwrite an existing playlist. Duh! Click OK and the next time you open the list, it remembers the changes you just saved.

Using the AutoDJ to Create a Playlist

If you don't want to be tied into selecting each song for your playlist, the MusicMatch Jukebox has an AutoDJ feature that can save you some time. To begin this process, click the AutoDJ button on the Music Library's toolbar. The dialog box shown in Figure 16.9 enables you to select the criteria that gets used to select songs for the playlist. Remember how we discussed the concept of track tags earlier? With the track tag you can include genre type, mood information, and so on for each audio track you add to your library. For AutoDJ to work effectively, it needs this information!

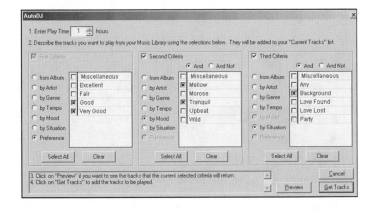

Figure 16.9

You can select music automatically by specifying the criteria the AutoDJ should use.

You can select tracks by artist name, album name, genre, and other categories, as you can see in Figure 16.9. You further subselect by breaking up your preferences into first, second and third criteria.

To make these selections, first determine the number of criteria you want AutoDJ to use by enabling or disabling the appropriate check boxes (you can't disable the First

Criteria section for, what are hopefully, obvious reasons). From here, select the First criteria from options like Album, Artist, Mood, etc. Once making that selection you must actually choose how AutoDJ will select from the category. For example, if you choose by Preference, do you want to hear only songs you've classified as Excellent and Very Good? Do you want to hear only songs that you think are just Fair? Use the checkboxes to make these selections and then do the same for the Second and Third criteria.

Between Tracks

Certain criteria selections require you to select either an And or And Not option. The default is And which specifies that you want to include tracks that fit the selected criteria. And Not means that you actually want to filter those matching tracks out of the list.

When you're finished selecting criteria, click the Get Tracks button; the AutoDJ then makes selections for you and adds them to the current playlist window. You can then use the playlist to start playing the songs, or you can save the playlist and give it a name. You also can use the playlist to burn a CD.

Using the Playlist to Burn a CD

If you look at the player window, the buttons beneath the Playlist pane include one labeled CD-R. Guess what this is used for. That's right; you click this button to start the recording process. This brings up the Create CD from Playlist dialog box, from which you can do several things. First, you can add more songs to the playlist or delete songs if your playlist takes up more time than your CD has to give. In Figure 16.10, you can see this dialog box with the Options button clicked to show additional selections you can make when creating a CD.

Figure 16.10

The Create CD from Playlist dialog box enables you to test or actually burn a CD.

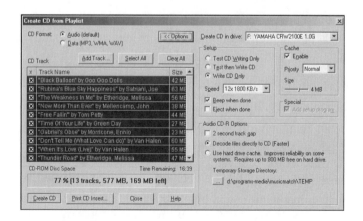

You can use this dialog box to create either an audio or a "data" CD. An audio CD, of course, means the files are converted to the CD-DA format compatible with any music CD player and written to the disc. A data CD is somewhat misnamed, in that you can still only write audio files, not perform system backups like you could in Easy CD Creator or CD-Maker 2000. In this case, MusicMatch writes the actual audio files (MP3, WMA, and WAV) to the disc, should you plan to play it on a computer CD-ROM or compatible CD player. Many of the other options, including write testing and eliminating the two-second gap between tracks, are similar to what you saw in Chapter 5, "Drag and Drop with Easy CD Creator," for creating audio CDs. The Print CD Insert button prints a single page that contains a front cover insert and a back cover insert. You can specify the text for the spines (edges) of the back insert, and you can either browse to find your own cover art or let the program choose something for you. Unfortunately, there is no option to print a label for your CD. While useful if it's all you've got, this program is nowhere near as elegant as the jewel case insert and CD label programs included with CD-Maker 2000 and Easy CD Creator. Given the choice, I'd recommend you just use one of those programs when making inserts.

Don't Get Burned

Just like Easy CD Creator, MusicMatch Jukebox has a cache that can store information so it can supply a steady stream of data to the laser burner. In the Create CD from Playlist dialog box, you see the Cache section at the top right. Leave the Enable check box selected. The Priority feature determines the amount of system resources MusicMatch Jukebox can use when burning the CD. The Size slider bar feature enables you to set the size of the cache. Unless you find that you are creating lots of coasters, leave both of these fields at their default levels—Priority: normal and Size: 4Mb.

When you're finally ready, click the Create CD button to start burning. Similar to Easy CD Creator, you see a dialog box; this one is called CD Creation Progress (see Figure 16.11).

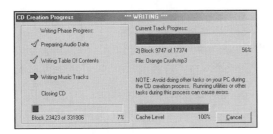

Figure 16.11

MusicMatch records music to CD just as well as any other program covered in this book.

The usual Preparing Audio Data and Writing Music Tracks are shown here. When finished, MusicMatch Jukebox tells you, with a small dialog box, that the CD is complete. Click OK to dismiss this dialog box and you've got a new CD!

A Perfect Match?

Whether MusicMatch Jukebox is worth the price of admission or effort to download really depends on your own needs. Certainly many Windows users would prefer to use the Media Player application that they can use for free. There are also other downloadable programs like WinAmp that draw rave reviews. However, I will say that I've used many an application for stockpiling my MP3s and none of them has held a candle to MusicMatch when factoring in ease of use, appealing interface and overall quality.

The Least You Need to Know

➤ Musicmatch is available as a free demo program from www.musicmatch.com. However, without the full version, certain key features are disabled.

➤ Tracks stored in the Music Library have tags that you can use to store information about a track, including your preferences for it, it's tempo and mood.

➤ You can use the AutoDJ feature to generate playlists very quickly, using track tag information to include only songs that fit your current mood.

➤ Use of the Recorder window is an easy way to get music from CD to your hard drive.

Chapter 17

Using NTI Music Café Lite

In This Chapter

➤ Playing CDs, WAV, and MP3 files with Café Lite

➤ Playing tracks from a playlist—in a predetermined or random order—with Café Lite

➤ Playing songs in a predetermined or random order using a playlist

➤ Loading more than one playlist at a time

➤ Burning a CD by dragging a playlist to an Audio Layout in NTI CD-Maker

---

If you're going to use your computer to store music files on, you'll need some program to play the songs you love to hear. NTI's Café Lite does just that. It looks just like a CD player, with the usual controls, but also allows you to create playlists so you can hear songs in any order you prefer. In this chapter you'll learn how to use this great audio player.

Overview of Café Lite

Unlike Microsoft Media Player, which extracts music from CDs, the Internet, or other sources and stores them on your hard drive, NTI Café Lite instead allows you to place your WAV, MP3 and other audio files (such as a CD-ROM drive containing a particular CD in CD-DA format) anywhere you want on your system. You can then create playlists to organize the order in which you want to listen to your audio files. You can create, edit, merge, and delete playlists using Café Lite.

You can launch Café Lite easily after you've installed the NTI CD-Maker software by clicking on Start/Programs/NTI CD-Maker Professional/Music Café Lite. In Figure 17.1 you can see the simple interface the application presents.

Figure 17.1

The Café Lite application window is a simple one.

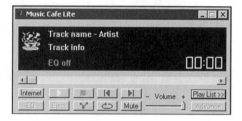

As you can see, the window looks just like an ordinary CD player at first glance. There's the usual play, pause, forward and backward buttons, and a volume control. However, if you click the Playlist button, then the window changes, as you can see in Figure 17.2.

Figure 17.2

Click the Playlist button to add audio tracks to Café Lite.

The left part of this window is called the Control Panel. This is where you use the standard buttons for play, pause, and so on. The right side of this window is called the Track Information Area, which is used to show information about the tracks being played. In the Control Panel, you'll see the name of an audio track when it's being played (as you'll see in just a minute), followed by a line of text that gives you information about the audio track, such as the length and the type of track. The third line of text that will appear in the Control Panel portion of Café Lite is used to give you information about whether the track is stereo or mono, and whether EQ (equalizer) is turned on or off, or if you're operating in shuffle mode (letting Music Café Lite randomly pick songs) or Repeat mode, where a track is played over and over.

The playlist area is where you get to add tracks and create playlists. Track filenames will show up here when you add them to a playlist.

Creating and Using Playlists

The first thing to do in order to create a playlist is to locate audio tracks. One of the really neat things about adding audio tracks is that while you can use the Add button, you can also open Windows Explorer and locate the files you want to add and click and drag them to the playlist window! If you're adept at navigating your computer using Windows Explorer, this is a very simple task. Just open both Music Café Lite and Windows Explorer and start dragging!

The second method you can use to add songs to a playlist is to use the Add button. As you can see in Figure 17.3, the standard Windows Open dialog box pops up, allowing you to locate the file or files you want to add to the play list.

Figure 17.3

The Add button allows you to select files using Windows' standard Add dialog box.

Just click on an audio track (WAV, MP3, or CDA) and then the Open button and the track will appear in the playlist. Keep in mind that this doesn't create a new copy of the song, just a pointer to its location. So if you move a song to a different place on your computer, the playlist won't be able to find it. If you want to use the Add button and the Open dialog box to add multiple songs, you can click on the first track, and then, while holding down the Shift key, click on the last track, and all of the tracks between the two will be selected and added when you click the Open button.

Similarly, you can use the CTRL key to select several individual tracks. Just hold down the CTRL key and click on each track you want to add in the Open dialog box; only those tracks will be selected and added to the playlist when you click the Open button.

Editing and Removing Tracks from a Playlist

You can easily remove any track you want from a playlist by simply clicking on it once and then clicking on the Remove button. You can also move tracks around to change the order of the playlist by clicking once on a track and holding the left mouse button down and then dragging it to a new position. A black line will be drawn across the screen as you move the track to show you where it will be inserted when you let go of the mouse button.

Adding Songs from a CD

If you want to add songs from a CD, you'll also want to see the song titles. In Figure 17.4, you can see what the Open dialog box looks like when you first select a CD drive that has an audio CD in it.

But don't worry. Music Café Lite uses the CDDDB/FreeDB database, so if you are online, just click the songs on the CD (or use the Shift+Click to select all of the tracks), and Music Café Lite will look them up for you. Now this isn't going to work for CDs you've put together yourself that consist of compilations of songs from other CDs.

And it isn't going to work if the particular CD you've chosen is an obscure one that's not listed in the database. But you'll find that most popular CDs of the past few years are in the database, so when you select them from a CD, the database will return the correct track titles for you.

Figure 17.4

At first glance, adding tracks from a CD to a playlist doesn't seem promising!

Once the database has been consulted, the tracks you've selected will appear in the playlist by name instead of Track 1, Track 2, and so on.

Saving a Playlist

Once you've selected the songs you want for a playlist, it's time to save the playlist. Simply use the Save button that is on the button bar above the playlist. In Figure 17.5 you can see the Save dialog box. Enter a name for the playlist and click the Save button. Note that a playlist is saved with a file extension of .m3u, which can be used by a lot of other applications that support playlists. This makes it easy to import a playlist into other applications, if you use more than one. You can also use a playlist to burn a CD.

Figure 17.5

Playlists are saved using the standard .m3u format.

Using Music Café Lite to Play Songs on a Playlist

To open a playlist, simply use the Load button on the button bar above the playlist section and locate the playlist you wish to listen to. Once you've loaded a playlist, you can open another playlist, and it will be appended to the one currently in the playlist pane. This way you can open multiple playlists, if you wish. Then, to hear the songs, just click the play button on the Control panel side to start enjoying the music.

Note that if you created a playlist for a CD, then you must insert the CD in your computer's CD-ROM drive so that the playlist can locate the tracks! One good use of creating playlists for CDs is that if you have a particular CD that has a few songs on it you don't care for, you can create a playlist that contains only the ones you like! So, when you play the CD, you hear only what you want to hear. Another reason is that you can select playlists when you burn an audio CD and add them to the audio CD layout pane. Thus, you can add files from your hard drive and from a CD at the same time when you burn a new audio CD.

Randomizing Playlists!

Want to hear those songs in a different order, but are too lazy to move them around? Load a playlist (or better yet, load several) and then in the Control Panel, click the Shuffle button and then the Play button. The Shuffle button is right under the Stop button (the big red square button) and looks like a "Y" with arrows pointing in three directions. This Shuffle button will cause Café Lite to automatically select songs from the playlist(s) you load, in a randomized order. If you load several playlists instead of just a single playlist, then you'll get hours of nonstop audio without having to worry about selecting which playlist or songs you want to hear.

Between Tracks

If you want to be able to add songs from your favorite CDs to playlists, and don't want to have to install a few hundred CD-ROM drives in your computer, then simply use NTI CD-Maker to extract the files to MP3 or WAV files on your hard disk and then add those files to the playlist!

Play It Again Sam

Want to hear a particular playlist over and over? Click the Repeat button on the Control Panel. It's the button that looks like an open circle with an arrow, directly to the left of the Mute button. And you can probably guess what the Mute button does. It's for when you see the boss walking down the hall and you're using Music Café Lite at work.

The playlist will continue to repeat until you stop it, so don't lock up the shop and go home at night without shutting it off, unless you want the creatures of the night to be able to enjoy your musical tastes.

Burning a CD from a Playlist

To create an audio CD, you need to click the Audio CD button on the NTI menu. This is discussed in Chapter 6, "NTI CD-Maker: Says What It Does and Does What It Says," which teaches you how to create your own customized CDs by creating an audio layout that consists of MP3, WAV, CDA, and other files. The neat feature about creating an audio CD in this manner is that you can also add a playlist as a single unit, and all the songs on the playlist will be added to the customized audio CD you create. When the CD-Maker window appears, you can add files as usual from the Explorer pane to the Audio Layout pane at the bottom of the window, or you can also add playlists (*.m3u) files to the Audio Layout pane. If the playlist contains MP3 files, don't worry. They'll be converted on the fly by CD-Maker when it burns the audio CD.

As you can see in Chapter 6, after you've produced an audio layout, you can save it for later editing, or you can use the layout to burn a CD. Using the playlist feature of Café Lite can allow you to create custom CDs by first creating the playlist and using it for a while, then burning the final CD when you've decided that you like the customized playlist. You might consider that Café Lite can be used as a "staging ground" for a CD you'll burn later!

The Least You Need to Know

➤ Café Lite is more than just your ordinary CD player, since you can play WAV and MP3 files also.

➤ You can create your own playlists for both files on your hard drive, as well as for CDs. For the latter, you can screen out songs you don't like on that particular CD!

➤ The music can go on forever—you can set Café Lite to repeat a playlist until you tell it to stop.

➤ You can drag a playlist to the NTI CD-Maker Audio Layout pane to burn a CD based on the playlist.

Chapter 18

Making Digital PhotoAlbums with Roxio PhotoRelay

In This Chapter

➤ Using PhotoRelay to create digital photo albums

➤ Adding audio to individual pictures in your photo album

➤ Sending pictures to friends and family via e-mail with the click of a button

➤ Burning your photo album to CD using PhotoRelay

Most people I talk to who have CD burners use them to make copies of CDs they already own or to store important files on CD for long-term storage. However, a lot of other fun programs are out there that you can use with your burner, which you might not have ever thought about. For example, you already know, if you've read this book from the beginning, that you can take all your graphic files—family photos and stuff like that—and store them on a CD. However, when you want to go back and use them, you must go through all the trouble of finding specific pictures and cranking up some graphic editor to look at them. After all, these picture files don't look different from any other data file you might store on the disc.

PhotoRelay enables you to create photo albums on your computer's hard disk and, if you want, burn those favorite albums to a CD, thus eliminating the need to use another program to view your photographs. When you make a PhotoRelay CD, all you have to do to view your digital photo album is stick it in your CD-ROM drive and it does the rest! This is really a great idea when you want to send some photos to friends who know nothing about imaging editors and the like. Just make a PhotoRelay CD and mail it to them!

Creating Electronic Photo Albums on CD—Using PhotoRelay

If you have lots of disk space on your computer, you can use PhotoRelay to create photo albums that can hold both photographs and audio files. Why audio? One of the niftier PhotoRelay features makes it possible for you to attach an audio file to any particular picture. So when the picture is viewed, the accompanying audio file gets played, too. If, for example, you happen to have a picture of yourself in the Rocky Mountains, would there be anything more appropriate than having Van Halen's "Top of the World" play when you view the picture?

PhotoRelay can be used sort of like a word processor—you can start creating the album, and when you get bored, you can save it. Later, you can come back and add more to the album or delete stuff that you've changed your mind about. In contrast to a real photo album, however, you won't run out space for your pictures (unless your hard drive fills up). You can also burn the album to CD when you have finished fine-tuning your project so that you don't have to waste that valuable real estate on your hard drive.

However, you must create the album before you can create the CD, so let's start with creating an album first.

Starting PhotoRelay

To start the PhotoRelay program, you can select it from the Applications menu in the Roxio Easy CD Creator 5 folder, or you can double-click the desktop icon Create CD to open the Roxio Project Selector (see Figure 18.1). From the Project Selector, hover your mouse pointer over Make A Photo or Video CD and then click Photo Album.

Click photo album to open PhotoRelay.

Figure 18.1

The Roxio Project Selector makes quick work of launching the PhotoRelay applications.

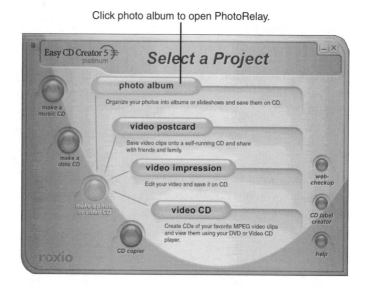

The PhotoRelay application window (shown in Figure 18.2) pops up, and you are ready to create a new photo album. By default, when you open the PhotoRelay application, a small dialog box also opens letting you know what the icons are that you use to add photos or videos to your album. Just click OK to continue.

Note that the Album field in this figure says New. You can use the pull-down menu for this field to open albums you've already created. By default there is a "Photos" album that contains several basic pictures already included when you install PhotoRelay.

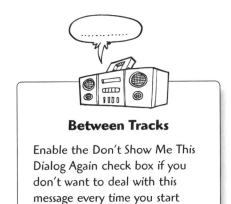

Between Tracks

Enable the Don't Show Me This Dialog Again check box if you don't want to deal with this message every time you start PhotoRelay.

Acquire   Print   SlideShow   PhotoIsland

Add   Save   Sort   Video Postcard

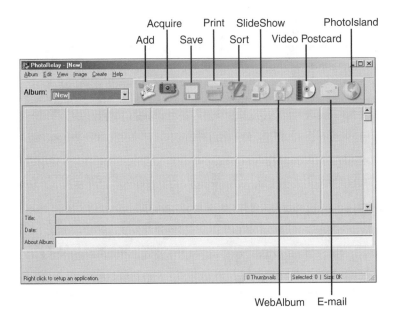

Figure 18.2

The PhotoRelay application enables you to create photo albums that can be stored on CD.

WebAlbum   E-mail

Notice also that next to this field is a series of icons, each of which represents a tool you can use with PhotoRelay. These tools are as follows (from left to right):

➤ **Add.** Adds files to the album you are creating.

➤ **Acquire.** Use your scanner to "acquire" a new photo to add to the album.

➤ **Save.** Enables you to save your work on the current active album.

➤ **Print.** Prints all or part of an album.

➤ **Sort.** Sorts your images.

➤ **MakeSlideShow.** Creates a picture slide show that you can play on any Windows 9x/Me or NT/2000 system.

➤ **MakeWebAlbum.** Creates a Web Album that you can send to friends and family, which displays *thumbnails* of your album in any Internet Web browser. Selecting a thumbnail opens the full image using whatever default picture-viewing program the user has available.

Arcane CD Speak

When you need to see several pictures on the computer screen at the same time, such as when working with PhotoRelay, it's impossible to display them all in their full-size format. This isn't just because of limited screen space, but because a large number of picture files takes up a lot of memory, too, which slows down your computer. A **thumbnail** is basically just a miniaturized version of a picture that takes up less screen space and considerably less memory. Although it has much less detail than the actual picture, it makes it easier for you to keep track of your work when dealing with many pictures, such as, say, in a photo album, maybe?

➤ **MakePostCard.** Creates a Video "Postcard" that you can play back on any Windows compatible computer.

➤ **SendMail.** Embeds a picture in an e-mail message using your default e-mail program.

➤ **PhotoIsland.** This button connects to an online Web site (www.photoisland. com), where you can sign up for storage space that you can use to upload and download your pictures to and from the Web.

Before we get into actually creating photo CDs and such, let's look at how you build a photo album in the first place.

Adding and Removing Photographs from the Album

To add a picture to an album, click the Add tool—the first icon in the toolbar after the Album field. The Add to Album dialog box appears and enables you to select the disk and directory that contains the photographs with which you want to work.

To select an image for the album, just double-click it in the dialog box or click once to highlight it and then click the Open button. A thumbnail for the picture is created and presented on the application window. In Figure 18.3, you see PhotoRelay with an assortment of images ready for recording.

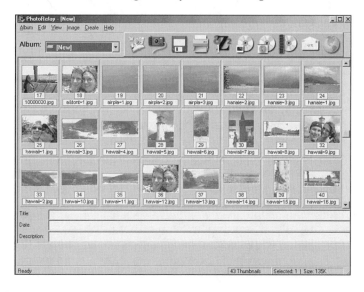

Figure 18.3

Thumbnails appear on the PhotoRelay window for each picture you select.

As you continue to add photographs to the album, you can use the scrollbar on the right side of the program to run through the album's contents.

Note that three fields are at the bottom of the PhotoRelay main window: Title, Date, and Description. (If you have no image selected the Description field is replaced with an About Album field.) You can fill in these fields for each picture as you add it. Or, later you can go back and click any picture to change this information.

Removing an image is just as simple as adding it to the album. Just right-click the image and select Delete from the menu that appears. When you select this option, PhotoRelay asks you to confirm the deletion. On this dialog box, you can also choose to remove the picture from your hard drive in addition to just the album. To do so, put a check in the Remove The Image Files From Disk check box. Once you're ready to proceed, click OK.

From the aforementioned right-click menu, you can also use the other standard editing commands that appear in this menu, such as cut, copy, and paste. You'll find these same capabilities in PhotoRelay's Edit menu.

Between Tracks

You can select multiple pictures from within a single folder. To select a range of images click the first one, hold down the Shift key and click the last image. To select individual pictures, click the first one, press the Ctrl key, and then select any other image in the folder you want selected.

Adding Audio to a Photo

You easily can add an audio clip to any picture or to the whole album that you create. If you add an audio clip to an individual picture, that audio clip gets played when the picture is displayed, such as in a slide show (which we'll get to later in the chapter!).

Don't Get Burned

Unlike the rest of the Easy CD Creator audio-related applications, PhotoRelay has not added support for WMA audio files. The only audio formats you can use are MP3 and WAV.

Simply select the picture on the workspace area and, on the Image menu, select Audio, Attach Audio. You are prompted to locate the file using the typical Open dialog box you see everywhere in Windows programs. Find and select the file; then, just click Open and you're done. Once you've attached Audio there's an icon that appears on the picture in your Photo Album to denote that it has an audio file associated with it. To preview the audio associated with a picture you can click the Image menu and select Audio, Play Attached Audio. A small audio player control box appears on the screen as shown in Figure 18.4.

Finally, if you decide you'd rather not have audio associated with a picture, you can choose to remove the attachment by clicking the Image menu and selecting Audio, Detach Audio.

Figure 18.4

It's a good idea to preview audio attached to a picture to make sure it's what you had in mind.

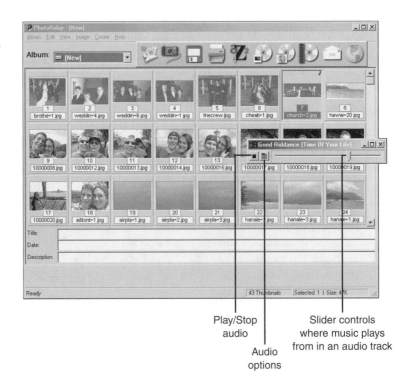

Play/Stop audio

Slider controls where music plays from in an audio track

Audio options

Other Miscellaneous Options

Before we get into the various ways you can distribute a photo album, let's deal with some of the other basic tools found on the PhotoRelay window.

The tool with the camera image is the Acquire tool. By clicking this button, you're presented with a dialog box, from which you need to select an available TWAIN device (like a scanner). Once you do, PhotoRelay steps you through the process of capturing that image.

The Print tool is obviously for printing from your album. However, when you click on it, you must make a choice. You can choose to print all or multiple thumbnails from the album or multiple selected images, or you can choose to print only the currently selected image.

If you choose to print all or multiple thumbnails, you must then select whether to print all of them, a grouping of selected images, or a range of images in numerical order. From there PhotoRelay takes you through a step-by-step process from which you must choose whether or not to include things like picture borders and background, the size of the thumbnails, and so on.

If you choose to print just one selected image, PhotoRelay sends up the dialog box shown in Figure 18.5.

Figure 18.5

From this dialog box you can choose to add such options as picture title, a border, print as a jewel case insert, and so on.

Once you've made your selections, simply click the Print button.

Finally, the Sort tool allows you to control how pictures are sorted in your album. When you click on this button, a dialog box appears with radio buttons, allowing you to sort by:

➤ File Name

➤ File Type

➤ File Size

➤ File Date

267

➤ Title

➤ Date

➤ Description

You can also choose to reverse the order of any of these sort options by putting a check in the Reverse Order check box.

Saving the Photo Album

You can save a photo album at any time during your work by clicking the Save tool (the floppy disk icon on the toolbar). You can also select Save Album from the Album menu. Either method brings up a small dialog box that enables you to give a filename to the album. After you've saved it, the "New" text in the Album field is replaced with this album's title.

Don't Get Burned

Note that saving the album *doesn't save all the photographic image files you've selected*. It just saves the thumbnail that was created of the photo and other information you might have entered into the album, such as the title. When you recall an album to look through or to edit, the original files should still be present if you want to burn the CD. Just remember that until you do burn the CD, don't touch any of the photographs you've selected for the album! Even moving them to a new folder on your hard disk makes it so your album can't locate them.

You can tell if PhotoRelay has a problem locating an image when you reopen the album. It indicates this by putting the universal symbol, the red circle with a line through it, at the upper-left edge of the thumbnail.

One very important thing I should also say here is that—in addition to using the Save option to save an album so you can work on it at a later time—until you save the album, you cannot proceed to the next step of burning the CD! You must "save" the album; otherwise, the CD burning option barks at you to tell you to do so first!

Burning an Album to CD

When you've gotten together an album of photographs, and perhaps some audio to go with it, that you want to put to CD, all you need to do is decide which kind of photo CD you want to create. As mentioned, your choices include:

➤ **SlideShow CD** shows the images in the order you decide and autoruns when inserted on a computer that supports that option.

➤ **WebAlbum CD** lets you create a CD that enables you to view thumbnails of your album in a Web browser.

➤ **Video PostCard** enables you to record a video using the AVI format on a CD.

In the following sections, we'll take a look at each of these methods.

Creating a Slide Show

After you click the MakeSlideShow button, a dialog box titled Select File pops up and prompts you to select the images from the album that will be recorded onto the CD. You can pick and choose using the Add or Remove buttons, or you can simply select the Add All button if you want all the pictures in your album on the CD. After you've selected what you need, click Next to continue.

The next dialog box (shown in Figure 18.6), is titled Audio Options.

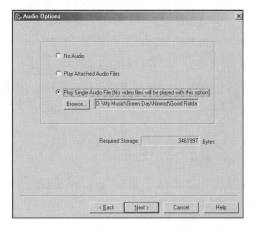

Figure 18.6

You can select how audio files are used when creating a slide show.

The Audio Options dialog box enables you to …

➤ Select that no audio be used on the CD.

➤ Play audio files attached to individual images. Just because you attached audio to the image when creating the album doesn't mean you have to record these audio tracks to the CD.

➤ Play a single audio file. This option enables you to play one audio file, and the slide show is timed to fit within it. Of course, as you can see in the Figure 18.6, you must select the audio file you want to add using the Browse button if you use this option.

Before clicking the Next button to keep going, do be sure to glance at the Required Storage field to make sure it doesn't exceed the size of your CD. If you've selected audio, it might take a few seconds or even a minute or two before the next dialog box pops up. This dialog box, titled Select Destination, enables you to copy the slide show to your CD burner and create a CD, or to copy the slide show to a hard disk location if you want to further edit it (see Figure 18.7). If you choose to first try out your slide show by storing it on the hard disk, you can also use the Directory field to tell PhotoRelay where you want it to place the files. If you are ready to burn a CD, then you also can specify a directory name. This can be handy if you want to give a descriptive name to the directory on the CD so you can tell what is on the CD when you view it using tools such as Windows Explorer.

Figure 18.7

You can select to burn the CD or to store the slide show in a hard disk location.

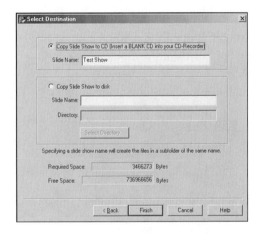

Because this book is about burning CDs, that's the option we'll choose now; then, click the Finish button.

The CD Creation Setup dialog box that you're used to seeing (assuming you've read up on any of the other Easy CD Creator programs) then pops up and enables you to make changes to several options. See Chapter 5, "Drag and Drop with Easy CD Creator," for more information about using this dialog box's advanced features. For our purposes, leave Track-at-Once selected in the Record Options section and choose Finalize the CD. To start the CD burning process, click the Start Recording button.

If you haven't inserted a blank CD-R into the recorder yet, you are prompted to do so. The CD Creation Process dialog box shows you the progress of creating the CD.

Again, if you've used Easy CD Creator, you're used to this dialog box. It shows you which step the program is currently working on in the creation process. When the

CD has been successfully completed, it tells you so and gives you the option to create a CD label or jewel case insert using the CD Label Creator program.

Creating a Web Album

This CD-burning option can be used to create a CD of photographs you can view using an Internet browser. If the computer supports the autorun feature, your browser pops up automatically and enables you to select from the thumbnails to see the full image. When selected, Windows opens whichever default program it's using to view graphic images (this will depend on what programs you have installed).

To create a Web album, select its tool from the PhotoRelay window. The next dialog box that appears is the same as for the slide show, asking you to choose the images you want to appear in the Web album CD. Make your selections and click Next. This will get you to the Layout dialog box, shown in Figure 18.8.

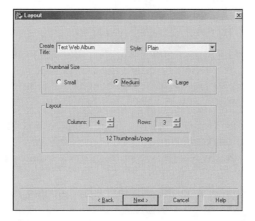

Figure 18.8

You can customize the layout of a Web album using this dialog box.

In this dialog box, you can select the size the thumbnails will be on a Web page (small, medium, or large) and the number of rows and columns for the display. Based on your selections, PhotoRelay tells you the number of thumbnails that appear on a page when it is displayed. You also can use this dialog box to give your Web album a title. Click the Next button when you are ready to continue.

Another dialog box asks you to select details you want to have displayed with each thumbnail. These include the title, date, and description of the image. Remember those three fields you had the option of entering information for each photo on the main PhotoRelay album window? This is where Web Album gets that information. Options are also available for including the picture's filename and file size. You can use check boxes to select which of these to display.

After you click Next, the Select Destination dialog box, which we saw back in Figure 18.7 appears and lets you choose to burn your Web album to a CD or to a directory on the hard disk. Make your selection and click, finally, Finish!

Once again, CD burners get the CD Creation Setup dialog box. Select to finalize the CD unless you plan to add more albums to the CD. Click the Start Recording button, making sure you have a recordable CD already inserted in your CD-RW drive.

The CD Creation Process dialog box will keep you company and show you the steps being taken to create the CD, along with the number of files and tracks that have been written. When the CD is finished, you'll see the usual dialog box confirming your successful recording of a CD.

Creating a Video Postcard

This option is a little different from the others in that it involves putting video data on a CD instead of still photographic images. Although creating a Video CD (VCD) is covered in Chapter 6, "NTI CD-Maker: Says What It Does and Does What It Says," this is quite a bit different. To make matters even more confusing, whereas VCD Creator is adamant that files use the MPEG-1 video format, a video postcard uses yet another type: AVI.

Another difference between a Video postcard and the VCD is that, for a VCD, you must use an editing program to produce your video and then burn it to the disc. A Video postcard, on the other hand, is a much simpler type of CD that just plays back a short video clip you select, against a postcard-type of background. You shouldn't use PhotoRelay's Video Postcard feature to burn your favorite TV show onto a CD!

Because this is going to be a postcard, you can see in the first dialog box that you must select a template to use as the background for the video (see Figure 18.9). PhotoRelay comes with several images in the library portion of this dialog box.

Figure 18.9

You first select the background for the postcard and the size of the video window.

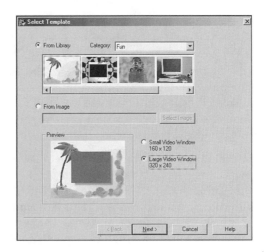

From this dialog box, you also can set the size of the window that is used to play back your video clip. Select small or large and then click Next to continue. You can experiment by simply clicking the Small or Large size radio buttons. The template image changes to show you the space your actual video will take up when it's played on top of the background you've selected for the postcard.

When you click Next, you get to the postcard section of this project. Here, as you can see in Figure 18.10, the dialog box looks just like a postcard. What you enter here appears after the video has finished playing.

You can use the Select Font button to use another font for your text or to change the font size to enable you to get more text on the screen. To enter your oh-so-poetic message, just click in the area of the postcard you want to type into and click Next when you're finished.

Between Tracks

Note that in Figure 18.9 that only a few images are shown in the library supplied with the program. Click the Category button, however, and you'll see that more libraries are available, with background images to choose from.

Figure 18.10

Fill in the typical postcard information, just as you would with the paper variety!

The Preview dialog box pops up next, showing the background image you've selected. You can use the Select Video button to select the video clip you want attached to this video postcard. You can select from several video file formats, including MPEG and AVI. If it's not an AVI file, the postcard program converts it to one, as necessary. *After* you've located the file, click it once to select it. You can now use the preview pane on this dialog box to preview the clip.

After you start previewing, the Play button turns into the Stop button, which you can use when you are satisfied that you've selected the correct video clip. When you've found your file, click the Open button, which returns you to the Preview dialog box. You can use the Play and Stop buttons found there to play the video again, or just click Next to continue.

Finally, the Select Destination dialog box appears, as was shown previously in Figure 18.7. To create the video postcard CD, select the option Copy Video PostCard to CD. Click the Finish button. The CD Recording dialog box appears and, as in the last two sections, shows you the progress of writing the CD. When it's finished, you'll see the usual confirmation; you can then use the video postcard CD.

When your newly burned CD is inserted into a Windows computer, the postcard is automatically started up and your video plays, followed by your postcard message.

Web and E-Mail Functions

There are two more functions of PhotoRelay to cover. Specifically, let's talk about the SendMail and PhotoIsland tools.

The SendMail tool is simple enough. Just select a photo (you cannot select a range of photos) and give the tool a click. A message window will open from whichever e-mail program you use as your default containing an attachment with the selected photo. Type in the recipients of the message, a brief subject and perhaps a quick message and sent it out across the Web to its awaiting recipient.

Between Tracks

If uploading, make sure you select the photos before clicking the PhotoIsland button.

The PhotoIsland option is a little trickier, although not by much. The first thing you need to do is go to www.photoisland.com and sign up for an account (click the Sign-Up Free link and follow the site's instructions). Once that's taken care of, you can feel free to click the PhotoIsland tool from within PhotoRelay (see Figure 18.11).

Figure 18.11

Before accessing the PhotoIsland Web site, you need to choose whether to upload photos to it, or download photos (you've sent previously) from it.

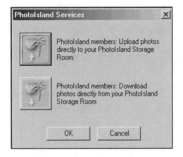

Once you select one of these options, you need to input your login name and password to gain access to your online storage space. If you're uploading files, the Upload to Photo Island dialog box also shows you which files you've selected for uploading. From there, just follow the on-screen steps to send up or retrieve your photos.

The question of whether or not you should actually use PhotoIsland really depends on your own personal tastes. Certainly I'd recommend you always be wary of freely giving out your name and e-mail address to, what amounts to, perfect strangers. This kind of information has a habit of turning up in databases that bombard your e-mail inbox with unwanted advertisements and service offers.

On the other hand, PhotoIsland is the ideal tool for sharing your photos with friends and family who have Web access, but who may not be the most savvy PC users out there. For the inexperienced, extracting and viewing an image file from an e-mail can be a monumental task and using PhotoIsland can save both you and those you're sharing photos with a significant number of headaches.

The Least You Need to Know

➤ You can use PhotoRelay to store pictures, along with audio files, on your hard disk or to burn a CD.

➤ You can create simple postcards that play video clips against a postcard–like background to send to friends using PhotoRelay.

➤ You can use PhotoRelay to create a Web album that can be viewed using a Web browser.

➤ You can sign up for free online storage space to and from which you can send and retrieve photo album pictures.

Chapter 19

Roxio's Sound Editor

In This Chapter

➤ Using the Sound Editor to modify WAV files

➤ Learn how to "read" a waveform

➤ Editing WAV files for the purpose of improving the sound quality, adding special effects, removing extended silences, and more

This chapter digs the Sound Editor utility that comes with Roxio Easy CD Creator 5 Platinum. Editing a book can be a difficult job; just think back to the term papers you had to write in school! However, the Sound Editor is an easy-to-use tool that can help you fix up some of the problems that come with burning CDs. For example, if you record from an LP using the SoundStream Disc Doctor utility, you can use the sound editor to remove that little bit of unwanted silence from the beginning or end of a track. If you have a music CD that has a bonus song included with the last track on the disc (where it's the same track, but recorded following a gap of a minute or two), you can use Sound Editor to break them up into separate music files. And yep, as you've probably guessed, there's more!

Using the Sound Editor

One of the best things about being able to put WAV files on your hard drive is the fact that you can edit them to suit various needs. After all, if you're recording "In-A-Gadda-Da-Vida," you might not want to eat up a quarter of your CD time on a drum solo. The Sound Editor packaged with Easy CD Creator Deluxe 5 Platinum is used to modify WAV files that you have extracted from other sources.

Between Tracks

Sound Editor can use only files recorded in the WAV format. It cannot open MP3 or Windows Media Audio files. However, you can use the SoundStream utility to convert any MP3 or WMA files you may have into WAV files. Once you're done making edits, you can use it again to change them back. You can find more information on using SoundStream in Chapter 7, "Your Very Own Recording Studio: Using Easy CD Creator SoundStream."

The Sound Editor enables you to add special effects, cut and paste sound clips, and perform a host of other features. There are a couple of ways to launch the Sound Editor, but for a change, using the Project Selector isn't one of them. You can either …

➤ Open SoundStream, click Show Options Drawer button and select Sound Editor (you may have to use the side-scroll buttons to see this option).

➤ Click Start, Programs, Roxio Easy CD Creator 5, Applications and Sound Editor.

Either way you do it, you'll end up at a screen like the one shown in Figure 19.1.

Figure 19.1

The Sound Editor enables you to make changes to WAV files before recording them to CD.

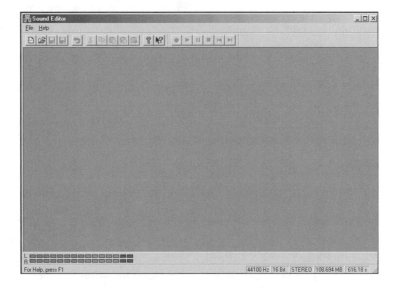

At this point, you can use the File menu to open an existing WAV file on your hard drive for editing.

Opening WAV Files So You Can Make Edits

To open a WAV file that you have just recorded or saved to your hard disk, use the File menu and select Open. Then, navigate your computer's directory structure to find the file you want.

Between Tracks

You can open multiple WAV files at the same time, but you have to open them one at a time. Unfortunately, the Shift+Click method won't allow you to select more than one file. So, if you plan to mix and match stuff from different audio files, just open the first file, then the second, and so on. Each appears as its own window within the main program. You can cut and paste portions of the wave form from one WAV file window to another.

In Figure 19.2, you can see the Open dialog box that is used to select the track(s) you want to work with in the Sound Editor. If you're not sure whether you've selected the correct file, click the Preview button to give it a listen. When previewing a song, the Preview button changes to a Stop button, which you can use to stop listening when you've heard enough.

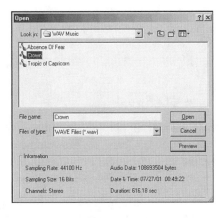

Figure 19.2

You can select to preview each track before you edit it using the Open dialog box.

Notice in this dialog box that there is an Information section at the bottom showing a lot of technical gobbledy-gook about the quality of the WAV file you are about to work with. In this example, the file is recorded using a sampling rate of 44,100Hz, with a sampling size of 16 bits. The only thing you need to know about these numbers is that this is approximately CD quality. If you see lower numbers, then the file in question would be something of slightly poorer quality.

After you have found the file you want, click Open. As you can see in Figure 19.3, this opens the audio track in the main program window.

Figure 19.3

After you've opened an audio track, the editor brings up a window for it so you can start editing.

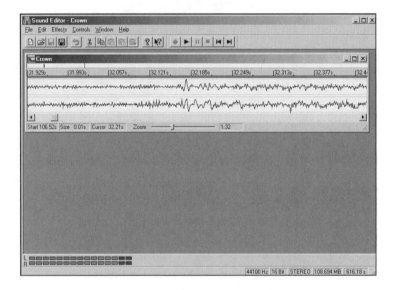

As you can see in this figure, two jagged lines are drawn—one for each channel—indicating a stereo effect. The lines are a graphic representation of the audio track, showing the *amplitude* of the audio signal.

Arcane CD Speak

I'll bet you've heard the word **amplitude** many times before, but perhaps have never given a second thought as to what it really means. Basically, it's the volume of the sound track. In Sound Editor, you can actually "see" the amplitude of the audio in the file. The sound track is a continuous line that goes up and down as the volume changes. The greater the distance between the high and low points, the greater the amplitude, or volume.

At the bottom of the window, you can see the data we just talked about concerning the WAV file. You can see the 44,100MHz, 16-bit stereo information here, along with the length of the track and how much space it takes to store this song. Although this 108.694MB file doesn't take up a large chunk of space on modern hard drives that often hold 20GB to 80GB, I can still remember, back in the days when the wheel was still a pretty nifty idea and when PC hard drives couldn't store more than 5MB of data. The march of progress, 2002 style!

Navigating the WAV (File)

When you first open a WAV file, you'll notice that a slider bar appears at the bottom of the window. Unless your audio track is only a few seconds long and fits in this small editing window, you can use this slider bar to move to various parts of the file. If you want to edit a portion of the song that is, for example, halfway through the track, just move the slider bar to about halfway. Of course, unlike text editors, this can be a little tricky. After all, it's not like you can look at a waveform and understand what it "says," like you can with text. To ensure that you've gotten to the part of the file you want to edit, you can select a part of the waveform, just as you would text in a Microsoft Word document and then use the Preview button on the toolbar to actually hear the selected portion. You also can click and drag across a selection, like you can with text, to preview a specific portion of the track. If you're not where you want to be, move the slider bar around (or use the arrows you find at both ends if you want to move only a little to fine-tune your location).

Another interesting feature you can use is the Zoom feature. The Zoom feature also uses a slider bar, but its function is radically different! Zoom, predictably, expands or compresses the visual representation of the audio track onscreen. In the last paragraph, I told you that unless your song was just a few seconds long, the whole thing will not fit into the window and you must move to the part you want to edit.

Don't Get Burned

If you select a "range" of a track to preview, be sure to verify that the selection is of a significant length. Depending on where the track's Zoom setting is, highlighting a section of the waveform may only be a half second of audio. You can tell how much time a segment of audio is by looking at the time indexes (shown in seconds) above the waveform.

Suppose all you want to do is chop off a little silence at the beginning of the track and a little at the end? Wouldn't it be nice to simply collapse the whole track so that it *does* fit in the window to enable you to see the whole file at once? Well, that's what Zoom does. If you move the slider bar the Zoom feature uses to the far right, the graphic representation of the WAV file is compressed and—usually—the whole thing fits within the space the editing window provides. Of course, you wouldn't want to do this if you're trying to just find one little annoying pop or click to delete. If you compress the track display too much, you'll have a much more difficult time trying to locate a tiny portion of the file.

Cutting and Pasting Audio Data

The two basic functions used for any kind of editing—cutting and pasting—are done easily in the Sound Editor. You can simply place your cursor where you want to start selecting the sound clip, hold down the left mouse button, and drag to the point where you want the selection to stop. In Figure 19.4, you can see that part of this WAV file has been selected using the cursor method.

Figure 19.4

You can select part of the WAV track just like you can with text when you are editing the file.

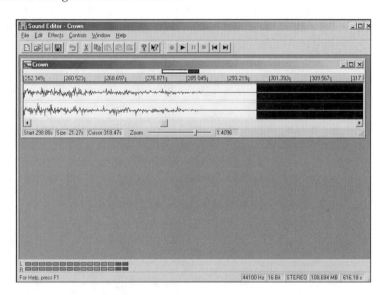

Consider the Edit menu your holy grail for making changes to a WAV file. If you want to cut out the selected part of the track, just select Cut from the Edit menu (or press Ctrl+X), click Copy (Ctrl+C) to copy the selection, and to insert a cut or copied piece of audio, place your cursor elsewhere in the track (or in another WAV file) and then use the Edit menu to click Paste (Ctrl+V). If you're unhappy with the results, the Undo command (Ctrl+Z) can turn back the clock, erasing your most recent change. From there, you can use Undo to remove the change right before that, too. Finally, you can put an undone change back in place using the Redo command (Ctrl+Y).

Between Tracks

At the start of this chapter, I told you that you could use Sound Editor to chop out parts of the audio file you don't need, such as too much silence at the start or end of a track. Those of you with a lot of "live" recordings should consider that you can use Sound Editor to remove some of the junk usually found on these albums, like the artist talking about solving the world's problems, long applauses, and so on.

In addition to the normal paste command that you would expect, the Edit menu also has a command called Mix Paste (sorry, no shortcut). This feature enables you to layer the sound clip on top of the other data at the point at which it is pasted. In effect, this is like having two tracks playing at the same time and can be useful for planting hidden messages into music, like, "Buy copies of this book for all your friends."

Using Special Effects on Sounds

Even though you're not going to find yourself using Sound Editor to create sound effects for the next *Star Wars* epic, you can apply some basic special effects to all or part of a clip. If the audio track you are working with is in stereo format, you can apply some effects to just one channel of the stereo track. You can find the different special effects you can use in the Effects menu. The effects that can be created using the Sound Editor are:

Between Tracks

If you want to quickly select the entire track without having to use your mouse, just use the Edit menu and click Select All (or double-click the waveform). This highlights the entire track so that any changes or effects you apply are for the entire WAV file.

➤ **Amplify.** The Amplify effect changes the volume of the track when it is played back. To use this effect, select part or all of the audio track using your cursor. Then, click Amplify on the Effects menu. A dialog box pops up and enables you to change the volume level for each track, if this is a stereo track, as you can see in Figure 19.5.

Figure 19.5

The Amplification Settings dialog box enables you to change the volume of the audio data.

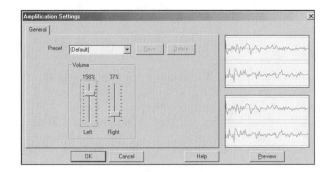

➤ **DC offset.** There are times when you might have hardware or other problems that cause an audio WAV file to be created with the waveform shifted from the baseline. This might be noticeable to you as a hissing in the background when you play the track. You can correct this using the Direct Current (DC) Offset effect.

➤ **Echo.** This is an audio effect that everyone is used to. It's just as easy to implement as the others. Select the part of the track you want to be echoed and then select Echo from the Effects menu. In Figure 19.6, you can see the dialog box you can use to control how this effect is applied.

➤ **Fade.** This effect enables you to slowly increase or decrease the volume of the clip. You can specify a fade-in at the beginning of a clip and a fade-out at the end. There are two sliding bars for the fade effect. The bar labeled Initial can be used to determine a fade-in at the beginning of the clip, whereas the bar labeled Final enables you to control the degree of fading out at the end of the clip.

➤ **Flange.** This is a strange audio effect. It works much like an echo, but the delay times are not fixed as in an echo effect. In Figure 19.7, you can see that the controls for a flange effect are also more complicated than those for the echo effect.

➤ **Format Conversion.** This Effects menu selection, which is best left alone if you don't understand things such as sampling rates, applies to the entire WAV file with which you are working. It can be used to change the format of the WAV file, such as the rate at which sound is sampled and whether or not the track is in stereo or mono. To use this effect, just select Format Conversion from the Effects menu; the dialog box shown in Figure 19.8 pops up to enable you to make the appropriate format changes.

Between Tracks

As you explore these effects options, notice that every screen has a Preview button that allows you to test an effect setting on an audio track before you actually apply it. Since adding effects to an audio track is very much a hit or miss process this button is invaluable as no changes are made to your wave form until you click OK.

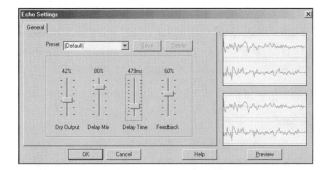

Figure 19.6

The Echo Settings dialog box has several parameters to configure for the effect.

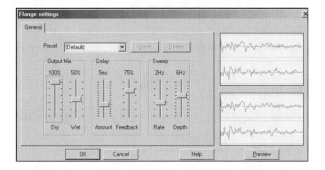

Figure 19.7

The Flange effect is similar to an echo effect.

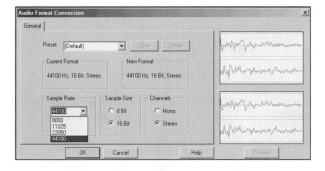

Figure 19.8

The Audio Format Conversion dialog box enables you to change the format type of the WAV file with which you are working.

➤ **Graphic Equalization.** This effect gives you a graphics equalizer on your desktop that can be used to manipulate the amplitude (amplification) of selected frequencies in the audio file. You might want to amplify a bass sound or lower the volume of a high-pitched sound.

➤ **Invert.** The Invert effect causes the waveform of the audio sound to be inverted vertically. This means that, if the original sound was increasing in volume, it will be decreasing after it is inverted, and vice versa. If you are pasting clips together into a single file, this might help by making one clip more compatible with another.

➤ **Pitch Shift.** This effect enables you to raise or lower the pitch of the track. This means you can take the audio track and change it from one musical key to another. If you are mixing two clips together into the same file, this can be useful by letting you match their pitches so that they blend together well.

What Are Effect Presets?

When you spend a lot of time fine-tuning something, isn't it nice to be able to save your settings so you don't have to go through that process all over again? For effects, some with complicated controls, this is accomplished by using *presets*. In all the dialog boxes for sound effects you've seen so far, there has been a field called Preset near the top, and it has always said Default. Of course, that's because, if you haven't changed anything, the dialog box pops up with the default values for that effect.

After you make changes to a particular effect, you can save those settings so you can recall them and use them again on another file. This does not save the audio information you are working on, though, just the positioning or selections made to the controls. To save a preset, place your cursor in the Presets field and enter something other than Default. After you've changed the text, the Save button becomes available; click it. The next time you use this effect, you can use the drop-down menu where the Default text appears to recall a particular preset you have created before.

The Least You Need to Know

➤ The Sound Editor is used to edit WAV files on your hard drive.

➤ If you want to edit audio stored in the WMA or MP3 format, use SoundStream to convert them to WAV. Then convert them back when you're done.

➤ You can cut and paste between various sound clips.

➤ You can apply various special effects to audio tracks that can improve or distort their sound quality.

Chapter 20

I Ain't Got No CDs, but You Should See All My New Coasters: Troubleshooting CD Recording

---

In This Chapter

➤ Nothing's perfect in a changing world, especially CD-recording technology!

➤ Check your source first

➤ If your source is okay, check the discs you are recording to

➤ Is your software and hardware up to date?

➤ Check your vendor's site for help specific to your products

---

Ready to throw your computer out a window, CD-RW drive and all? Okay, but make sure the window is, in fact, open ... or you can look to this chapter for a fix to your problem. Before you begin to troubleshoot, remember that any new technology is always prone to problems. With luck, and the use of this wonderful book, you are going to succeed.

When you run into any problems on the way, consult this chapter.

Hey, Nothing's Perfect!

No matter how good the technology, there are always going to be gremlins working themselves into the machinery here and there. In a field such as CD recording, where there are standards, but in which many companies produce equipment of varying capabilities, you can expect even more gremlins. There will likely be enough of them to have a party that could fill the Metropolitan Opera House!

A typical example is the CD-R or CD-RW blank discs you use. Different dyes and metal alloys are used in various brands. Some might work better on your drive than others. Some might not work at all. As drive technology continues to improve, and as manufacturers keep working at getting the perfect media, these kinds of problems will go away. But I wouldn't hold my breath for that happening any time soon. The most important factor here is just to make sure you get discs rated to burn at a speed equivalent to what your CD-RW drive is capable of.

The remainder of this chapter provides both a few tips and a few typical trouble-shooting procedures that can help you as you exercise all the capabilities of the software you are using.

Don't Get Burned

In a couple of recent online articles, it's been reported that some music publishers have begun testing a new method of preventing pirating of their material. Obviously, copy-protection schemes of all kinds have been proposed, and most are successfully hacked (broken) in test environments before they even reach the public testing stage. However, there's a new one out there that might even be a part of your newer CDs and you might not even know it!

Certain newer CDs currently on the market (details on which ones were not available) contain "hidden" pops and scratches that you cannot hear while playing the CD in a normal CD audio player, but become painfully apparent if you should attempt to rip it to an MP3 or WMA file on your hard drive or portable audio player. It's rather like playing a scratched LP.

Needless to say, this scheme is a classic example of punishing everyone for the sins of a few. Honestly, I rarely even listen to published CDs anymore. I copy them to my hard drive, weed out the tracks I decide I don't like, and burn them to compilation CDs. All of this is, of course, perfectly legal. The attitude of certain music publishers however is that just because there's no law saying you can't do this, it doesn't mean you have the right to. I say if they're really that worried about it, perhaps they could just hire a rent-a-cop for each CD they sell. Then if you should do something with it they don't like, they could just cuff you on the spot. What a wonderful world that would be!

It Helps to Start with a Perfect Source

Whether you are making a simple copy of a CD or are undertaking a more complex project, such as creating a video CD, the first rule of thumb should always be to start with a good source. Although you can use the cleaning options that Roxio Sound-Stream provides, you won't get a crystal clear, brand-new-sounding CD from an old LP that has been treated badly.

The same goes for CDs. Although CDs have a nice protective coating on the bottom to help shield them from abuse, deep scratches can still cause problems. CDs can tolerate some degree of fingerprints and other contamination before becoming noticeable when you play the CDs. So, before you even begin troubleshooting a problem with CD recording, make sure your sources are clean and in good condition. You can find all sorts of products at audio and discount stores that can be used to clean almost any kind of media. Don't forget that the media player itself might need some cleaning or tuning up. When recording from a phonograph LP, don't use a player that has a needle in it that's 20 years old. If you're recording from tape, clean those tape heads!

Between Tracks

Like all recording media that has come before them, a new industry is forming to provide for the need to clean or repair CDs. Check the local record shop or software retailer and you'll probably find a lot to choose from. There are even products that can be used to fill in scratches. In my opinion, if you have to go that far, just buy a new CD. Or if you've made a backup copy and have been playing the backup copy, your new, barely used CD wouldn't have that scratch to begin with. It would be stored safely in a closet somewhere!

Assuming that you start with a good source, you also should end with a good product. So in this chapter, we'll look at some specific problems that can occur and how you can avoid them.

Who Can Read What

One frequent problem is that you'll create a CD and take it to a friend's place, only to have him/her complain that it doesn't do anything in their player. When using recordable CD media, remember that older audio players, and older computer CD-ROM drives, might not be able to use your CD-Rs. At this point, it's a hit-or-miss thing, because people tend to keep a working machine, such as a CD player around until it breaks, which can be a very long time. Just about all the newer, and many of the older, audio players can read closed CD-R discs, and you shouldn't have any problems related to format if you buy a new audio player.

Whenever I hear from someone who can't play a newly created CD in his audio player I first tell him to insert it in his computer's CD-ROM drive and see whether he can play it from there. Most likely, his computer is newer than his stereo system, so he can quickly determine whether the problem resides in the CD or the player. There is always the possibility, too, that you forgot to close the CD! You can use Easy CD Creator or CD-Maker 2000 to look at the properties for the CD to determine if this is the problem. If you did not close the CD, then it won't be playable in an ordinary CD audio player. Of course, the way this technology is changing all the time, that might not be true in the near future.

Also, remember that some kinds of discs can be read in only one kind of drive. For example, read-write discs that you can use over and over again aren't readable in CD-R drives. If you try to use a mixed-mode CD (as we talked about in Chapter 2, "The Machine Behind the Curtain: How CDs and Recordable CDs Work") in your car CD player, you're going to get a big surprise when a loud grating noise comes blasting through your speakers as the player tries to interpret the first data track that comes before the audio! Note that this very kind of event has been known to actually ruin speakers, so be careful which CDs you place in your audio player!

Another thing to remember is that if you use multiple sessions on a disc, then usually the last session is the one that's readable by a CD-ROM player, by default. To change sessions and access the data there, you'll need a product such as Roxio Session Selector, which is a part of Easy CD Creator 5 Platinum.

A Look at Common CD-R and CD-RW Recording Problems

Remember that although specific standards exist for the way data and audio are recorded onto CDs, there are many manufacturers and each might come up with a different method of creating a CD burner or a CD reader. Little differences between manufacturers can be significant problems for some people. For example, some people like using the 80-minute CD-R media instead of the standard 74-minute discs. Suppose you want to use these discs and find that your software says no way, can't use them. You upgrade your software to a version that does allow 80-minute recording, only to find out that it's your hardware CD burner that has a built-in 74-minute limit! It doesn't care what the software tells it to do, it's just a dumb machine!

This is a reminder of what I was referring to at the start of this chapter. The state of this industry is changing so rapidly that you can always expect the unexpected when you begin to troubleshoot. It could be the media. It could be the recording drive. It might be some silly program running in the background using up computer resources that you've forgotten about! For example, even if you have a large, fast system, be sure you disable things that start themselves up automatically. Such programs include screensavers, power management utilities, task schedulers, and the like. If you have a product like this, watch out! If it kicks in when you're burning, you might get burned, so to speak.

In the following sections, we'll look at some of the more common problems and some ways you can fix them.

Between Tracks

Although they don't all appear here, the easiest way to disable a background program is to look at the list of icons in your system tray (next to the clock on your desktop). Right-click each of these icons; you should see an option for closing or disabling them. Doing so prevents them from running and taking up resources your CD-burning program might want.

To disable power management or a screensaver, right-click the Windows desktop, choose Properties from the menu, and then click the Screen Saver tab in the dialog box that pops up. Here, you can turn off your screensaver and access any of the power management functions (which work a little differently depending on your flavor of Windows and computer hardware).

Buffer Underruns: The Ultimate Coaster Creators

When we were looking at creating or copying CDs in previous chapters, we saw that Easy CD Creator and CD-Maker 2000 have a progress dialog box that keeps you posted on the progress of the CD burn that is in progress. You can see a copy of the Easy CD Creator dialog box in Figure 20.1.

The reason I mention this dialog box is that it has a field that shows you the amount of data available in your CD-RW drive's write buffer. Because the laser burner has to receive a constant stream of data telling it how to make burns through the dye layer of the CD-R blank, problems occur if an interruption of data occurs. For this reason, a buffer in the computer's memory is created to store part of the data stream. If the hard disk from which the file is coming is partially fragmented, there might be milli-seconds here and there that are wasted while the disc heads look for the next block of data. During this seek time, the buffer is used to supply data to the laser. If the CD burner looks to the buffer for data and nothing is there, you'll get more use from your disc by setting a cold drink on it than you would trying to put data on it.

Figure 20.1

The CD Creation Process dialog box is common to many applications and shows you the buffer usage.

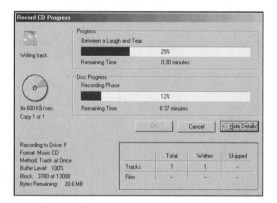

So a buffer underrun, as you can see, is a serious problem. Watch this indicator closely and be sure it stays near 100 percent. If it drops a bit, you should be okay, but you might start to see problems if the buffer drops even to the 75 percent mark (de-pending on the total buffer size). If you have a newer computer that runs at least as fast as 500MHz or a CD-RW drive with some form of BurnProof technology, you probably won't have any problems with buffer underruns. If you do, the remedies you can try are varied. Some might work; some might not work because the source of a buffer underrun is rarely perfectly clear. Here are some possibilities:

➤ Stop using the computer for anything else while the CD is burning. Don't use up the computer's resources while it's trying to keep that buffer full!

➤ If you're burning a disc on your work network or you have a home network then, for goodness sakes, don't use a network drive as your source! The network is gazillions of times slower than accessing your hard drive.

➤ If necessary, *defragment* your hard disk drive. If you are copying CD to CD, this won't help. But if you are copying WAV, MP3, or image files to your CD burner, a defragmented disk reads much more quickly, keeping that buffer full.

➤ Execute the Scandisk program (Start, Programs, Accessories, System Tools) to see if it can locate and fix any problems that might exist on your hard drive.

➤ Check for viruses on your system! If you're on the Internet and you don't have a virus checker, you're just waiting around for trouble! A virus can hide in the background, unnoticed, using up valuable system resources.

➤ Turn off any background processes that might be running (as described in the previous section).

Arcane CD Speak

The term **fragmentation** sounds kind of scary, doesn't it? No, it doesn't mean that part of your disk is broken! Instead, it is a condition that occurs naturally because of the way computers write data to the hard drive. If your computer just wrote one file after another to your hard disk and never deleted anything, you would (in an ideal world) have a disk on which similar blocks of data are located next to each other. This ordering would make them read more quickly because the computer wouldn't have to go looking to different parts of the hard disk for them.

However, when you delete a file, you leave a hole in your stored data. Because that space is now available, the drive eventually writes to this recycled space. When that space runs out, it just looks in its little index and finds some free spots elsewhere on the disk and continues writing the file at that location, and so on. Over time, you end up with a lot of data that's scattered, or fragmented, all over the disk! This, of course, can cause your data to take more time finding the files it needs. This includes files you want to write to a CD!

Most versions of Windows have a disk **defragmenter** utility, which examines how files are stored on the disk and attempts to rearrange them in a more orderly manner. Click Start, Programs, Accessories, System Tools to see whether your version of Windows has this program.

If you decide that you need to defragment your hard drive then, for Windows 98, you can do so using the following steps:

1. Click Start, then Programs, Accessories, and System Tools.

2. Click the Disk Defragmenter icon in the System Tools folder.

3. The Select Drive dialog box prompts you for the drive to defragment. Choose, of course, the one on which you have stored WAV or MP3 files (or disk images of CDs you want to create), and click OK.

4. A Defragment Drive dialog box keeps you company as the information on the drive is rearranged, block by block, to make as many like files as close to each other as possible. The larger the hard drive, the longer this will take, which can last up to several hours.

For Windows Me, NT/2000 and XP users, the procedure is similar. If you have Windows 95 or some other operating system, you can always purchase a disk defragmenter utility, such as Norton SpeedDisk; however, it might not be an inexpensive proposition.

Pops and Clicks That Weren't on the Source

Sometimes the actual burning process produces pops and clicks in the output CD you create that sound as if you were recording from an FM radio station that was too far out of range. This can be due to many causes, such as a bad WAV file to begin with. If you extract audio CD-DA tracks to WAV files, be sure to listen to them using Sound-Stream, the Windows Media Player, or some other applicable program before you record to a blank CD. If these turn out to be the problem, try extracting the WAV files at a slower rate or try recording them using a different CD-ROM drive (for this, you could even record from your CD-RW drive).

Between Tracks

You might think that recording at the fastest rated speed of your recorder drive might be the best thing. However, most media is rated as 1× through something-×. If you find it doesn't work well at the highest rate, then back down. Even though it takes a lot longer, almost everything works at slower speeds like 1× through 4×.

The reasons for failure can be numerous. Remember that on a CD-R disc, the laser is burning through a dye layer. It will do this differently at various speeds. If this dye layer acts differently at different speeds, so will your recording abilities.

As a matter of fact, a general rule I always use when extracting audio tracks to WAV files is to do so at only 2× speed. I've got time to sit around and read while the extract takes place. Why extract at 12×—unless you're really sure your drive can handle it and you never have problems—when good old 2× still works just fine and can keep other problems from cropping up?

This problem can also occur when copying from a CD-ROM drive to your CD recorder. If your CD-ROM drive is an older one, and it passes the digital audio extraction test to see if it can extract data at a fast enough rate to keep the recorder supplied, problems can still occur if you have a source CD that has minor errors on it.

You might not be able to detect these sounds when you play the CD, but when the track is being extracted and the data sent to the recorder, these problems can become magnified. To find out whether this is the cause, try using your CD burner itself as the source, copying the CD image to a disk image file, and then burn the CD from that image. If this doesn't work, try cleaning the CD to eliminate the possibility of minor errors caused by a dirty disc.

The CD Recorder Drive Wants a Bigger Disc!

Sometimes we bite off more than we can chew! The same goes when trying to use an Easy CD Creator layout that goes past the 74-minute limit. (Weren't you watching the indicator at the bottom of the application window that tracked your time?)

Sometimes, however, it's because we want to use Easy CD Copier to make a copy of a commercial CD that was actually created at a length greater than 74 minutes. I've run into several of these *overburned* CDs myself during the copying process. CD-burning fans of Frank Sinatra or Yoko Ono surely know what I'm talking about.

The solution? If your drive works with them, go out and buy a box of 80-minute blank CDs and try using those. Blank CD media doesn't come any larger than that yet, so if the 80s don't satisfy your burner's hunger, nothing will.

Another alternative is to look at the total time on the CD layout, if you're using Easy CD Creator, and try to remove one or more files or tracks to get back down under the 74-minute limit. If you are using Easy CD Copier, you might consider using the Easy CD Creator instead and selecting only the number of tracks that will fit onto a 74-minute blank. If it's a music CD and you're very close in time, you might even want to consider using Sound Editor to cut or fade out a few seconds of a music track or two.

I Used Audio Cleaning Options to Reduce Noise, and I Get a Dull Sound!

Options that allow you to "clean out" pops, hisses, and scratches from recorded audio must be taken with a grain of salt. Although they do work, they're not the most perfect tools you could use to do this. And remember, when filling in a pop or a click in the record, the sound has to come from somewhere. When you take away some of the bad, you also take away some of the good.

Cleaning and pop-removal tools should be used on WAV files on your hard disk so you can preview the output before committing it to a CD-R blank. I've found that when I've recorded some old LPs to CD, it actually doesn't sound that bad to have an occasional noise distortion here and there. To us old-timers, songs recorded with pops, hisses, and scratches is what nature intended! Besides, it brings back memories.

If you use the cleaning tool to its extreme value, which might be necessary for a record from the early part of this century, you get a very dull output. Experiment!

However, light applications of this tool seem to improve some records significantly. Try it at your leisure, pretending you're cutting your latest album and trying to get that groovy *sound*, man! Can you dig it?

Another option is to try a more sophisticated sound-editing program. Many are available; just check your local computer store and look for product reviews in magazines and on the Web.

Don't Overlook Hardware and Software Problems

In the changing scene of technology that CD recording is, you should always check with your vendor(s) on a regular basis. If you are a hobbyist and are having great results from your computer and the applications you are using to make CDs, just skip this chapter (until the next Microsoft update, of course!). However, as new patches are issued for operating systems, such as Windows, and new devices are created and brought to market, the possibility always exists that, to get your parts all working together in unison, you'll need to download something from somebody.

The first place to start is your software vendor. Publishers like Roxio and NTI are usually pretty consistent about issuing updates and patches that fix bugs and increase their program's compatibility with different hardware setups. Next, check your other software vendors, and then go to the hardware sites for the manufacturer of your CD-R or CD-RW drive. You never know what you'll find. However, when new operating system patches or versions are released, shortly thereafter you'll probably find a device driver file on your hardware vendor's Web page that should be downloaded and installed.

Another aspect of software as applied to hardware devices is *firmware*. This is software code, which usually is stored in your device's memory, that can be used to modify the operation of the hardware without having to actually change the hardware! In other words, firmware is the code that runs on the card or drive you've attached to your computer, but it's stored in a special kind of memory on the card or adapter, not the computer's memory.

Sometimes the update for hardware devices—such as CD recorders—are updates to firmware. Installing these kinds of updates varies based on who made your drive. Don't worry, these updates are usually very simple to apply and usually come with good directions. When you download them, just look for a file called "Readme" and open it up with Windows WordPad or Notepad!

Last, you might just have a drive that is either getting old or was defective from the start. For example, one common problem I hear about is the "power calibration area" error. When the CD burner starts to record a CD, it first performs a quick test near the very beginning of the CD (the center, remember!) to test how much power the laser will have to use to punch holes through the dye layer. Different blanks, different manufacturers, and different drives all add up to make this test necessary. If you get this error from the very start, try using a different brand of blanks. If that doesn't solve the problem, you might have a bad burner. If it's new, return it! If it's an older burner, the laser might simply be having trouble focusing correctly. One other possibility could be your computer's power supply (that hunk of metal in the back of the case with a large fan in it that the power cord plugs into).

When you see complete systems being sold cheap, you have to know that corners are being cut somewhere. One of the easiest targets for a hardware vendor is to include a cheap power supply in your computer. Cheap power supplies can cause all sorts of odd Windows errors, including system lockups and blue screen errors. They can also cause power calibration errors when burning CDs! If you think you need a new power supply, visit PC Power and Cooling's Web site (www.pcpowerandcooling.com). They're simply the best!

The Least You Need to Know

➤ Go slow if you have problems recording. Use a speed in the 1×- to 4×-range for difficult discs or recorders.

➤ Clean up your sources before you record! A dirty LP vinyl album isn't going to improve in quality just because you transfer the dirty track to a digital format.

➤ Defragment your hard disk drive if you're using it as the source for audio files being burned to CD.

➤ Update your software frequently by visiting the home pages of software vendors. The same goes for hardware vendors who might have to issue new driver software as operating systems continue to evolve.

Installing Roxio Easy CD Creator

Getting to Know Easy CD Creator 5 Platinum

Installing Roxio Easy CD Creator 5 Platinum is a somewhat time-consuming, but mostly painless process. The sections in this appendix outline the software package as a whole and go through all the ins and outs, including updating the program, you need to get your system kicking with Easy CD Creator.

Different CD-RW drives inevitably come with some form of CD-burning software. By far, the most common software that's shipped with these drives is Roxio Easy CD Creator. Because getting something for free is just so un-American, usually this software is disabled or missing certain features (like the copy contained on this book's CD). Regardless, most folks who get this demo version also end up buying the full package, so that's why it's one of the key products we focus on in this book.

Even though this book covers certain aspects of Easy CD Creator that may not be present in a demo or light version, don't be too disappointed. Even the demo version is still just fine for creating music or data CDs, or for making copies of other CD-ROMs. Just remember that the examples in this book are based on Easy CD Creator 5.0 Platinum. For those of you using the 3.0 or 4.0 versions, all is not lost! This book can still be of great use to you; the majority of the programs covered here work the same way in versions 3 and 4 as they do in version 5 (even if they look a tad different in some cases).

However, if you've been trapped in the demo dungeon or are stuck with an older copy of Easy CD Creator and are looking to upgrade to Easy CD Creator 5.0 Platinum, you can find it in most every computer store. If you are thorough, you might be able to find it with a rebate coupon or on sale, as well. Keep your eyes on those weekly circulars found in most consumer electronics outlets!

Remember, however, that Easy CD Creator is by no means the only player in the CD-burning market. We use it and NTI's CD-Maker in this book because they're the most common, have a broad array of features, and are generally quite user-friendly.

In addition to the Roxio software, we do talk a little about a couple of other programs you can use to burn CDs. These you'll find in Part 7, "Wait! There's More, So Buy Now: More Fun Software and Utilities!" we do discuss a couple of other options, like MusicMatch, that you also have at your disposal.

Installing Easy CD Creator 5.0 Platinum

Before you first install Easy CD Creator 5, you should double-check to make sure your computer meets its hardware requirements. Obviously, you must have a CD-RW drive installed, but if you don't know that then you might just be the first person an *Idiot's Guide* was too technical for. Aside from that, your computer must also have:

Between Tracks

If you're using a version of Easy CD Creator that bears the name Adaptec instead of Roxio, you need not worry. Roxio is a relatively recent spin-off of Adaptec, but *is* part of the same big happy family. Outside of changes between the 4.0 and 5.0 versions, Easy CD Creator operates the same whether your title screen bears the Adaptec or Roxio name.

➤ A 200MHz or better Intel Pentium, AMD K6, or equivalent processor.

➤ A modern version of Windows, like 9x/Me, NT4/2000 or the brand new Windows XP (which is well worth the upgrade for owners of newer computers).

➤ 32MB of system memory, but 64MB is a more preferable sweet spot. Though between rock-bottom prices for system RAM and with both Windows and other applications getting more and more hungry it's definitely worth your while to get yourself up to at least 128MB of RAM or more.

➤ At least 205MB of free space on your hard disk.

➤ Windows-compatible audio built into the motherboard or on an audio card (virtually any PC that meets the above specs should have this).

While in this "wonderful new millennium" (or so marketing folks tell us) most PCs should have no trouble meeting these requirements, if you're unsure about your system there's an easy way to check.

Making Sure Your Computer Measures Up

In response to the question, "What kind of computer do you have?" I'm always a little shocked by how often someone tells me that they either don't know or that it's, "A Dell of some kind," or "A Compaq something or other." Checking to see what type of computer processor you have, how much system RAM you have, or how much space is available on your hard disk is actually a very simple process. To check your processor type or amount of system RAM:

1. Simply start Windows and right-click the My Computer icon at the top right corner of your desktop (Windows XP users may have to look in the Start menu for this icon).

2. Click Properties from the shortcut menu that appears and Windows will present you with a dialog box like the one in Figure A.1.

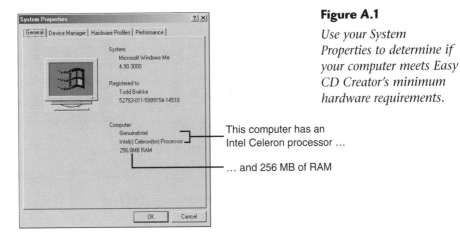

Figure A.1

Use your System Properties to determine if your computer meets Easy CD Creator's minimum hardware requirements.

This computer has an Intel Celeron processor ...

... and 256 MB of RAM

3. On the General tab, the section labeled "Computer:" shows your computer's processor and RAM information.

If you're unsure as to whether or not your hard drive has enough space to install Easy CD Creator, rather than right-click the Windows My Computer icon, double-click it. My Computer then opens with a listing of various icons of all the drives in, or connected to, your system. Click the hard disk drive icon to which you want Easy CD Creator installed and you'll see information about how much space it has available (see Figure A.2).

Once you're satisfied that your computer is ready to rock and roll with Easy CD Creator, it's time to insert the installation CD into your CD-ROM drive and take your first real steps toward mastering the CD-burning process.

Between Tracks

If you don't see any information about your drive when performing these actions, try right-clicking your drive icon in the My Computer window and choosing Properties instead. The dialog box that appears will show you what you need to know.

Figure A.2

The My Computer window can be used to determine whether or not you have enough free hard disk space to install Easy CD Creator.

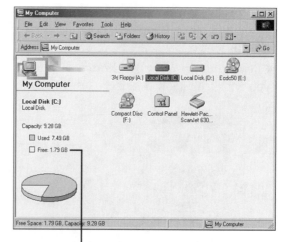

This hard drive has just under 2 Gigabytes of free space
and can easily contain an Easy CD Creator installation.

Starting the Easy CD Creator Installer

Before you install Easy CD Creator, first exit all other programs you may be running, just in case one of them doesn't play nice with the other kiddies. Once you insert the Easy CD Creator CD, Windows should immediately recognize it and ask you if you'd like to, "install the product now." There are buttons for Yes and No. Presumably, you're going to click Yes, in which case Easy CD Creator runs various checks on your system (verifying drive space and requirements) before launching its InstallShield Wizard, which makes installation a breeze. Click Next to continue.

Between Tracks

If you find that the installation menu does not pop up automatically when you insert the installation CD, you might not have your computer set to use the autorun feature. In that case, double-click My Computer on your desktop and then the icon for your CD drive. Depending on your flavor of Windows, this will either launch the autorun process described above or open up a listing of files on the CD. If it's the latter, look for a file named, "Setup," and double-click it.

This being the modern age of legalisms and technical gobbledy-gook the first thing you'll have to endure is agreeing to Roxio's licensing "agreement." This "agreement" basically tells you all the things they don't want you to do with your software (and is found in any software package you install). Some choice. Either you agree to its terms or try to take the software back to your local software retailer, who's likely to not accept a return of opened software, for a refund. Assuming you're willing to agree to the license (or willing to pretend to), click the radio button next to the option for I Accept The Terms In The License Agreement and click Next.

The next screen asks for your name, organization and CD key that helps ensure you're not running someone else's copy of the software (see Figure A.3).

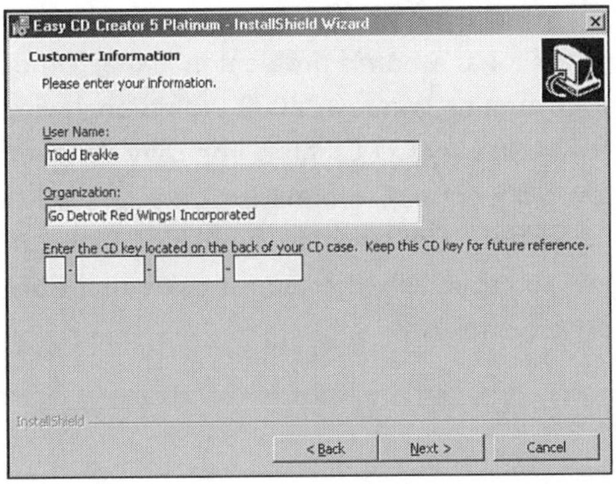

Figure A.3

Roxio tries to ensure its software isn't being pirated through the use of a CD key that you must enter before the program can install.

While you can ignore the Organization field, you must enter your name and the CD key number, which is located on the back of the CD's packaging. When ready, click Next.

The next dialog box asks you what kind of setup you'd prefer to use. If you want to keep it clean and simple, select Complete and click Next. If you select Custom, you can control which Easy CD Creator programs are installed on your computer. The list for the Platinum edition consists of:

> ➤ **SoundStream.** For creating compilations of music from various sources like MP3s, WAV files, and even LPs. SoundStream is covered in Chapter 7, "Your Very Own Recording Studio: Using Easy CD Creator SoundStream."

> ➤ **Sound Editor.** Allows you to edit audio files encoded in the WAV format. Sound Editor is covered in Chapter 19, "Roxio's Sound Editor."

Don't Get Burned

Make sure, when entering CD key, also called the TSID number that you enter exactly what is shown on the label. Even one incorrect digit will prevent Easy CD Creator from installing.

➤ **CD Label Creator.** Allows you to create killer CD and jewel case labels. CD Label Creator is covered in Chapter 14, "Making Killer Labels with Easy CD Creator CD Label Creator."

Don't Get Burned

The shipping version of Easy CD Creator 5 has a horrid problem in it that Windows 2000 Professional users must take note of. If running Windows 2000 Professional with certain removable-drives, the Take Two software in Easy CD Creator, ironically designed for backing up data, can seriously and irrecoverably corrupt information on your hard drive. Roxio does have a patch to fix this, see the section "Finishing Touches: Using Web-Checkup" later in this appendix to find out how to get it. Whether or not this patch truly works for everyone is a matter of debate in certain circles.

➤ **Easy CD Creator.** As the name suggests, the core Easy CD Creator 5 Platinum application. Use it to create audio and data CDs from scratch. Making audio and data CDs with Easy CD Creator is covered in Chapter 5, "Drag and Drop with Easy CD Creator."

Between Tracks

If you get to this point and are unsure as to whether you have room on your hard disk to install the Easy CD Creator Platinum programs you've selected, click the Space button on this dialog box and you'll see a screen that breaks down your available hard drives, how much space is required and how much you have available.

➤ **Take Two.** A program that allows you to back up your hard drive's data. Because Take Two's stability in Easy CD Creator 5 is somewhat suspect and because you can use the main Easy CD Creator to backup your most important data, this application is not covered in this book.

➤ **DirectCD.** Lets you write files to your CD-RW drive from Windows Explorer or My Computer, just as you would when moving files around on your hard drive. DirectCD is covered in Chapter 11, "Dial Direct with Easy CD Creator DirectCD."

➤ **Video Impression.** Lets you Spielberg and Lucas wanna-be's edit and burn video to CD. Video Impression is covered in Chapter 9, "Toss Your VCR: Using Video CD Creator to Create Video CDs."

➤ **PhotoRelay.** Gives you the ability to store digital pictures in virtual photo albums and burn them to CD so you can amaze (or bore) your friends and family with pictures from your vacation to the set of Ponderosa. PhotoRelay is covered in Chapter 18, "Making Digital PhotoAlbums with Roxio PhotoRelay."

By default, all of these programs are installed in a Complete or Custom setup. However, if you left-click the icon next to the program you don't want installed, you can click the red "X" on the shortcut menu that appears. If you change your mind later, bring up the menu again and click This Feature Will Be Installed on Local Hard Drive.

Finally, if you prefer to control the locations to which programs like Easy CD Creator are installed, click the Change button on this dialog box. From the window that appears in Figure A.4, you can either use the buttons and scroll-box at the top of the dialog box to navigate to (or create a new folder for) the disk location you where you want the program installed or type the location into the Folder Name: field.

Once satisfied with your selections, click Next to continue and Easy CD Creator will ask you confirm that you're ready to begin installing its applications. In case you haven't already guessed, click Install.

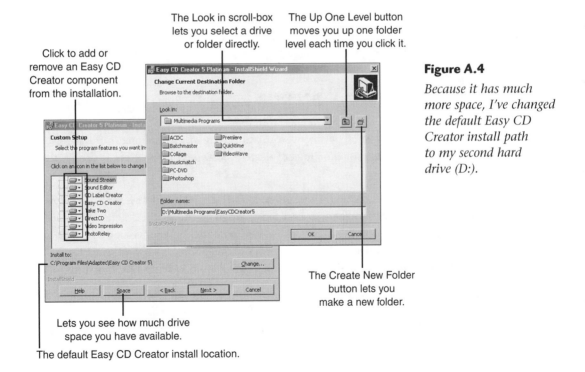

The Look in scroll-box lets you select a drive or folder directly.

The Up One Level button moves you up one folder level each time you click it.

Click to add or remove an Easy CD Creator component from the installation.

Figure A.4

Because it has much more space, I've changed the default Easy CD Creator install path to my second hard drive (D:).

The Create New Folder button lets you make a new folder.

Lets you see how much drive space you have available.

The default Easy CD Creator install location.

Finishing the Installation

Once you click Install, Easy CD Creator finally begins the installation process shown in Figure A.5. At this point it should only take a couple of minutes to install.

Figure A.5

After several mouse clicks, Easy CD Creator finally begins installing.

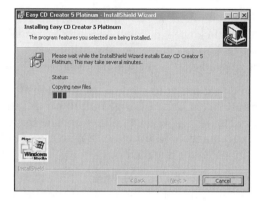

Between Tracks

Like many other programs, Roxio commits a sin that's sure to annoy any user who puts their computer's performance over convenient launching of applications. In this case, it puts background programs for the Project Selector and DirectCD functions in your system tray (refer to Figure A.6).

You can rid yourself of these icons, and others like them, in several ways. Using Windows 98 or Me, my method of choice is to click Start, Programs, Accessories, System Tools and select the System Information Utility (these steps vary based on your version of Windows). In the window that appears, click Tools, System Configuration Utility, and select the Startup tab. Here you'll see a list of all the programs that load when Windows starts.

To prevent these two programs from loading on startup, remove the checkmarks from the options for AdaptecDirectCD and CreateCD50. While doing so does mean you'll have to launch these programs manually when you do want to use them, I think most people prefer to have the choice.

Once installation is complete, yet another dialog box opens to let you know. Click Finish and you'll get one final gotcha, as you must now restart your computer so that certain files can load properly during your computer's boot process. If you're not ready, you can click No and reboot later, but it's better to take the time to do so now, so click Yes.

Finishing Touches: Using Web-Checkup

Once your computer reboots after installing, there are a few new things to take note of. First, note the new icons that appear on you system's desktop and system tray. You can use the desktop icon to launch the main Easy CD Creator screen as shown in Figure A.6.

When you first reboot your computer after installation, Easy CD Creator takes the liberty of opening to its main menu. Most of these options are covered in other chapters throughout this book, however, there is one to take note of: Web-checkup.

The Roxio Project Selector

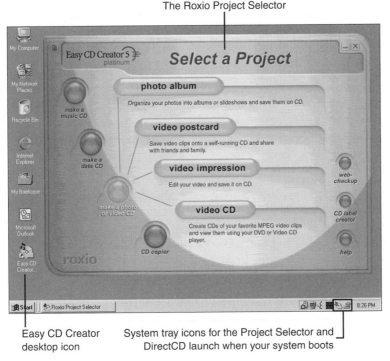

Figure A.6

Use the Roxio Project Selector to launch Easy CD Creator programs and to update the product with Web-checkup.

Easy CD Creator desktop icon

System tray icons for the Project Selector and DirectCD launch when your system boots

Roxio is vigilant about posting larger updates to the software on their Web site. You can use the Web-checkup feature to make sure you are running the most up-to-date software. True, that's one more thing that gets in your way of actually doing something useful, however, like rebooting, it's a pretty good idea to check for these updates so you can be sure you're working with as bug-free a program as possible.

Arcane CD Speak

A **bug** is a mistake in a program that slipped past a publisher's quality assurance testers. Because of how complex these programs are, very few ship completely bug-free. While some bugs are as innocuous as spelling errors or a button that goes nowhere, others can be so bad as to crash the program you're using or even Windows itself (newer versions of Windows, like 2000 and XP are better equipped to deal with these kinds of bugs). That's why many programs come with features like Web–checkup, so users can easily obtain fixes that kill bugs dead.

To use Web-checkup, ensure that your PC is connected to the Internet and then click the Web-checkup button on the Project Selector. When you do, it opens your default Web browser (such as Internet Explorer or Netscape Navigator) to the update portion of Roxio's Web site.

This page has some basic instructions for how to update your product. The long and short of it is that you must click the link on this page for the version of Easy CD Creator you have (likely version 5). When you do, a list of updates available appears. Click the links applicable to your installation to download available updates.

In general, after you've made this initial check for updates, you'll need to use this Web update feature only every once in a while. Besides, if your burner is working just fine and you're producing a lot of great CDs, why mess with success?

Installing NTI CD-Maker

CD-Maker is a CD-authoring program created by NewTech InfoSystems (NTI). Like many software applications of the modern computer era, it's really a suite of several different programs bundled into multiple editions (think Microsoft Office XP and its editions for Standard, Professional, and so on). The version of CD-Maker 2000 we're focusing on in this book is the Professional Edition.

Getting to Know NTI CD-Maker 2000

Think of NTI's CD-Maker 2000 as the lesser-known sibling of Easy CD Creator. We chose to cover the Professional Edition of CD-Maker 2000 because its suite of applications rivals Roxio Easy CD Creator in quality, usability, and depth. Tasks you can accomplish with CD-Maker 2000 Professional include ...

➤ Making copies of various CDs.

➤ Creating audio CDs from WAV and MP3 files or even live audio on the fly.

➤ Using FileCD to record to your CD-RW disc as if it were just another hard drive on your PC.

➤ Creating a video CD or SuperVideo CD.

➤ Producing killer CD labels and jewel case inserts.

Overall, CD-Maker 2000 doesn't come off looking as polished as a program like Easy CD Creator. Nor is it quite as powerful a tool as Nero. But unlike Nero, which we don't cover in this book because of its complexity, CD-Maker 2000 is a snap to use. And while it may not glitter in the sun like Easy CD Creator, it's actually a much deeper program that gives you more control over the types of CDs you want to burn.

Between Tracks

NTI also publishes a Standard Edition of CD-Maker 2000 that doesn't have as many features as the Professional iteration. Specifically, you won't be able to ...

➤ Burn audio to a CD-R or CD-RW on the fly.

➤ Convert WAV and CD audio files to MP3s and vice versa.

➤ Master your own video or SuperVideo CDs.

Getting Ready to Install NTI CD-Maker 2000

Installing NTI CD-Maker 2000 is a relatively painless process. A double-click here, a single click there, and you'll suddenly find it copying itself onto your hard drive more quickly than *ER* can turn over cast members. Heck, if this program weren't so darned useful, its user-friendliness might just draw some comparisons to Microsoft BOB!

Before you install NTI CD-Maker for the first time, it's always a good idea to double-check to make sure your computer meets its hardware requirements. If your computer falls short of the following requirements, you'd best hope that the software retailer where you made your purchase has a liberal return policy. This possibility is, however, unlikely, as CD-Maker's modest hardware requirements are even less than those for Roxio Easy CD Creator. In addition to the obvious requirement of a CD-RW drive and audio card (for burning audio CDs), running CD-Maker requires ...

➤ An Intel 486 33MHz processor or better (any Intel Pentium or Celeron-class processors' owners, or those with AMD's K6, Athlon, or Duron line of processors are very much in the clear).

➤ A modern version of Windows, like 9x/Me, NT4/2000, or the latest Microsoft operating system incarnation, Windows XP (which is well worth the upgrade for owners of newer computers).

➤ 32MB of system memory, but 64MB is preferable.

➤ At least 35MB of free space on your hard disk.

If your PC can't match these almost pathetic system requirements, you shouldn't be worrying yourself about burning CDs. Instead, you should immediately do yourself a favor and place a call to Gateway, Alienware, or Falcon Northwest and get yourself a new PC (deep bank accounts not withstanding, of course).

Installing NTI CD-Maker 2000

Generally before installing a new program, it's best to close out of any other programs you might have open. It's probably not necessary, but you never know when having too many cooks in the kitchen ... err ... too many programs on your desktop will lead to conflict.

Once you insert the CD-Maker 2000 CD, Windows should immediately recognize it and present you with an installation screen. If Autorun fails to launch the CD-Maker install wizard, you can launch it manually. Open Windows Explorer (click Start, Programs, and Windows Explorer—some versions of Windows put this program in the Accessories folder) and select your CD-ROM drive. Double-click the Install File.

From here, you must choose Install Products, which takes you to a nice bland Welcome dialog box, like the one shown in Figure B.1 (if they really wanted to welcome you to the installation, I think they should include a cash rebate form on this screen).

Cross Reference

If you have no idea what kind of PC you have, check out the section "Making Sure Your Computer Measures Up" in Appendix A, "Installing Roxio Easy CD Creator."

1. To get the installation party started, click Next and immerse yourself in the End User License Agreement (EULA).

2. Once satisfied that you can honor the terms of the EULA, click Yes. If you click No, the installation cancels.

3. At this point, CD-Maker wants your User Information. Give it your real name and organization (if you're a home user, typing "Personal" for your organization will do). Or if you've really got a Jones for protecting your privacy, type in the name you always wished your parents had given you—something really cool, like Moonbeam or The Dude. Click Next to proceed.

Arcane CD Speak

An End User License Agreement is essentially your pledge to use this software without copying and distributing it to 5,000 or 6,000 of your best friends.

Figure B.1

If you've reached this in-stallation's Welcome dia-log box, you know you're on the right track.

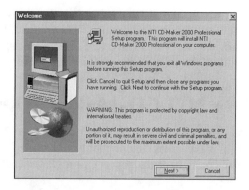

4. Now it's time to decide where to install CD-Maker 2000 (see Figure B.2). The default directory they have provided will do for most users. However, if you'd like to change this location, click the Browse button.

Figure B.2

The Choose Destination Location dialog box lets you customize where to install CD-Maker 2000.

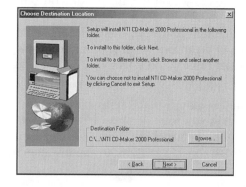

Between Tracks

If you do choose to install CD-Maker into a custom location, make sure you create it using My Computer or Windows Explorer before clicking Browse. Unlike most installation wizards, this one does not let you create a new folder from within the Choose Folder dialog box.

5. The next screen lets you customize where the CD-Maker 2000 icons appear in your Start menu after installation. Unless you have some other master plan, in which case I'm of no use to you, take the default selection by clicking Next.

6. Finally, NTI will begin copying files to your hard drive. When it's complete, a dialog box will ask you to reboot your computer. While you can do so later, it's best to just get it over with by selecting the Yes, I Want to Restart My Computer Now radio button and then clicking Finish.

Once your computer reboots, notice that you'll have a couple of new desktop icons to play with (see Figure B.3).

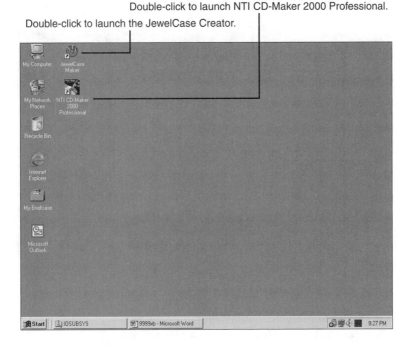

Double-click to launch NTI CD-Maker 2000 Professional.

Double-click to launch the JewelCase Creator.

Figure B.3

The CD-Maker 2000 in-stallation program places two new shortcuts on your Windows desktop after installing the prod-uct and rebooting your computer.

Now that your installation is complete there remains one final step.

Finishing Touches: Using Web-Checkup

Any time you install new software, and especially if that software has been on the market for a while, it's always good to check for free updates prior to using it. No soft-ware program of any size or complexity gets through testing without a few broken or bugged features, and CD-Maker is no exception.

Fortunately, NTI makes it easy to check for and download these updates. To do so, take a stroll through the following steps:

1. Open the NTI CD-Maker 2000 application by double-clicking its desktop icon (refer to Figure B.3).

2. When the application opens, select the Help menu and click the option for Software Update Download Page (see Figure B.4). If you connect to the Internet with a dial-up modem, be sure to establish your Internet connection first.

3. Your default Web browser then opens (probably Internet Explorer or Netscape Navigator) to the NTI downloads page. To see if any upgrades are available, click the Free Updates link on this page.

Figure B.4

Checking for updates in NTI CD-Maker 2000 is as simple as clicking the mouse a couple of times.

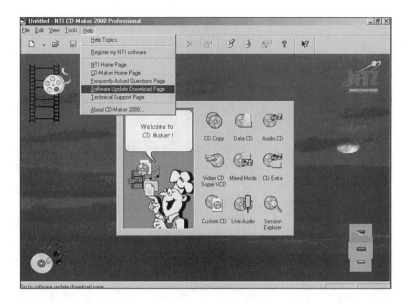

4. If you spot a newer version of you NTI software, use the accompanying scroll-box to select your language and click Download.

5. At this point Windows prompts you to choose a save location for the file. Once you select the location and click on Save, the file downloads. When complete, you are prompted to either open the file or close the File Download dialog box.

Between Tracks

It is possible that the version of CD–Maker 2000 you have on CD is newer than any of the "updates" on the NTI Web site. To compare the available update version numbers with your own, click About CD-Maker 2000 on the same Help menu where you elected to open the NTI download page.

If the version number in the dialog box that appears is higher than the one listed on the NTI update Web page, stand pat with your current installation.

6. To immediately install the update, click Open. To install the update later, click Close to close the download dialog box. Then, when you are ready to install, locate the folder you downloaded the file to using My Computer or Windows Explorer and double-click it.

Now that you've got CD-Maker installed and updated with the latest batch of fixes, you're finally ready to start burning some CDs!

The Colorful Books of CD Standards

While those of us who grew up with phonograph records and black-and-white televisions never thought of the complicated technologies that were to come, we thought much less about standards. That is, until the famous VHS/BetaMax wars came along! Surely, some of you remember going to a video store and having to choose between the VHS and BetaMax sections? How horribly expensive Beta's death must have been for those who thought it would be the winning technology. Compact disc manufacturers were wise enough to avoid this by creating standards for the various kinds of CDs you use today. This appendix provides a brief overview of the books that define the standards that apply to your CD-burning lifestyle, all of which are known by the color of their covers. So, if you're ever in a conversation with some cyber-geek and someone mentions the Orange Book or the White Book, you'll know what he's talking about.

Because my aim here is really just to give you a basic idea of what these standards represent, you're not going to come out of this appendix a scholar in the field. In fact, you'll likely find that some of the numbers and specifications I'm bandying about are just way over your head. Don't worry about it—this is strictly an FYI for those who want a few more tidbits about the various CD specifics. That's why this is just an appendix!

For more information on the contents of these specification documents, just call up your local international manufacturer and ask for a copy … and expect a big bill! These aren't like Internet standards, which are developed by standards organizations comprised mostly of volunteers. These are the hard facts from the companies who developed the technology and now make it so "cheaply" available to us. If, for some reason, you do want the actual documents, be warned—they'll cost you a pretty penny (and then some) to obtain!

The first compact disc standard was designed with the music industry as its target. Today many standards exist, but these were not developed to satisfy the consumer's brand of a particular playback device; instead they were developed to include new kinds of data that could be stored on the disc. Of course, this doesn't mean that all CDs will work on all CD hardware devices. For example, although you can play an audio CD (more correctly called CD-DA), you obviously cannot insert a photo-CD into an ordinary CD player made for playing back audio recordings and expect to see your photos. Audio players don't have display screens or video-out ports to your television! You can use that same CD, however, in a player meant to interpret the data as photographic images. The point is that when you buy an audio CD-DA disc, you can be assured, because of the standards, that it will play in your CD player.

So for this discussion, we focus on the "book" specifications that were created to specify how certain types of discs should be created. Each book is used to define a different purpose for the compact disc, and each is identified by the color of the cover of the book.

The Red Book—the Audio CD Format

In 1982, Philips and Sony released the "Red Book," which set forth the specifications for creating audio CDs (also called CD-DAs). This is the CD with which most people are familiar. This type of CD uses an error-correction scheme called *CIRC*. When using Easy CD Creator, you can choose to record MP3 files in addition to the CD-DA tracks you can find on a Red Book CD. The program, however, converts the MP3 file to a WAV file, which is almost exactly the same as the Red Book CD-DA method. Either way, you won't be able to tell the difference.

The Yellow Book—the Computer CD-ROM Format

This standard was released in 1983. As you can probably figure out, the term CD-ROM stands for "compact disc read-only memory." In other words, you can only read from it, not write to it. It would be years before we'd see the birth of a recordable CD.

At the time this standard was created, computer manufacturers had been creating faster systems with larger storage capacities (both in hard disks and in memory chips), which in turn led to software applications that grew in size. This process is still going on today! Installation files for an application that used to fit on one or two floppy disks now require many more. The first version of Microsoft Office that I purchased came on, I believe, more than twenty floppy disks! Yet, all that could easily be stored on a single CD-ROM today, along with a lot of other data.

The CD-ROM disc is the same size as a CD-DA disc, 120mm. However, the method used for storing data on the disc is much different, which is why the two formats are incompatible.

318

Between Tracks

As computers continue to become more powerful, and as software developers continue to develop larger applications, it is easy to see that the typical business or home computer is already outgrowing the limitations of the CD. It is easy to see that just a few years down the road, the CD will be thought of much as we do the floppy disk today. If you don't believe this, look in your local computer store—or search the Internet—and you will find that some software packages and applications are already available on DVD as well as CD-ROM. Even the venerable Microsoft Office has outgrown the format. Have you seen the number of discs that come with the Premium Edition for Office XP?

The Green Book—Interactive Multimedia Format

Just as computer manufacturers realized that an immense amount of data could be stored on a CD-ROM, companies specializing in multimedia came to the same conclusion. Thus, the interactive multimedia (CD-I) format was released in 1987 to enable video, audio, and other files to be stored on the CD-ROM and to be used in special interactive devices or in a standard computer.

This kind of disc is usually found in those self-repeating product demonstrators found on kiosks in shopping malls. The ability to allow the user to interact with a program and incorporate multimedia features makes it ideal for this purpose. This reminds me, when was the last time you saw such a kiosk? This goes to show you that sometimes standards get developed for an anticipated usage that materializes only briefly, if at all.

The Orange Book (Parts I, II, and III)—CD-R

This kind of CD differed in its development from the others in that it was the first "recordable" CD. Actually, two kinds of CDs are defined in this book—called CD-WO (CD write once), which is now called CD-R, and CD-MO (CD magneto optical), which is usually found in high-end installations such as large computer rooms. These standards, which form parts I and II, were released in 1990.

Part III of the Orange Book was released in 1995. It takes the CD-R concept and adds the ability to erase and re-record on a CD-ROM. The actual CD-R and CD-RW (which started out being called CD-erasable or CD-E) discs are, however, not manufactured in the same manner, and the reflection of the laser light is different on the two discs. If you have a recent model of a CD-ROM disc drive, it should be able to read CD-RW discs on the CD-ROM drive, but many older models cannot. CD-RW drives are now the industry standard (you'd be hard-pressed to find a CD-R-only drive anymore) and are backward-compatible with most other compact disc formats, so you will most likely be able to read any kind of CD on a CD-RW drive.

Originally CD-R drives were so expensive as to be beyond the reach of most consumers, inexpensive recording devices did not start to come on the mass market until about 1995. At this time, CD-RW drives that are much better than their earlier counterparts are now so inexpensive that you can get one on sale for less than $200. If you're buying a new computer, more than likely it will already come with a CD-RW drive. Even laptops are more and more frequently becoming equipped with CD-RW drives as a standard feature.

The White Book—the Video CD

This standard was defined in 1993 by Philips, Sony, and JVC to enable storing about 70 minutes of video on a CD-ROM. It was based partly on a karaoke CD that JVC had developed earlier. This was version 1.1 of the White Book. In version 2.0, released in 1994, Philips, JVC, and Matsushita developed a more versatile version of the video CD that could be used for standard video content, as well as provide support for interactive applications.

The drive used to read these kinds of discs is called CD-ROM/XA.

The *XA* in this disc's name stands for *extended architecture*. This kind of disc is an extension of the Yellow Book standards and enables several kinds of data to be stored on the same disc, including the following:

➤ Audio

➤ Video

➤ Computer data

➤ Compressed audio

You will usually need a special kind of player to read a disc that is of the CD-ROM/XA type.

The Blue Book—CD-Extra

This format was released in 1996 and has been known by other names, such as CD-Plus and Enhanced CD. It contains multisessions, each of which can contain various kinds of data. For example, most audio CD players can recognize only the first session, and the music recorded there will play just as if the CD were of the CD-DA variety. However, a second session could be added to contain computer data. Because most audio CDs usually contain only 50 to 60 minutes of music, a second session could be added that could store a few hundred megabytes of computer applications or data. When played in an ordinary audio player, you would hear the music. When played in a computer, you would listen to the musical selections *or* play with the multimedia applications stored in the second session.

Packet Writing Formats (Sorry, No Color)

In many cases, you either copy an entire CD or at least select data from several sources and write a CD-R disc during one session. A technology called packet writing enables you to write in much smaller increments to a disc over time. Two standards have been developed for packet writing. The CD-RFS format is a Sony-developed format, whereas the CD-UDF format is a more standard format for packet writing.

Index

329

331

Top Ten Things to Do with Your CD Burner

1. Make copies of all your audio CDs and play them instead of the originals. You can always make extra copies if the CD-R disc gets "loaned out" to a friend or finds its way into the coaster stack after time.

2. Using the programs discussed in this book, you can create your own compilation CDs from MP3, WAV, and CD audio files.

3. If you have a collection of vinyl records, use Spin Doctor to record what's left of those priceless items! Listening to a CD made from a vinyl record album won't have the same quality as a new CD, but playing the CD doesn't hurt your vinyl collection. Remember, you can't buy everything on CD!

4. Got photos? Got lots of photos? If they're priceless objects, you should take the precaution of scanning them into electronic format and making backup copies to store for your kids. No matter what happens to the film negatives or the prints you have, you will always be able to upgrade most common digital formats to newer ones in the future.

5. Okay, you've got photos. Got a bootable disk? You can create a bootable CD-R disc that can be used to boot when something goes wrong with your hard drive or your operating system.

6. You can use programs such as Ghost to create an image file or snapshot of your system disk (or any other important disk) at significant times. Ghost and other programs of its kind can restore from a CD a lot faster than you can imagine.

7. Create backup CDs of projects in the work environment. This is an ideal way to create backups of important documentation, data structures, and especially code files for in-house developed applications.

8. Use DirectCD or FileCD when you need to copy files to a rewritable disc instead of performing a full backup. For a home user, having several CD-RW (rewritable) discs that contain important data can be a very efficient backup method.

9. Use the VCD capabilities of both Easy CD Creator and NTI CD-Maker to create CD-R discs that play in some DVD players. Start converting those VHS tapes to digital files, before it's too late!

10. Make coasters—it's fun! Actually, it's a learning experience. Don't worry, just when you're most confident, you'll find out. There's not a single person on this planet who has a CD burner who hasn't made a coaster or two! Just be certain to learn something from your failed attempts.

CD-ROM included in back of
    book.

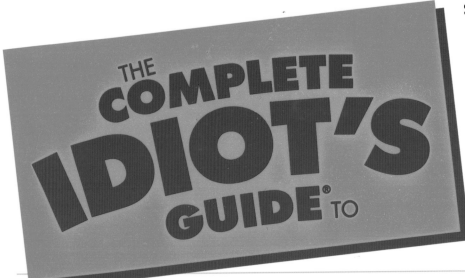

THE COMPLETE IDIOT'S GUIDE® TO

Creating Your Own CDs

SECOND EDITION

♦ **Easy-to-follow instructions** on duplicating and creating your own video, audio, and data CDs

♦ **Essential features** to look for in a CD burner

♦ **Idiot-proof information** on popular software programs

Terry William Ogletree
and Todd Brakke